MORE PRAISE FOR SETH LEVINE AND ELIZABETH MACBRIDE'S *THE NEW BUILDERS*

"Across various chapters of my professional career, one of which as head of Investment and Innovation of the U.S. Small Business Administration, I've seen first hand the seismic changes our entrepreneurial economy is going through. *The New Builders* perfectly captures these important and interconnected trends – trends that many people fail to see."
—JAVIER SAADE, Former Associate Administrator, Chief of Investment and Innovation, U.S. Small Business Administration

"As a woman entrepreneur in a field dominated by men, I know what it's like to have to work harder to be taken seriously and to win respect. Women have power, as these stories make clear. They don't need it lent to them. They need and deserve a fair shot – and we'll all benefit from giving them one."
—EVA SHOCKEY BRENT, Author, TV Personality, Bow Hunter, Conservationist

"*The New Builders* is a masterpiece of investigation and insight. Joe Biden and everyone in his administration needs to read this book NOW! It is both an inspiring and troubling glimpse at the changing nature of entrepreneurship in America."
—DAVID SMICK, Global Macro Hedge Fund Strategist and NYT Bestselling Author

"Pay attention to this book: Entrepreneurs may not look like you expect them to, but they're always at the forefront of where we need to go, next."
—JIM SHOCKEY – Naturalist, Outfitter, TV Producer and Host of Jim Shockey's Hunting Adventures and UNCHARTED on Outdoor Channel

"Elizabeth MacBride and Seth Levine have done it again! Discerning fact from fiction and really getting to the heart of how the 21st century entrepreneur is thinking and responding in the ever-evolving landscape of "innovation ecosystems" domestically and globally. This is a must read book for those intrigued or looking to better understand how entrepreneurs and small business owners will ultimately reinvigorate the American and Global economy in a post COVID-19 landscape and channel the spirit of America's Founders whom were the original entrepreneurs that founded one of the greatest countries of modern history ... "
—G. NAGESH RAO, 2016 USA Eisenhower Fellow

"As entrepreneurship becomes democratized, the characteristic of entrepreneurs is rapidly changing. Seth and Elizabeth do a brilliant job of explaining these changes by telling specific stories of the next generation of entrepreneurs in *The New Builders*. Anyone who cares about the future of entrepreneurship, or the future of the American economy, needs to read this book."
—BRAD FELD, Foundry Group partner, Techstars co-founder, author of The Startup Community Way

"We're about to experience a profoundly different and exciting economic future – one where community will matter more than ever. This book is an essential guide to what's ahead for anyone who cares about reinventing the American economy."
—ELAINE POFELDT, journalist and author, The Million-Dollar, One-Person Business

"Entrepreneurs translate society's values into reality. *The New Builders* is a fascinating (and heartening) window onto the next generation of entrepreneurs and the products and services they're building in communities across the country."
—FELICE GORORDO, CEO of eMerge Americas, Miami

"Thanks to Seth and Elizabeth for this clear, concrete roadmap on how to drive entrepreneurship and innovation in the U.S. economy. Their stories and messages show how the face of American entrepreneurship is changing and how entrepreneurs on Main Street are key to job growth and prosperity. I hope the new team in Washington checks out "New Builders" and follows many of its recommendations."
—AMBASSADOR JOHN HEFFERN (ret), Fellow, Georgetown University

"Elizabeth and Seth have uncovered the power and unlimited creativity of the human brain personified by the new generation of creators helping a new ecosystem which will conquer this planet … Inspirational to all including governments and their leaders. It tells you how to take and give and shows how to embrace the philosophy of problem solving rather than complaining."
—ZAHI KHOURI, Palestinian/American entrepreneur and philanthropist

"The vitality of Lancaster City is in larger measure because of its New Builders, the mosaic of peoples from across the globe who have made Lancaster their home – whether in the 1600s or the 2000s. To see this concept reflected by MacBride and Levine is to understand what is special about our city – and no doubt, many others."
—DANENE SORACE, Mayor of Lancaster, PA.

"Journalists who write about the Arab region tended to cover stories of conflict, security, destitution and hardship. The region is so much more than that. Elizabeth decided to write a different narrative, about the opportunity and hope in entrepreneurs who are innovating and driving change. I would argue that many of those stories became known because of her tireless efforts. Now, she and Seth Levine have turned a similar, powerful lens on *New Builders* in the United States – I can't wait for these stories to be known, too."
—DINA SHERIF, Executive Director, MIT Legatum Center for Entrepreneurship & Development, and Partner, Disruptech

"Leveling the playing field for all entrepreneurs is crucial to our country's economic future. The increasingly diverse and dynamic people starting businesses today are closing the opportunity gap and developing innovative products and services to address some of our most pressing problems. *The New Builders* brings their stories to life. It is critical reading for anyone who wants to understand the future of business in the United States."
—STEVE CASE, Chairman and CEO of Revolution, LLC, Co-Founder of AOL, Founding Chair, Startup America Partnership

THE NEW BUILDERS

Face to Face with the True Future of Business

THE NEW BUILDERS

Face to Face with the True Future of Business

◇

SETH LEVINE

ELIZABETH MACBRIDE

WILEY

Published by John Wiley & Sons, Inc., Hoboken, New Jersey.
Published simultaneously in Canada.

For general information on our other products and services or for technical support, please contact our Customer Care Department within the United States at (800) 762-2974, outside the United States at (317) 572-3993 or fax (317) 572-4002.

Wiley publishes in a variety of print and electronic formats and by print-on-demand. Some material included with standard print versions of this book may not be included in e-books or in print-on-demand. If this book refers to media such as a CD or DVD that is not included in the version you purchased, you may download this material at http://booksupport.wiley.com. For more information about Wiley products, visit www.wiley.com.

Library of Congress Cataloging-in-Publication Data is Available:

ISBN 978-1-119-79736-4 (Hardback)
ISBN 978-1-119-79738-8 (ePDF)
ISBN 978-1-119-79737-1 (ePub)

COVER DESIGN: Paul McCarthy
COVER IMAGES: All Photos Considered Photography | Allie Atkisson Imaging | Photo Portfolio, Highlights | Cathy Sachs | Claire Hibbs-Cheff | Donald "Diz" Zanoff | Emil Kuruvilla | Eric Elofson | Rope Line Media | New Hampshire Community Loan Fund | Montgomery County Chamber of Commerce | Philip Vaughan Photography | Scott Suchman | Seth Goldman

SKY10026234_041321

For Greeley: Love. Always.

and for Sacha, Addy, and Amanuel – our *New Builders*

———

For Lillie and Quinn

My marvelous daughters

CONTENTS

FOREWORD: OWN YOUR FIERCE POWER

"Wow, what an innovative concept. I love this."

"I've never heard of anything like this before. It's so creative ... so thoughtful."

"It's genius. I believe in it and I believe in YOU."

Beautiful words, right? Ego building. Pride boosting. Words every budding entrepreneur wants to hear.

Wrong.

Because after all of that praise comes ... Nothing.

Welcome to my world. OUR world. I don't invite you in to garner pity. But I thank you for RSVPing to the plain, hard truth – the truth that I and so many have to endure. Yet still we rise and rise again because we believe – no, scratch that – we KNOW that what we have to offer society can truly change the world.

But how do you change the world when someone won't even lend you the change from their pocket?

There are many kinds of beauty in the world, many kinds of entrepreneurs, and many kinds of power. I'm a *New Builder*. I'm a Black woman, with decades of experience across industries, launching new businesses and working on new next-level ideas.

But just like it is for many *New Builders*, the struggle to raise money is real. I have watched my White, male peers raise serious capital with ease, with ideas that are far less developed. And I know what you may be thinking – but just because my name may appear on billboards doesn't mean business boards respect my business acumen. And nor should they. Celebrity does not automatically equal a sharp business mind. But mine is. And so are the minds of so many *New Builders*, yet we struggle to be taken seriously because we don't fit that mold of what an entrepreneur "ought" to look like.

Entrepreneurship, for me, is not just about financial success. It's about leaving something that lasts beyond my time on Earth. A true legacy. From expanding the definition of beauty to teaching personal branding at the Stanford Graduate School of Business, I believe my profit must have a purpose. My companies reach people around the world and delight, entertain, and educate them in out-of-the-box ways. We are obsessed with storytelling, and everything we do must have some funny, some fierce, and lots of heart, whether it's a worldwide television franchise or a tasty food product.

You've been reading my words for a bit now, so speaking of food, I think you deserve a treat. What about a scoop of ice cream? And what if I hid a yummy, chunkalicious, *Surprise* in it?

Okay, while you enjoy your ice cream, let's get back to business.

Becoming an Entrepreneur

When I was a model, I answered to the people behind the camera. But I always wanted more than that. I wanted control. Every single day of my modeling career, I encountered prejudice because I was Black or because I was curvy. People said I couldn't do this runway show, or couldn't be on that cover, or star in that campaign. I heard a lot of "no" and "you can't" and even "you'll never."

Oh, it hurt. Bad. I cried. Lots. But I'm happy to say, it didn't break me. The tears turned to hunger – a famished feeling in my tummy to show naysayers that I could and I would. (I can hear the "models don't eat" jokes running in your head right now, but I was the rare one who lived off of barbecued ribs and coffee ice cream milkshakes. And I was carrying about 30 pounds more body weight than my colleagues. Oh yeah.) I was also eager to show people that my skills expanded way past runway walking and magazine posing. And yes, when I spoke those aspirations aloud, the "nos" from the powers-that-be flowed again.

But I'm writing this Foreword, so we all know that those "heck, nos" turned into some "hell, yeses." Without struggle there is no progress, said Frederick Douglass. And without progress, there is no power. Entrepreneurship is a way to create and hold onto your own power. *Your fierce power.*

Power Moves

I have messed up a lot through all this. And learned plenty of what-the-heck-was-I-thinking lessons that I now excitedly pass along to others. One of my favorite things to do is mentor young entrepreneurs over a hearty lunch while I teach them how to draw strategic mind maps to chart the path to their B.F.O.G.s – their Big Fierce Outrageous Goals.

Here's a bit of what I tell them:

- **Different is better than better.** Tiny improvements on someone else's product or service ain't gonna get you far. What about your business is unique? And don't force a unique narrative when you know you're derivative. VCs and PEs see straight through that ... and you.
- **Hone your personal brand.** People don't just invest in companies, they invest in people. What's your personal origin story? What do you stand for? How are you letting the world know that? You're competing with so many others for capital, community, customers, and team members. The clearer you are about how you want to present to the world, the more ownership you have of your own narrative and the more attractive you become to attract others.

- **Find some shoulders ... to cry on.** Entrepreneurship is no joke. Wins, losses, setbacks, unpredictable craziness.... You need someone you can just be vulnerable with. You also need that someone who shakes you and says, "Okay, enough with the wallowing in self-pity. Get your butt up. Get your funky butt in the shower. And then get back at it!" This "E-life" is damn hard sometimes, but don't easily give up or stop trying. Life has no mercy on you when you stop stepping up. And if you're not experiencing failure in your work life or business, you're playing it way too safe. Shake it up and take a risk ... and yes, a shower, too.

- **Make freezing-cold calls.** Reach out to people who inspire you. Keep it short and to the point. Compliment them on something recent they've accomplished and give it context on how it has inspired you. You just may get a mentor out of it. That's how I established a meaningful relationship with somebody we lost this year, Tony Hsieh. I was obsessed with his book, *Delivering Happiness*, and picked up the phone. That cold call turned into a rewarding mentoring and business friendship. I miss him. We all do.

- **Reward people who disagree with you.** One thing that terrifies me is a *yes* person. Where everything I think up is perfect and flawless and they would never dare disagree with me. Yikes! Just writing about this type of person feels like a horror movie to me. In meetings, I often insist on hearing dissenting voices. About 50 percent of the time, there's a nugget (or a boulder) of truth that positively influences some of my decisions.

- **Turn up your mic.** Reach out. Speak up. Make yourself heard and seen. Don't sit there and say, "I'm going to work really, really hard and one day they're going to notice." Because they won't. They're not thinking of you. Make them.

Hope you enjoyed my tips. Oh ... how's that ice cream tasting? Magnificent? Wonderful. It's from my new business, SMiZE Cream. And yeah, you heard me say this already, but the "*nos*" thrown my capital-raise-way were dizzying.

I pitched my ice cream business to this one investor, and even though I felt beaten down by all the passes, I pitched with all of my heart and soul. I shared how we are not just an ice cream company but that we are in the business of goal setting and goal getting and teaching others how to be the same. That we don't just scoop an amazing-tasting super-premium frozen treat, but that we are an IP company with a suite of revenue streams that don't just bring in the bucks but delight customers to the max and help them make their dreams come true, too.

"Wow, what an innovative concept. I love this."

"I've never heard of anything like this before. It's so creative ... so thoughtful."

"It's genius. I believe in it and I believe in YOU."

And then he said, "I'm in."

What?!

Okay, okay. So he didn't say those words *exactly*, but pretty close. But the point is, he said "yes"! And his *yes* was so refreshing. This guy wasn't full of empty, ego-stroking words. He didn't flatter me. He saw me. I spent months digging into the details with him, and the idea evolved into one with true enterprise potential.

New Builders like me need to be seen for our true power. That's why I'm so happy to be connected to them in this book – all of them across the country, through this tome you hold. And I say to all of them, when they're judged unfairly for the color of their skin, or the shape of their body, or any damn thing else, find that shoulder, let the tears flow, then get your shower and go pitch again and again and again. The world is changing. And you are a part of that change. The world needs your idea. You can change the world.

And you know who else can change the world? The financial community peeps who have the big bucks to enable, support, encourage, and uplift the change makers. How do they do that? By not trying to just be better. But by being DIFFERENT. Seek out entrepreneurs who don't look like you. When they have a product or service you don't quite understand, don't pull in the one person who looks like them from your office expecting them to be an expert. Dig deeper. Staff up your team to culturally represent and be able to identify opportunities that are outside of your own reach and understanding. The world needs your leadership to make real change.

Now, back to the man who lent me the change from his pocket for my own biz. He is the co-author of this book. Yep. Hi, Seth. Thank you so very much for seeing my power.

Okay, back to you, reader. Turn the page. And experience how, together, we can turn the world around. Elizabeth and Seth, thank you for giving voice to this community, to these amazing change makers, to these *New Builders*.

–Tyra Banks

INTRODUCTION: THE REBIRTH OF THE GREAT AMERICAN ENTREPRENEUR

The definition of success in America today is increasingly corporate, built around the concepts of growth, size, and consumption. Big companies – large in terms of revenue, profits, and mindshare – frame the way we think about what is important and powerful. But our current overweening love affair with big poses a fundamental problem for America and what has been our uniquely dynamic economy. In this environment, entrepreneurship is dying. We've lost touch with the critical part of our society that is created by smaller businesses, which are responsible for much of our innovation and dynamism, most of the job growth, and produce nearly half of US Gross Domestic Product. Where entrepreneurship is thriving, it is so narrowly, among brash, young, typically White and male, technology company founders on their way to becoming big.

The needs of most entrepreneurs and small business owners are increasingly being overlooked and, as a result, they are being left behind in the economy and left out of the conversation. Entrepreneurship in the United States has declined over the last 40 years. As we narrow our definition of entrepreneurship, we narrow our opportunities and limit our economy.

It doesn't have to be this way.

The future is always coming to life *somewhere*. Luckily for us, we happened to be witness to it.

In the summer of 2019, we – Seth Levine, a venture capitalist, and Elizabeth MacBride, a business journalist – set out to tell the stories of entrepreneurs beyond the high-tech enclaves we both know well. What did entrepreneurs look like in the middle of America and in communities outside the halo of traditional technology startup hotbeds?

What we discovered surprised us. The next generation of entrepreneurs doesn't look anything like past generations, and defies the popular image of an "entrepreneur" as a young, white founder, building a technology company. In fact, almost the opposite is true. Increasingly, our next generation of entrepreneurs are Black, brown, female, and over 40. They are more likely to be building a business on Main Street than in Silicon Valley. They typically start businesses based on their passions and rooted in their communities. In many cases, they are building businesses in areas left behind after the uneven recovery that followed the Great Recession of 2008–2009.

In this book we tell the stories of a wide range of entrepreneurs, from a man who revitalized an entire community through sheer stubbornness, to a family of guides in the Montana wilderness, to the first chocolatier in Arkansas, to a baker for the Dominican community of Massachusetts.

We call these entrepreneurs *New Builders*. They are the future of America's entrepreneurial legacy. This book tells their stories and explains the financial systems and power networks that must change if we are to help them succeed.

Yet, when we took our initial findings to our peers in the worlds of venture capital and journalism, people didn't believe us. They thought, based on what they saw about entrepreneurs in the news, that entrepreneurship in the United States was thriving. Most people have missed the fundamental changes that are taking place in our entrepreneurial landscape. As the people starting businesses have changed, our systems of finance and mentorship have failed to keep up. For the first time in history, the majority of entrepreneurs don't look like either the past generation of entrepreneurs or the people who control the capital and systems of support that are enablers of entrepreneurship.

New Builders are a diverse group, but they share one trait: they don't fit the mold of corporate success. In a business world that increasingly values conformity, *New Builders* defy it.

But being overlooked is a superpower of *New Builders*. Because of racism, sexism, and ageism, or because they saw ways to create new systems outside the ones they couldn't change, many *New Builders* turned to entrepreneurship – starting businesses and creating successful lives on their own terms. They often start businesses based on their values, and they are unusually resilient, possessing an extra dose of grit and determination.

New Builders are disconnected from the systems that accelerate new businesses and propel business growth. Those systems were built for past generations of entrepreneurs. *New Builders* are undercapitalized, and when they try to access networks that control capital, they often face systemic racism and sexism.

Entrepreneurs have been the bedrock of American business since before our country was founded, and entrepreneurship is deeply rooted in our country's history. Entrepreneurs were the women and men who explored and settled the vastness of the United States, and who built the infrastructure that stitched it all together – from rail, to industry, to the internet, to the goods and services needed for our everyday lives. But unlike past generations of entrepreneurs, who upended yesterday's big companies, today's *New Builders* don't have the support they need to be the dynamic engine of our economy. The Covid-19 pandemic unfolded while we were in the midst of writing *The New Builders*, accelerating trends already in motion and bringing the harsh reality of our country's declining economic dynamism to the surface. When the final numbers are tallied, we will have lost millions more small businesses from what was already a shrinking base.

But *New Builders'* optimism is infectious, and their success in the face of obstacles gives us hope for the future of small companies and their crucial role in the American economy. In *The New Builders,* we argue for a better future. One that celebrates and supports the next generation of entrepreneurs and creates a more dynamic, egalitarian, and equitable society.

Our economic future lies in some surprising places – surprising only because we cling to a mistaken narrative of entrepreneurship. America needs a resurgence of these small businesses and the entrepreneurial spirit they embody, especially as we emerge from the Covid-19 economic crisis. Renewal and change come to life in small companies – from Main Streets to office parks, from kitchen tables to back-alley garages.

In *The New Builders*, we call for a new mission that embraces the next generation of American entrepreneurs. Just as Silicon Valley was born out of a national mission to embrace mid-twentieth-century innovation and expand democracy's reach around the world, so too must we come together to build a network of support for our next generation of entrepreneurs. *New Builders* will play a critical role in helping rebuild communities, and in so doing will help bring forth a new vision for the United States. *New Builders* are not add-ons to our mental map of business in the United States. **They are the map**.

In our time meeting and interviewing *New Builders*, we found compelling examples of new networks and support structures springing up across the country. But those efforts need to be expanded, and too many focus on changing *New Builders* to adapt to the existing system, rather than on adapting the system itself.

New Builders are the bedrock of the economy and the strongest part of the fabric that holds our communities together. Individually, they are strong; together, they are mighty. Their resolve – and ours – was tested in 2020 and 2021 as the pandemic raged across the country. This resolve will continue to be challenged. In this book, you will meet many *New Builders* and in doing so, gain a glimpse into the future of American business.

Our focus is on the amazing individuals we call the *New Builders*. Their stories offer hope and promise. Their passion, dedication, and grit inspire. We hope *The New Builders* makes you think differently about entrepreneurship, about the businesses you support, and about the policies that help drive our economy. Perhaps this book will invite you to consider the role you might play in supporting *New Builders* in your community.

Fundamentally, this book describes the urgent need for those with power in our society to change their thinking and their actions. We all benefit by creating a more robust society where a greater number of people have access to the capital and know-how necessary to create and grow businesses.

Most of all, we hope this book inspires you with the potential for our shared future.

–Seth Levine
–Elizabeth MacBride

PART I

WHO ARE
THE NEW BUILDERS?

"This is not just a grab-bag candy game."

Toni Morrison

CHAPTER ONE

A New Generation

Danaris Mazara opened the door at Sweet Grace Heavenly Cakes the day after the governor lifted the Covid pandemic lockdown on "nonessential" businesses in late May 2020.

"Thank God," she said. Her 12-year-old bakery, which had been conceived of when she was lying on her couch staring at the ceiling with $37 to her name, was back in business.[i]

Eight women were already back at work on Essex Street in Lawrence, Massachusetts, making cakes in the back of the shop. The Sweet Grace bakers turned out cakes, from five silver-festooned tiers for a wedding to two-layered dreamy dark and milk chocolate affairs. On any given day, a cake as grand as a two-foot-tall Noah's Ark birthday cake, complete with a giraffe peeking over the top, might hold pride of place in the window.

It was a parade of life events, decked out in butter and sugar, for the Dominican community that Sweet Grace served.

Twelve orders came in the day before. But a week usually brought more than 100 orders. Danaris worried whether sales would be strong

---

[i] Quotes from Danaris are from six interviews conducted between May 2019 and December 2020. Elizabeth visited in person in summer 2019, a visit that included a lunch in a lively Dominican restaurant.

enough to make the payroll, the mortgage, or payments on the loan she had taken to expand late last year. She recalled what the space looked like before she remodeled it. Its transformation mirrored her own, from bankrupt and nearly out of money to business owner and community leader. The space had been dim and cluttered, with abandoned fixtures and trash left by the hair salon that was its previous occupant. Now it looked like it smelled – soft, sweet, and full of energy. But not as busy as it was before the pandemic and economic crisis hit.

"I think it's normal to be afraid," she said. "You don't know what's going to happen in the future. I'm trying very hard to … " she trailed off. "Just wait and keep working," she finished.

Around the corner, the family-owned Italian bakery also opened its doors that morning. But unlike Sweet Grace Heavenly Cakes, it had been able to stay in business through the Covid-19 shutdown because of a historical relic: it baked bread. Somewhere, somebody in the state's bureaucracy had decided that bread was essential. But not cake.

That's not how Danaris saw it. For people who love to dance and sing, and who live for their families and communities, cake *is* essential. Now, she wondered if everything she had built – for her family, her community, for her workers, and their families – would survive.

Danaris and her husband had arrived in Lawrence in 2002 from Puerto Rico. Born in the Dominican Republic, her mother had moved the family to Puerto Rico when Danaris was a young girl. There she had grown up and met her husband, Andres. Moving to the mainland after they were married, Danaris and Andres started their life in Lawrence, in her brother's attic. The room had no air-conditioning, which meant it was sweltering in the summer, and had little insulation, leaving them to huddle together in the winter. But there were jobs in the factories in and around Lawrence, and the opportunity for a better life.

At the factory where she first found work, Danaris tried, tentatively, to speak a few words of English. "I didn't know that when people eat American chicken, they start speaking English," mocked the assistant manager on the production line.

She was so humiliated she couldn't bring herself to go back the next day. Instead, she found a language school. The lessons paid off and when she eventually found another job, they were impressed enough to quickly promote her to assistant manager. Right before her daughter, Grace, was born, the Great Recession of 2008–2009 hit. Her husband was laid off from his job at Haverhill Paperboard, a local manufacturer that had been operating for over 100 years. The layoff cost 174 people their jobs and livelihood.

"I was very depressed because I had a newborn baby, something I was waiting to have for many, many years. But I couldn't stay at home to take care of her. I didn't know what I was supposed to do," she told us.

Sweet Grace Heavenly Cakes was born in that moment of desperation, from the mind of a woman who, typical of today's entrepreneurs, had little in the way of resources, or even a well-resourced network, to help. The bakery succeeded in the early days because of the help of an unlikely trio of benefactors: an Indian-born billionaire, a Harvard-educated tech executive, and a banker from Brazil. They were all engaged in programs to help Lawrence, a city of old and new immigrants, come back to life. In 2018, they had pulled together to help the city recover from a gas line explosion that destroyed 40 homes and caused the immediate evacuation of 30,000 people (from a city of 80,000). Now, as the Covid-19 pandemic dragged on, Danaris wondered: if things were really bad, could she turn to them for help?

In better times, before the pandemic hit, Sweet Grace's reputation was so good, people lined up to pay $2 just for a cup of the crumbs. Even the Immigration and Customs Enforcement (ICE) agents, whose office was menacingly outside the back door, sometimes stopped in for a cup.

"We have many customers coming from far, far away to get our cakes," she said. "Dominican people, you have to know us. We are always celebrating."

Danaris made it through seven weeks of pandemic closure by using her personal savings to pay both the mortgage on her house and the payments on her building renovation loan. She paid her employees – four of whom were women with children still back in the Dominican Republic – for a week. But she was stretched thin, both financially and emotionally.

She had been right before to trust in her ability to build a business. Her prayers had worked in the past. Now, she trusted they would again.

The *New Builders*

Danaris is a *New Builder*. She is one of the next generation of entrepreneurs defining the future of American business. These entrepreneurs are increasingly Black, brown, and female. Many are older than entrepreneurs of previous generations and, as a result, today's entrepreneurs are older than many people realize. They are talented innovators and businesspeople with an extra dose of grit. They're passionate about what they do, and their motivations are often more complex than our current definition of *entrepreneur* allows. They're apt to be driven by the idea of contributing to their community as much as by the idea of profit, though they often believe they can do both.

The entrepreneurs of today are a much broader group than the entrepreneurs that dominated our old mindset, the high-tech founders of Silicon Valley and Boston. Very few *New Builders* have businesses that fit the idealized Silicon Valley model of fast-growth, highly profitable (or at least highly valued) enterprises – but out of their ranks, we will find winners in the post-pandemic recovery. You'll find them in places as varied as Main Streets, redlined communities, and technology parks everywhere. And they come up with ideas for their businesses not tinkering in the fabled garages of Silicon Valley but in teenagers' bedrooms and around kitchen tables. Some are building technology businesses with the goal of hyper growth. Most are not. If we want them to win in greater numbers, we need to understand better who they are and how to support them. Our idea of entrepreneurship has been overtaken by a particular myth – that important entrepreneurs are White, male, and Ivy League–educated, and that the only truly worthwhile businesses are software-driven companies with the potential to grow into huge businesses. *That image doesn't reflect the reality of entrepreneurship across America*, or the fact that small businesses are not just a sentimental cause – they are critical part of our economy. It's time to take back the idea of entrepreneurship to include the incredibly rich and wide variety of businesses that are being started in America today. By not seeing *New Builders*, not supporting them and helping them thrive, we risk letting go of the entrepreneurial edge that has long set America apart from other countries.

The *New Builders* are out there. They're an invisible army, working to further themselves and their communities as they turn their business ideas into reality.

Entrepreneurs Are Everywhere

Danaris, like many *New Builders*, didn't come to start and build a business from a whiteboard or as part of a class exercise. It was her lived experience, combined with the kind of motivation that comes from the knowledge that you're not going to succeed any other way – at least, not on the terms you want. Quiet but forceful, and fiercely proud of her culture, Danaris spent years putting other people before herself, including her husband and her children. Like the mother who inspired her, she knows how to carry on through tears. But in the company of people from cultures where tears are a sign of weakness, she also knows how to hold them back. If you passed her on the street, you might not give her a second look. You almost certainly wouldn't think this Dominican woman was a community leader and small business owner.

In today's economy, an estimated 60 million people are entrepreneurial in some way. There were 5.6 million employer firms in the United States in 2016, the last year for which complete data are available. If you include the number of "nonemployer" businesses (sole proprietorships – what we now like to call "solopreneurs") this share goes up to 98 percent. Overlapping with these businesses are the 57 million Americans who freelanced in 2018 as part of the *gig economy*.[1]

It's easy to underestimate the impact of grassroots entrepreneurs on the economy, especially in a country that's become consumed by a fast-growth, high-tech business narrative. But recent World Bank research found that it's almost impossible to predict which companies will eventually turn into "gazelles" – their term for firms that take off quickly, grow rapidly, and employ large numbers of people. High-growth firms aren't just technology businesses (though some are). Nor are all startups in the classic sense. Rather, they are firms between one and five years old, and they're found in many sectors across our economy.[2] Likewise, important innovations are as likely to happen in Danaris's kitchen – the low-calorie cake she's been playing around with, for example – or a lab in the Midwest, as in the head of a Silicon Valley computer coder.

Early data suggest that the number of entrepreneurs is growing in the midst of the Covid-19 pandemic, as people become entrepreneurial out of necessity. As the pandemic started, the average small business had just two to four weeks of cash on hand, a fact that explains why so many folded (already numbering in the several million, as of the time of this writing).[3] Our economy needs more *New Builders*.

If the past is any guide, unless something changes, fewer and fewer Americans will choose to become entrepreneurs after the pandemic aftereffect fades. The long-term slowdown in new business activity contributes to the phenomenon of what one might describe as *ghost startups* – businesses that never got started because the founders didn't have the opportunity to get their ideas off the ground. The Ewing Marion Kauffman Foundation calls them *pre-entrepreneurship leavers*.[4] We'll never know the names of these businesses, nor the impact they might have had on a local, national, or even global scale, unless we pause to recognize how many ghost startups our current economy is missing.[ii]

The startup rate in America, the share of companies zero to two years old, fell from more than 12 percent in 1980 to about 8 percent in 2015.[5] Meanwhile, the number of people employed by small businesses – while still more than 40 percent of the workforce – fell by one-third between 1987 and 2015. The Covid-19 pandemic is exacerbating these trends and, at the same time, highlighting why small business entrepreneurship is so essential to our economy.

What we found as we interviewed dozens of entrepreneurs and small business owners – we use the terms almost interchangeably – across the

---

[ii] This is actually an area of emerging research. The Kauffman Foundation, in particular, has started to look more closely at those who have business ideas but don't end up starting companies. You can find a link to their initial report on this subject in the endnotes.

United States is that several elements are merging to make it hard to be a *New Builder.*

The systemic racism, sexism, and ageism that pervades our culture means that today's entrepreneurs often don't get enough support. Our systems of capital and networks are dominated by White men, many of whom consciously or unconsciously look for other White men to invest in. But today's entrepreneurs are increasingly women and people of color. And many of our best entrepreneurs are older.

Consider:

- Women will soon make up more than half of all business owners in the United States because the rate at which women are starting businesses is growing at more than four times the rate of business starts overall. And women of color are responsible for 64 percent of the new women-owned businesses being created, making them the fastest-growing segment of business owners in the United States.
- The entrepreneurship rate in the United States has been driven by people of Hispanic origin, whose rate of entrepreneurship is almost twice that of the average of other groups.[6] Immigrants, as well, are twice as likely as native-born Americans to start businesses.
- The average age of the leaders of high-growth startups is 45.[7] And the highest rate of entrepreneurial activity in the United States is among people aged 55 to 64.[8]

Entrepreneurs can succeed in today's economy – you'll meet many in this book – but many are struggling because our business landscape has fundamentally changed. We find ourselves in an age dominated by big business and powered by software and the consumer movement. Our current business environment is driven by a pursuit for profit, above all else, and enforced by a government that, under both Democrats and Republicans, has increasingly shifted the rules of the game to favor size. Society has become obsessed with the ability to order any item at any time on demand, the convenience of everything under the sun being delivered to our front door, and the comfort of knowing that you can get the same coffee, burger, or taco in just about any large city in our country. We have started to devalue people who pick another path, who want to be producers, rather than consumers. Even among technology companies – which most perceive as thriving – fewer people are launching new businesses. Now is the time to focus on these changes and start to do something about them.

This long-term decline in entrepreneurship has terrible implications for the health of our society. Twenty-five years ago, a child born in the bottom 25 percent of the economic bracket had a 25 percent chance of making it into the top 25 percent. This was the basis for the American dream – through hard work, determination, and likely a bit of luck, anyone, regardless of the circumstances from which they came, could rise up the economic ladder. Today, someone born into the bottom 25 percent of the economic ladder has only a 5 percent chance of making it into the top 25 percent. The American dream is slipping away, and we're simply watching it happen.[9]

Hope

But this is fundamentally an optimistic book, because *New Builders* are optimistic people.[iii] In a cynical age, they still believe in the American dream. In researching and meeting *New Builders,* we found a group of people across the country engaged in building a new future for themselves, their communities, and, collectively, the country. We also discovered communities that are picking up the challenge of growing their own local support networks for these entrepreneurs. The people we met in researching this book show us how fulfilling it is to own a business, how meaningful it is to be part of a community of entrepreneurs, and how rewarding it is to be responsible for your own future.

We spend a lot of time in the United States today celebrating individual spirit, but also looking to the government for help. What we found is that most things of consequence today happen in the space between

---

[iii] This point can't be emphasized enough. Over and over again we were taken back by just how optimistic the *New Builders* we met in researching this book are. It's an infectious optimism that clearly rubbed off on us as well. While it would be easy to look at some of the trends and feel a sense of dread, we feel exactly the opposite. We've seen firsthand the power grassroots entrepreneurship can have on a community. And it has left us feeling hopeful about our future.

individuals and government, in relationships between people who create change, in new networks, and in communities that are leading their own revivals.

In the coming chapters, we'll explore places like Staunton, Virginia, which is home to a local angel network that has invested more than $1 million and is home to a makerspace that has helped rejuvenate the downtown. The story of the Staunton Makerspace shows what happens when the spirit of *New Builders* takes root in a community and is nurtured there. About a year after it was opened, a fire destroyed the fledgling operation in downtown Staunton. A 92-year-old former machinist, George Saugui, read about the fire in the newspaper. "I thought we lost everything," Dan Funk, the founder of the Makerspace told us. "But he showed up." The duo hoisted George's old workbench into a truck and brought it down to the ruined Makerspace. "He sat for four weeks, repairing all of our woodworking equipment," Dan recalled. The Makerspace was rebuilt with the help of George and others in the community who turned up to rally around this important asset. It is now back in operation and has since expanded to include members working on a variety of hobbies, as well as entrepreneurial ventures in everything from textiles to 3D printing (which quickly became important during Covid-19).

Indeed, entrepreneurs, especially those with unexpected success stories, have given the United States much of our identity as a nation of builders and doers, risk-takers, and innovators, of economic prosperity and deep community identity. The story we tell ourselves about America, although part myth and part reality, is inexorably linked to this entrepreneurial spirit.

Choosing What to See

You've probably never heard of Elizabeth Keckley. Born an enslaved person in 1818 in Virginia, she learned a skill, dressmaking, which her White owners used to help support their families. As is the case with many women – especially Black women – the value of her work was not her own. Through sheer grit and determination, she scraped together $1,200 (roughly $35,000 in today's currency) and purchased her freedom. In 1860, she made her way with her son to Washington, DC, where she met and befriended Mary Todd Lincoln, becoming her personal modiste. She eventually chronicled their close friendship in her book, *Behind the Scenes: Or, Thirty Years a Slave and Four Years in the White House*, a remarkable history of her escape from slavery and her time inside the highest echelons of American political society.

Hers is an almost unbelievable account of the power of the entrepreneurial spirit to change one's life and a testament to the determination required to succeed. It's also a reminder – and something we'll explore over and over as we meet more *New Builders* – of the power of network and mentorship. It's a story of promise and a beacon to this day for the power of American entrepreneurship. But it's also a reminder that *New Builders* and their predecessors have been fighting for hundreds of years for recognition and support in our entrepreneurial landscape. One of the reasons we don't value Danaris Mazara is that we haven't valued Elizabeth Keckley. Former US Secretary of State Condoleezza Rice – the first Black woman to hold that position – described this fight for universal dignity and respect that many dominant communities take for granted, but that others are in a constant struggle for, in a commencement address to the College of William & Mary in 2015:

> *I grew up in Birmingham, Alabama, the Birmingham of Bull Connor and the Ku Klux Klan and church bombings, a place that was once quite properly described as the most segregated big city in America.* **I know how it feels to hold aspirations when your neighbors think that you are incapable or uninterested in anything higher** … *We have not and will not quickly erase the lasting impact of our birth defect of slavery, or the follow-on challenge of overcoming prejudices about one another (emphasis added).*[10]

Rice reminds us that our past is something that we can't, and shouldn't, simply forget or tuck away in some dark corner. At the same time, our history does not need to define us.

As in every other sphere of American life, racism and misogyny are critical parts of the story. Too many women and entrepreneurs of color have been written out of our entrepreneurial history – from the earliest days of our country to the present day. Immigrants played, and continue to play, a critical role in building America's entrepreneurial identity. The truth is that the entrepreneurial fabric of our country has always relied on women, people of color, and immigrants. They built great businesses and helped develop the diverse Main Streets that flourished throughout much of our history as a nation. To see the potential of present-day *New Builders*, we need to understand how easy it has been to discount entrepreneurs who don't fit the prevailing model. Because now, more than ever, we need to recognize the role these diverse business owners play in our economy and change how we support and enable them. Our economy has always relied on the success of small businesses, some of which grow and others that stay small. But we're quickly losing sight of that and, in so doing, jeopardize not just our economy but along with it our national identity.

To understand how we got to this place, where we've nearly abandoned the people who are our best hope for building a better future, we need to start with a short trip into the past, on the shoulders of that too long, too complicated, and now seemingly co-opted word: *entrepreneur.* We need to understand how, in the late twentieth century, Silicon Valley and the tech world became, first, the gold standard, and then the *only* standard that mattered for entrepreneurship. And we need to understand that our love affair with size is causing us to forget the power of small. We've also lost sight of one of the most inexorable rules of money: it will flow along the path of least resistance and highest return, which is often to the people who already have it.

What Is an Entrepreneur?

Entrepreneur comes from a French root, *entreprendre,* which means "to undertake," according to *Merriam Webster Dictionary.* The modern concept of an entrepreneur is thought to have originated with French economist Jean-Baptiste Say in 1800. In Say's telling, an entrepreneur is an "adventurer," someone who "shifts economic resources out of an area of lower and into an area of higher productivity and greater yield."

Even before Say, Richard Cantillon, an Irishman living in France at the time he published *Essai sur la Nature du Commerce au General (Essay on the Nature of Commerce),* referred to "entrepreneurs" as those

who produce something at a fixed cost with the intention to sell it at
an unknown price. He also referred to entrepreneurs as "adventurers,"
which maps closely to the language that Say used and is perhaps where
Say took his idea. Cantillon's book was likely the first to outline a complete economic theory – coming some 50 years before Adam Smith's
more famous *Wealth of Nations* (Cantillon's book was published posthu-
mously around 1750, but sections of the work were reportedly widely
read in the 20 years leading up to its publication).[11] Unlike Smith, who
didn't mention the role of entrepreneurs in his seminal work, Cantillon placed entrepreneurship and the role of disruptors at the center of
his economic theory. Cantillon was, in many ways, the pregenerator of
modern economic theory as it relates to entrepreneurship. In his thinking, entrepreneurship stood at the center of economic activity and was
the core from which broader economies developed.[12]

The first serious modern-day academic to think about entrepreneurship was Czech economist Joseph Schumpeter, who identified people –
"wild spirits," he called them – who engaged in what he termed
"creative destruction" in the business sector. It was these individuals
who were responsible for virtually all of the innovation and much of
the growth in the economies he studied. Schumpeter moved to the
United States in 1932 and taught at Harvard University. His ideas of
these wild spirits captured much of what America loved about small
businesses of the middle of the century. He believed change came from
individuals, from within. And the wildness he described suggested this
entrepreneurial spirit could come from anywhere. Indeed, in his view,
anyone could start a business and succeed. This idea fit nicely with
the American ethos of the day and played directly into the long and
deep-seated narrative of America as a land of opportunity, a place of
adventure and risk. It was a land where people were not bound by
the circumstances from which they came, but rather, by what they
made of their natural abilities. It suggested a certain boundlessness to
opportunities and an ability to make or remake oneself. It played to
Americans' love of risk and to our celebration of individualism.

For much of America's history, the vast majority of Americans were
entrepreneurs. Wild spirits colonized the West, built America's cities
and towns, and created the infrastructure that supported commerce and
domestic society. The early days of America found most people pursuing

entrepreneurial ventures. Being industrious didn't set one apart in that time – it was table stakes for survival. And owning a small business, such as a tannery, bakery, or farm, was seen as a pathway to a better life. Consider the many early American novels that revolve around small business owners and entrepreneurs (not always successful ones!) such as Willa Cather's *O Pioneers!* or Booth Tarkington's *The Magnificent Ambersons.*

As in every other sphere of American life, race and gender have always been part of the story – and often a hidden part. It wasn't only Elizabeth Keckley who disappeared from the narrative. William Leidesdorff (1810–1848) was a Black hotel builder who owned an import/export business and a chandlery shop, as well as lumber and shipyards. By the time of his death, Leidesdorff was worth an estimated $1.5 million, and he is believed to have been the first Black American millionaire. Stephen Smith (1796–1873), an enslaved person, eventually became a successful Pennsylvanian lumber merchant and prominent abolitionist. These early, important stories of the success of people of color are often lost in our narrative, as are the stories of the many who have come after them and found success based on their entrepreneurial efforts.

Women-run ventures disappeared from the story in another way: they became part of the backdrop. Many early women-led enterprises, operations like laundry services, boarding homes, and dressmaking shops, were seen simply as an extension of normal household work, not as legitimate enterprises of their own. This has always been a mistake: these women-owned businesses could be sizable, and many required skilled labor, including dressmaking and millinery, that were learned through workplace apprenticeships.

By the late 1800s, patents obtained by women grew at three times the rate of patents issued to men. At least a tenth of urban businesspeople in the mid-nineteenth century were women, and by the early 1900s, there were tens of thousands of women-owned businesses in the United States. The sectors of our economy dominated by women were, and continue to be, undercounted and undervalued meaningful parts of the overall US business landscape.[iv]

[iv] Women have always started businesses across every economic sector imaginable, especially so in today's economy.

Small businesses were their own economic engines, turning people from workers into owners, offering prosperity and a chance to be
an agent of social and economic change. Collectively, the economic
power of these small businesses was enormous, and in some cases, a
threat to larger corporations that tried to use their pricing and sometimes near-monopoly power to dominate industries. These monopolistic
impulses were countered by government and legal action that, while
varied in their effectiveness and intensity, over time largely kept some
semblance of balance between large corporations and small businesses.

This has been the imperfect, sometimes challenging, sometimes
wonderful story of small business and entrepreneurship in America,
right up until the middle of the twentieth century.

Silicon Valley and the Rise of the Giants

By the 1950s, the United States was in the middle of the Cold War and
on a mission to beat the USSR. That effort meant that a firehose of
government funding landed on new and crucial innovations developed
around Stanford University and the defense-related businesses located
nearby. Research and development (R&D) made up 10 percent of the
entire US federal budget for the first half of the 1960s, with the US
federal government spending more on R&D than the rest of the world
combined.[13]

Over the next few years, the pace of innovation in Silicon Valley
meant that investors who poured dollars into the new companies alongside the government were making money at an enviable rate. This was
also true for the other technology hotbed at the time, the area surrounding Boston known as the "Route 128 corridor" because of the
cluster of technology businesses that set up in the office parks just off
the highway. The technology companies spawned during this time by a
scientific establishment that was overwhelmingly White and male were
small businesses, too – but they were a new breed of small business, with
access to endlessly deep pockets, an insatiable appetite for growth, and a
new way of delivering returns to investors.

Ronald Reagan, who owed his rise to power to his ability to
draw support from libertarians and freedom-loving evangelicals, was

well aware of what was going on in the Valley and how he might use it to his political advantage.[v] He declared the 1980s the "decade of the entrepreneur." In 1988, speaking to a crowd of 600 computer scientists in Russia, he said that freedom of thought and information enabled the surge of innovation that produced the computer chip and the PC. "No one better demonstrated the virtues of American free enterprise – particularly the low-tax, low-regulation variety beloved by Reagan – than high-tech entrepreneurs," historian Margaret O'Mara writes.[14]

To turn high-tech entrepreneurship into the perfect vehicle for a newly powerful libertarian ideology, one has to ignore some crucial facts, like the role of government in establishing Silicon Valley and the role of support systems of all kinds in building businesses. But since when have facts ever bothered marketers, politicians, or myth-makers?

As a politician, if you could equate software – easy and cheap – with innovation and job growth, it could safely be outsourced to entrepreneurs and venture capitalists. Democrats could reserve money for social programs. The newly libertarian Republicans could argue for across-the-board budget cuts or a shift in power to the states. And both could take advantage of a new, romantic, politically expedient American hero. An updated version of the lone cowboy: the risk-takers; the entrepreneurs.[vi]

The word *entrepreneur* came to take on a new meaning, a high-tech meaning. And the companies that were important in this new age of entrepreneurship were high-tech companies that often seemed to have one overriding purpose: to deliver returns to investors. They needed to look as if they can be very profitable at a considerable size. They needed to, in the language of the Valley, "scale."

Today, America is home to many big companies, many of them technology businesses that grew out of the Silicon Valley machine. They dominate our country's headlines, mindshare, and financial markets. And the very word *entrepreneurship* has been seemingly co-opted by this tech

---

[v] Reagan was governor of California from 1967 to 1975 and had witnessed first-hand the early rise of what became known as Silicon Valley.

[vi] These ideas were developed in conversations in Spring 2020 with historian Margaret O'Mara and Robert Atkinson, founder of the Information Technology and Innovation Foundation.

elite. We no longer think of the corner shop owner, restaurateur, or tailor as an entrepreneur, as they once were considered. This shifted our thinking about who really drives our economy and who deserves our support. The success of high-tech entrepreneurs hides both the truth and some of the alarming trends taking shape at the small end of the American economy.[vii]

One of the reasons that high-tech entrepreneurship has taken such a hold on our imaginations is that its rise is entwined with the idea that free markets produce the greatest benefit for the most people. Now, the consequences of libertarianism are becoming clearer in the first decades of the twenty-first century, including the negative economic consequences of a society without a safety net. If the underlying assumption is wrong we should question what innovations and founders are being ignored because of a mistaken idea that today's big businesses are the product solely of the private sector and unfettered free markets.

Because, as we discovered when we went out to find and talk to *New Builders*, the real story of American business is about small. Some of the most important businesses stay that way and become part of a collective whole that is far greater than its individual parts. Other businesses grow and create success on a different scale, sometimes measured in terms of profit or sales, and sometimes in other ways, like employment, technological advancement, or influence – but it's very difficult, if not impossible to predict which companies will grow. An environment that supports small businesses, not just a subset of them, is necessary for the economic vitality of the American economy. This is not to take anything away from tech companies, or successful larger businesses from across the business landscape and the convenience they bring to our lives. But it is worth taking a step back to consider what happens to society if the balance between big and small business gets too far out of kilter – if, in our search for convenience and lower prices, we fail to recognize what we're

---

[vii] Both Seth and Elizabeth know the world of technology startups well. Seth is the co-founder of a venture capital firm, Foundry Group, that has been an investor in many successful technology companies. Elizabeth is a long-time business journalist. We celebrate the innovation that comes out of this world at the same time sounding the alarm that our conception of entrepreneurship has been overtaken by it in a way that is counterproductive to our overall economy and hides fundamental truths about the state of our broader entrepreneurial ecosystem.

losing when we give up on small businesses and the unique relationship those businesses have to our communities and to our society as a whole. It will take some work to bring our economy back into better balance. It will also take a realignment in our thinking about entrepreneurship and about the role of small business in our economy.

To start, it will require a new understanding of who the next generation of American entrepreneurs actually are, and how critical it is to support them.

Endnotes

1. "Facts & Data on Small Business and Entrepreneurship," SBE Council, copyright © 2018, https://sbecouncil.org/about-us/facts-and-data/
2. Arti Grover Goswami, Denis Medvedev, and Ellen Olafsen, *High-Growth Firms: Facts, Fiction, and Policy Options for Emerging Economies* (Washington, DC: World Bank, 2019), https://openknowledge.worldbank.org/handle/10986/30800 License: CC BY 3.0 IGO
3. Diana Farrell, "For Small Businesses, Cash Is King," JPMorgan Chase & Co., September 2016, www.jpmorganchase.com/institute/research/small-business/insight-cash-is-king.htm; Alexander W. Bartik, Marianne Bertrand, Zoe Cullen et al. (2020), "Impact of COVID-19 on Outcomes and Expectations," *Proceedings of the National Academy of Sciences* 117, no. 30 (2020): 17656–17666, www.pnas.org/content/117/30/17656
4. Sameeksha Desai and Travis Howe, "Who Doesn't Start a Business in America? A Look at Pre-Entrepreneurship Leavers," *Ewing Marion Kauffman Foundation*, December 3, 2020, https://www.kauffman.org/entrepreneurship/reports/pre-entrepreneurship-leavers-in-america/?utm_source=newsletter&utm_medium=email&utm_campaign=currents-newsletter12_08_2020
5. "The US Startup Is Disappearing," *Quartz*, 2018, https://qz.com/1309824/the-us-startup-company-is-disappearing-and-thats-bad-for-the-economy/
6. Gonzalo Huertas and Jacob Funk Kirkegaard (2019), "US Entrepreneurship Rate Is Mostly Driven by Hispanic Population," *PIIE*, February 11, 2009, www.piie.com/research/piie-charts/us-entrepreneurship-rate-mostly-driven-hispanic-population
7. "Attention Millennials: The Average Entrepreneur Is This Old When They Launch Their First Startup," *Inc.*, 2018, www.inc.com/melanie-curtin/attention-millennials-average-entrepreneur-is-this-old-when-they-found-their-first-startup.html
8. "Older Workers Are the Economy's Most Underrated Natural Resource," *Quartz*, 2018, https://qz.com/1490044/older-workers-are-the-economys-most-underrated-natural-resource/

9. David M. Smick, *The Great Equalizer: How Main Street Capitalism Can Create an Economy for Everyone* (Perseus Books, 2017)

10. Condoleezza Rice, "College of William and Mary Address – May 16, 2015," Commencement address, Iowa State University Archives of Women's Political Communications, https://awpc.cattcenter.iastate.edu/2017/03/09/college-of-william-mary-commencement-address-may-16-2015/

11. Christopher Brown and Mark Thornton, "How Entrepreneurship Theory Created Economics," *Mises Institute*, 2014, https://mises.org/library/how-entrepreneurship-theory-created-economics

12. Ibid

13. American Association for the Advancement of Science, "Historical Trends in Federal R&D," https://www.aaas.org/programs/r-d-budget-and-policy/historical-trends-federal-rd

14. Margaret O'Mara (2019), *The Code: Silicon Valley and the Remaking of America* (New York: Penguin Books, 2019)

CHAPTER TWO

How Change Really Happens

"Come down to my store," Steve Murray said, urgently, one day in the mid-1990s. He'd reached Elizabeth, who at that time was a reporter with the *Lancaster Sunday News*, handling the cops and business beat on a small news staff.

Steve's store was about six blocks up Queen Street, one of the two main streets in the small city of Lancaster, Pennsylvania, about an hour-and-a-half west of Philadelphia. Once prosperous, by the 1980s and 1990s, this historic city in the middle of tobacco country was struggling, having fallen into the familiar narrative of Main Street decline.

Steve never seemed to notice that the world around him didn't match his style. He stood in the middle of his vintage shop in a historic storefront, loving the Deep Throat role he'd given himself. Zap & Co. was filled to overflowing with brooches the size of lobster claws, hats like flying saucers, and floor-length gowns and psychedelic shirts. Inventory that brought to mind Wallis Simpson, Lena Horne, and Cher, all at once.

And to an enterprising reporter, he was about to hand over the super-secret plan for the economic revival of Lancaster City, prepared by business owners involved in a group called the Hourglass Foundation.

The group was goodhearted but blind, Steve thought. Most of them longed for the patriarchal presence of Armstrong World Industries, a giant flooring manufacturer that produced enough linoleum in the mid-twentieth century to pave to the moon. But Armstrong was shrinking, replaced as Lancaster's largest employer by the local hospital. And, as in other cities, Lancaster's downtown was suffering from the lingering effects of White flight to the suburbs.

Steve thought the plan concocted by the big business leaders was *all wrong*. They wanted to tear down the beautiful old department store that anchored the town square for – "get this," he said, his voice dripping with derision – "a chain hotel."[1]

He was a renegade business owner who believed deeply – passionately – that Lancaster was a beautiful place. That the fading Victorian buildings could regain their former glory, that people from big cities would flock to the small downtown if there were good restaurants and more shops like his. Twenty-five years later, and only after Steve's point of view influenced the powers that be, he would prove to be right. Lancaster is in the middle of an economic renaissance.

Today's Lancaster is a vibrant small city, complete with an active downtown, a progressive mayor, and a growing national reputation as a place that has welcomed refugees without abandoning its conservative roots. In February 2018, *Forbes* named Lancaster one of the "10 Coolest US Cities to Visit," describing it as "one of the US's best-kept secrets" and "a cultural hotbed."[2]

Former mayor Rick Gray gave credit where it was due, speaking to the Lancaster newspaper: "Without Steve's foresight a decade before the convention center was built, downtown would not be what it is today."[3]

Dynamic economies are those that are in a constant state of change and motion. Businesses are continually being started, while others are failing and going out of business.[4] A dynamic system is often propelled by innovations and inventions, as well as by new ideas and new ways of doing business. Dynamism is a key ingredient to the overall health of an entrepreneurial ecosystem as well as to our broader economy. But dynamism isn't just defined by growth, as it is often misunderstood to be. It also isn't solely the purview of big businesses or large industries. In fact, it is often the interplay between the small end of the economy and larger companies that provide an economy its dynamic traits – small firms nip at the heels of larger ones, forcing them to be more nimble and innovative; large firms force upstarts to search for new products and markets to gain a toehold. Dynamism is more appropriately understood as change that happens across many dimensions. Size is one dimension, of course, but so are changes in terms of quality, value, and experience, as measured by scales *other* than size and profit.[i]

Steve Murray, like another entrepreneur we'll meet in this chapter, Fred Sachs, was dynamism in action. Zap & Co. never grew large, but Steve was a key actor in creating the long-term vision that would power the city's economy. Without him, the revival of an entire city might never have happened. A vibrant economy thrives on a certain amount of turnover, regeneration, and risk-taking. Old ideas are replaced by new ones, and past ways of thinking and working are overtaken by novel approaches. Dynamism lives in people like Steve: entrepreneurs who run businesses at the smaller end of the business spectrum, but who bring passion and life to new ideas. We have been taking these small businesses – these engines of dynamism – for granted.

Today's *New Builders* share this trait with Murray: they are change-makers and trailblazers. And the numbers bear this out. "Small businesses create two-thirds of net new jobs and are the driving force behind US innovation and competitiveness," reported the SBA in 2018, which tracks business trends for the US government. Small businesses accounted for 44 percent of all economic activity in the United States and were responsible for $5.9 trillion in GDP in 2014, the last year for which complete data are available.[5]

As Steve's story shows, size has only a minor bearing on the power to create change. Sometimes, a small business owner acts alone to create change as an inventor, innovator, or leader. More often and more powerfully, owners act collectively, as employers and community builders, with the results of that collective action being powerful community change.

---

[i] A 2014 Brookings Institute study by Ian Hathaway and Robert E. Litan described business dynamism as "the process by which firms continually are born, fail, expand, and contract, as some jobs are created, others are destroyed, and others still are turned over." Importantly they note that "[r]esearch has firmly established that this dynamic process is vital to productivity and sustained economic growth. Entrepreneurs play a critical role in this process, and in net job creation." See endnote 4 for further information.

But in our collective search for convenience and lower prices, and in our embrace of size, we hardly see small businesses as the economic and community powerhouses they actually are. They are an irreplaceable part of the American experience, often finding creative solutions to everyday problems and bringing energy and focus to critical causes. Small business owners are the people whose passion for something is so crazy that they'll build a livelihood around it. And while they certainly don't have a lock on ethical business practices, you will often find them melding compassion and good business, doing good while doing well, and in many cases employing people on the margins of our society.

These are the reasons supporting *New Builders* is so important. We risk losing so much more than just economic output if we abandon these businesses. We lose a key part of what is in effect the soul of America.

Main Street USA

According to the statistics site FiveThirtyEight, "Main" is the most common street name in America, with 10,902 streets carrying this moniker. Strangely, the second most common street name in America is 2nd Street, followed by 1st Street – which seems counterintuitive but is backed by the data.[6]

The name Main Street has expansive connotations. It evokes nostalgia for smaller towns and simpler living. But, importantly, the idea of Main Street USA isn't just a part of our history and days gone by. It turns out that thriving Main Streets and the robust set of local entrepreneurs who line them, or who operate out of office parks, strip malls, and other clusters, are critical to our economy's future.

The high-tech entrepreneurs who garner so much of our collective attention are a tiny sliver of the small businesses that drive the US economy. Fewer than 1 percent of entrepreneurs are backed by venture capital. Less than 250,000 businesses are "high-tech."

America's army of entrepreneurs includes many Main Street entrepreneurs – people whom we like to think of as grassroots entrepreneurs. Many *New Builders* come from their ranks and create much of the entrepreneurial activity across our nation. In the United States, small business *is* big business. Small businesses employ nearly half of the US workforce, over 60 million people. Smaller firms created over 1.6 million jobs in 2019. Importantly, firms that drove the most job growth were those that employed fewer than 20 people – a trend that matches that of prior years.

In a widely cited 2010 report, The Kauffman Foundation's Tim Kane argued that startups – companies less than a year into their existence – were responsible for essentially all of the job creation in the US economy.[7] In other words, without entrepreneurs, our economy would not add new jobs. The report further notes, "Gross job creation at startups in the United States averaged more than three million jobs per year during 1992–2005, four times higher than any other yearly age group."

There already was a cloud over the US small business economic engine. Even before the Covid-19 pandemic, that same 2018 SBA report that described small businesses as the "driving force behind US innovation and competitiveness" showed that the percentage of overall economic output produced by smaller firms was declining relative to that of larger companies. In the 16 years from 1998 to 2014, the small business share of GDP fell to 43.5 percent from 48.0 percent, according to the report.

This shift away from recognizing the value of small business and the entrepreneurs who build them has occurred over the last 40 years. The Silicon Valley/high-tech narrative is part of the reason. But there have been other changes in our economy that are important to understand as well.

How Big Became Beautiful

On September 13, 1970, economist Milton Friedman published one of the most influential essays in the history of business, "The Social Responsibility of Business Is to Increase Its Profits," in the *New York Times Magazine*. It was, as the *New York Times'* DealBook staff noted in a retrospective published in 2020, "a call to arms for free-market capitalism that influenced a generation of executives and political leaders, most notably Ronald Reagan and Margaret Thatcher."[8]

DealBook's retrospective included reflections from Nobel Prize winners, corporate executives, and entrepreneurs who had grown large companies, but not a single small businessperson. This is the nature of reporting about business today. Serious opinions are the purview of those who have size on their side. That in itself is but one influence of Friedman's essay.

A lot of attention has been paid to Friedman lately, but too little has been paid to the effect of his thinking on the small business economy. In 1970, Friedman posited that shareholders were the most important stakeholders in the business world and, in his view, distributing profits to them was the most efficient economic system. At the time, Americans were becoming owners of public companies' stocks in increasing numbers, a trend that peaked in 2007 with about 65 percent of Americans owning public stock according to the polling firm Gallup. Lately this trend has reversed, with just over half of Americans – 55 percent – owning these securities.[ii]

Friedman's thinking changed the way corporations acted. It was common up until the 1970s for firms to reinvest their profits back into their businesses – into R&D and employee salaries and benefits. In his *Harvard Business Review* paper, "Profits without Prosperity," Professor William Lazonick argues, "From the end of World War II until the late 1970s, a retain-and-reinvest approach to resource allocation prevailed at major US corporations. They retained earnings and reinvested them in increasing their capabilities, first and foremost, in the employees who helped make firms more competitive. They provided workers with higher incomes and greater job security."[9]

After Friedman's seminal paper, the mantra quickly changed to become one that favored reducing costs and distributing the cash gains from those cost reductions to shareholders. Lazonick termed this new management imperative *downsize-and-distribute*.

The new approach favored value extraction over value creation (literally, taking cash out of businesses and putting it into shareholders' pockets). Along with the weakening of the power of labor, the rise of technology, and the increasing use of stock-based compensation, this

---

[ii] A fairly large portion of those who report owning stocks do so through retirement accounts, and most of these holdings are relatively modest, in the range of $25,000 to $30,000.

approach has contributed to increased income inequality and overall employment instability.

As Friedman famously put it, the only "social responsibility of business is to increase its profits." Exacerbating this was the increasing use of stock-based compensation for executives, which, while in theory aligning their interests with those of shareholders more broadly, in practical application served to drive short-term profit-seeking behavior. Not surprisingly, the largest component of the income of top earners (the top 0.1 percent) since the 1980s has been driven by stock-based pay. This has also led to some unwanted market perversions. For example, from 2003 to 2012, the 449 companies of the S&P 500 listed through that entire period of time used the majority – 54 percent – of their earnings (a total of $2.4 *trillion*) to buy back their own stock. If you include dividends paid out during that period, 91 percent of earnings went to shareholders, leaving little left for reinvestment into these businesses.

This profit seeking behavior also had an effect on small business and the overall dynamism of the economy.

Why a Dynamic Economy Is Important

Milton Friedman's theories reshaped corporate practices, resulting in companies that were huge, not in terms of employees but in terms of resources, power, and access to capital. In 1964, the nation's most valuable company, AT&T, was worth $267 billion in today's dollars and employed 758,611 people.[10] Today, Apple is worth more than $2 trillion but has only about 147,000 employees – less than a fifth the size of AT&T's workforce in its heyday.[11]

Simply put, today's entrepreneurs face a nearly impossible uphill climb because large businesses are increasingly unchecked in their market power and profitability. At the same time, rising income inequality means fewer and fewer people have the savings to start businesses, a process that often means forgoing income for several years.

Almost like a living organism or a healthy forest, economies stay healthy by constantly building and changing. New firms are created, established firms grow, and outdated firms fail and close down. It's a balancing act between growth and consolidating market power and new businesses and new ideas nipping at the heels of incumbents. As just one example of this process in action, consider that the half-life of companies on the Fortune 500 list of America's largest corporations is just 20 years, meaning that 20 years from now we can expect 250 from today's list to no longer be among the top 500 companies in the country. This is dynamism at work, and it's a powerful force in our economy.

But there are signs that dynamism in the United States is waning. A 2019 recent study by Ufuk Akcigit, a professor of economics at the University of Chicago, and Sina T. Ates, a senior economist at the Federal Reserve Board, developed a theory as to why dynamism is slowing.[12] They noted 10 factors:

1. Market concentration has risen.
2. Average markups have increased.
3. Average profits have increased.
4. The labor share of output has gone down.
5. The rise in market concentration and the fall in labor share are positively associated.
6. The labor productivity gap between frontier and laggard firms has widened.
7. Firm entry rate has declined.
8. The share of young firms in economic activity has declined.
9. Job reallocation has slowed down.
10. The dispersion of firm growth has decreased.

All of these factors are important, but several have direct implications for *New Builders*. Specifically, increasing market concentration, increasing profits, the correlation between the rise in market concentration and the fall in labor share, new firm entry rate, and the declining share of economic activity from newer firms all describe how larger firms are making up a greater share of the market and wielding more market power.

Many of these factors reinforce one another. Economic activity from newer businesses is going down (factor 8), which is related to the fact that fewer newer firms are being formed and entering the market (factor 7). This leads to a greater concentration (factor 1) and the consolidation of power of incumbent firms (which is causing profits to be increasing – factor 3 – at the same time these firms are relying less and less on labor — factor 4). It's a virtuous cycle. Or perhaps more aptly put, a vicious cycle.

Harvard economist Larry Katz described the increasing concentration of American business as one of the leading factors in the decline of dynamism as well, describing to us that "there has been really big growth in economies of scale ... many traditional businesses can't compete with the large firms."[13]

Of course, businesses create and shed jobs all the time. Critics of the idea that small businesses are an irreplaceable piece of the dynamic American economy have argued that studies that profess the power of small business job growth gloss over job losses incurred by those same startup firms after their first year of operations. The net job numbers for startups include only companies adding jobs; after year one, they include companies that are adding new jobs and companies that go out of business or shrink, in each case, shedding jobs.

Robert Atkinson and Michael Lind argued the case in their book, *Big Is Beautiful*. It's a provocative work that argues that small businesses are in fact not responsible for most of the country's job creation and innovation. In Atkinson and Lind's worldview, the only kind of small firm that contributes to innovation are technology startups – who, they point out, ubiquitously have the goal of becoming big businesses. They believe that the idea that small businesses are the foundation of our economy is a relic of past times and nostalgic thinking. They argue that both consumers and workers are better off buying from, and working for, large businesses. In their view, new small businesses create new jobs; however, they argue that these jobs are lost over time as those businesses eventually close.

While important to acknowledge differing views – especially ones that are well formulated and argued – for us, these arguments fall short and ring hollow. It is absolutely true that businesses fail at a relatively high rate. To us, that is not a limitation of small businesses but, in some regards, a feature to them. Of course, new businesses create a large share of jobs. But to argue that if they simply didn't exist, larger companies would create those same opportunities defies logic and sense. If that were true, larger businesses would be creating new jobs irrespective of what is currently taking place at small companies. Big businesses

would be setting up shop on Main Streets, financing the first chocolatier in Arkansas, or starting a guiding company in the Bob Marshall
wilderness. They are not.

Small businesses have a larger appetite for risk, and by virtue of their
owners' passions, are sometimes willing to live with lower profits. An
economy devoid of small businesses is a flat, uninspired landscape of
sameness. To continue to thrive, America needs both big and small business and grassroots entrepreneurs of all backgrounds to create a living,
vibrant entrepreneurial economy.

To be clear, large companies are important to our economy as well,
and nothing in our experience meeting *New Builders* or in our work
as a venture capitalist and journalist suggests that they're not. But by
abandoning our startup economy, by failing to support *New Builders*,
we risk a critical part of America's economic engine. Importantly, the
struggle we're describing is not one of big business in conflict with small
business. In fact, many of today's biggest businesses sell products and
services to small businesses, which makes the danger even greater. Our
economy is not a zero-sum game and we don't need to choose sides.
In fact, our economy should be viewed as *positive-sum*.[14] The American
economy has thrived with both big and small businesses in balance. That
balance ebbs and flows over time, but we need to recognize that we're
in danger of letting that balance get dangerously, perhaps irreconcilably,
out of whack. Stories of well-loved small businesses closing their doors
because they cannot compete with larger, and larger-than-life, businesses
have become all too common.

Over the past 50 years, the US regulatory and political landscape
has changed significantly. Those changes have generally helped larger
businesses and hurt smaller ones. As much as politicians love to talk
about their love of Main Street and the importance of small businesses,
their actions largely have shown otherwise. So while we don't subscribe
to the blanket "'big is bad" mantra that some in the media like, even
as they celebrate "scale" and high returns, we recognize through our
research and reporting that our systems have become skewed too much
in favor of large businesses. And in the places we've tended to support
smaller enterprises, we've been overly focused on that tiny portion of
new companies that have both the goal and the potential to become
large businesses. In doing so, we've destroyed the level playing field that

fits the entrepreneurial mythology of the American Dream and created one that stacks the odds against grassroots entrepreneurs.

There is another cost to our love affair with big. Over the past decades, we've narrowed our focus as to where innovation happens, and in doing so, we miss seeing where creativity occurs. Especially if it's on a smaller scale.

Innovation Comes from Surprising Places

In our economy many, if not most, innovative breakthroughs are born in small businesses. A few big businesses have defied the odds to remain innovative over time, but almost by definition, big companies work on incremental innovations – an effort to build upon the value of what they already own and often to protect the economic value of past innovations.[15] The importance of small businesses in the process of innovation is one of the reasons that American government and media have showered so much time and attention on Silicon Valley and the technology industry. For a while, the Valley appeared to have a lock on the process of innovation, spawning thousands of small businesses – renamed *startups* in the high-tech world. With a purpose-made system of finance (venture capital, private equity, and the like), Silicon Valley has specialized in killing the startups that don't have fast-growth potential and nurturing the ones that do into big companies – sometimes very, very big companies.

But like our dynamic economy, our much-vaunted engine of innovation is showing signs of slowing down. Today, there are fewer entrepreneurs picking up the baton. We have a much less efficient system for funding ideas and companies because most of our systems of finance remain focused on a particular kind of new business founder: White males starting software or internet businesses. The barriers to women and people of color, as well as those from the lower rungs of our socioeconomic ladder, in particular, remain high, whether they are starting a technology company with the goal of scaling quickly or a business with different, yet equally important, goals. Additionally, class (perhaps better defined as caste) and age are also limiters of entrepreneurship and entrepreneurial vitality in the United States. In the long game of becoming an innovator/entrepreneur, almost the only people who succeed are those who are either born into privilege, or those who are so good at what they do, and so passionate about it that they are able to overcome the systemic barriers stacked against them.

Can You Tell an Innovator When You See One?

Fred Sachs is an inveterate entrepreneur. He bought his first company, a Main Street enterprise in Alexandria, Virginia, called Smoot Lumber, in his late thirties, and started a second one, a commercial door and hardware company, in time to ride Washington, DC's building boom in the 1980s. He sold them both, the first in 1996 and the second in 2008. He then started his third and invested in his fourth venture. In the first, a farm he owns in rural Virginia, he's experimenting with new strains of organic wheat. The second is a Canadian-based startup that is working on developing medical diagnostic devices.

He learns something every time around, he told us. At 76, he's every bit a *New Builder* – and one of his key qualities, which perhaps surprisingly seems to sharpen with age, is the ability to innovate. When Fred interviewed with the consulting firm McKinsey back in 1972, they asked whether he was more innovative or creative. Over the years, he's learned that being an entrepreneur requires both. "Sometimes you have to create a solution to a particular problem; and in other situations you have to innovate in order to get around a particular hurdle. And if you're not going to deal with the problem, you're going to be left behind. You have to continue to change."

Many successful entrepreneurs are older, in their forties, fifties, and beyond – a fact that has been obscured by our obsession with technology entrepreneurship, where founders often skew younger (certainly our myth of the startup founder does). Paul Graham, an investor in entrepreneurs and a co-founder of the famous Silicon Valley accelerator Y Combinator, once quipped that "the cutoff in investors' heads is 32 ... After 32, they start to be a little skeptical."[16]

This certainly maps to how the media portrays startup founders, but a closer look tells a different story. The average age of entrepreneurs when they start their companies is 42, researchers at MIT and the US Census Bureau found. And, perhaps bucking the conventional wisdom of Silicon Valley, the average age of a technology founder is nearly the same: 40.[17]

Interestingly, the time we spent with *New Builders* suggests that entrepreneurs might actually get more innovative as they get older. Early successes free older entrepreneurs to play with ideas, and they often have extensive networks built up over time that they can leverage in new ventures. Innovation and entrepreneurship for many older entrepreneurs seem to become something of a habit.

After Fred Sachs sold his first two companies, he planned to spend time on his small farm in Eastern Virginia. But an entrepreneur's mind is hard to disengage, and before long he was producing organic flour from Virginia-grown grains. First it was a hobby, but quickly his entrepreneurial juices began to flow. By 2018, Grapewood Farm was producing tons of flour, which it sold to regional bakers for upwards of $7.00 a pound, depending on the variety.[iii]

"I think we could probably do twice as much business as we're doing now, because it's unique and people are interested in eating healthy foods and buying local," he said. Meanwhile, he's also working on and investing in his medical diagnostic device business.[iv]

Innovation and Invention; Entrepreneurship and Science

Innovation has a fuzzy definition, and it's often confused with *invention* (also not always crisply defined). For our purposes, we think of innovation as a broad term. Many, if not all, entrepreneurs and especially *New Builders*, are engaged in our innovation economy. Breakthrough

---

[iii] Our interview was conducted outside at Sachs's home in downtown Alexandria, during the early months of the pandemic. Sachs and his wife split their time between Alexandria and the farm, and their sons are also involved in the business. Elizabeth and Fred sat outside a historic brick home, built by Albert Smoot, the grandson of the founder of the Smoot Lumber Company, in the 1930s. Seth joined them on Zoom.
[iv] Sachs runs his businesses using a set of what he calls "Management Musts." These are: (1) spend time identifying, and going after unique market segments rather than embarking on broad assaults on entire industries; (2) segment your business by products, customers, customer services, location; and (3) emphasize profits rather than sales growth.

innovations, like the silicon chip that laid the foundation for Silicon Valley, often take a long time and large amounts of money – from the first germ of an idea in a scientist's lab to market. But once they're realized and in the market, they create huge amounts of economic energy, spawning follow-on breakthroughs and incremental innovations. The spirits of science and entrepreneurship are often entwined, especially in pursuit of these breakthrough innovations. Thomas Edison is a classic example. The phonograph, the motion picture camera, and the light bulb grew out his ability to turn invention into a business process. He found likeminded funders – including Henry Ford (an innovator in manufacturing processes) and Harvey Firestone (the rubber and automobile tire magnate). In the mid-twentieth century, Otis Boykin,[18] who was Black, invented electronic control devices for guided missiles, IBM computers, and pacemakers. It's a sign of how much harder Black innovators had to work that he ended up in a lawsuit with his employer, Chicago Telephone Supply Corporation, claiming the company was trying to steal his early research for the pacemaker. He lost the lawsuit but left CTS Labs to work on his inventions through his own research and consulting company.

While it's easy to pick through history for stories of the genesis of inventions and innovations that we often take for granted in everyday life, it's much harder to imagine innovations that didn't happen. We described a version of this phenomenon in Chapter 1 when we talked about *ghost companies* – those businesses that never got off the ground and whose impact on our society will never be known. That these companies are invisible (they quite literally don't exist) is one of the reasons that they have been easy to ignore.

Much of America's innovation comes from companies at the smaller end of the spectrum. That many of these businesses are failing to come into existence is alarming from an economic perspective, but perhaps even more so as seen through the lens of our innovation pipeline. For example, early in the pandemic, researchers in bioscience and health spoke to us of innovations that they hadn't been able to develop, not because the science wasn't promising, but because they lacked support for projects. These included fast-growing tissue samples for vaccine testing and better ways to build trust for testing and vaccination programs with minority populations. That America is producing fewer new businesses suggests that large swaths of innovation are simply not occurring. Whether it's due to lack of resources, lack of investment in education, training, or a changing relationship with failure that is dampening our entrepreneurial spirit, the fact is by producing fewer new companies our economy is missing out.

The government plays a significant role in funding innovation of the breakthrough kind, especially because breakthrough innovations often don't have the obvious near-term market applications that private-sector investors or corporations like to see. But we have been systematically and methodically underfunding research through government channels over the past decades. In his book *Jump-Starting America*, MIT professor Jonathan Gruber found that although total US spending on research and development remains at 2.5 percent of gross domestic product (GDP), the share coming from the private sector has increased to 70 percent, up from less than half in the early 1950s through the 1970s.[19] Federal funding for R&D as a share of GDP is now below where it was in 1957, according to the Information Technology and Innovation Foundation (ITIF). Measured by government funding for university research as a share of GDP, the United States ranks 28th of 39 nations. Twelve of those nations invest more than twice as much as America does on a proportionate basis.[20]

In other words, the private sector, with its focus on fast profits and familiar patterns – and in the corporate sphere, on maintaining power – now dominates America's innovation spending. Today, even promising entrepreneurs with ideas that lack immediate commercial applications are often abandoned in favor of those with more near-term promise. And evidence is emerging that big companies may be buying smaller ones in order to control (and perhaps time) their innovations.[21]

The Easy Story of the Big Movers

Historically, Americans see themselves as champions of the underdog. There has been a special place in American history for those individuals who, through sheer determination and grit, forged ideas that changed industries and ultimately laid the foundation for new parts of the American economy. We've honored the Main Street entrepreneurs who spent their energy in the interests of building healthy communities, and in so doing, helped keep our economy dynamic. But in recent years, we've seemingly lost that part of our story. We've forgotten to value it. Even worse, we often seem to be actively devaluing it in favor of big business.

A few years before Steve Murray, whose story starts this chapter, died, he helped put on a fashion show at a local nursing home. The elderly ladies put on glamorous floor-length gowns, all silk and taffeta, with peplums and the long silhouettes of the World War II era. A woman named Vanda waltzed down the aisle of folding chairs in a fawn-colored number with sequined shoulders that looked like it ought to be brushing the floor of a New York City nightclub to Tommy Dorsey music. And there, in the back of the room, was Steve, leaning on a clothing rack. He'd lent the dresses to the ladies, and from the smile on his face, it was clear that he was loving every minute of it. He really did have a rare eye for beauty – a gift he lent to his community.

After the story about Steve Murray's role in Lancaster's revitalization was published, the economic development director for the state of Pennsylvania wrote his boss, then Pennsylvania Treasurer Joe Torsella. "Maybe we've been doing economic development all wrong," he said.[22]

But strangely, Steve is being written out of the Lancaster narrative in other places. *New York Times* columnist Thomas Friedman wrote a story about Lancaster's revitalization that celebrated the role of big business people – the very Hourglass Foundation Murray had battled – as the changemakers.

"They realized that the only way they could replace Armstrong (World Industries) and reenergize the downtown was not with another dominant company, but by throwing partisan politics out the window and forming a complex adaptive coalition in which business leaders, educators, philanthropists, social innovators, and the local government would work together to unleash entrepreneurship and forge whatever compromises were necessary to fix the city," Friedman wrote.[23]

The famous anthropologist Margaret Mead acknowledged our propensity to believe that big institutions create change and the reality that they don't when she said, "Never doubt that a small group of thoughtful, committed citizens can change the world; indeed it's the only thing that ever has."[24]

In truth, Lancaster's transformation needed both Murray's cussedness *and* the support and deep pockets of the powers-that-be. But it's the role of the influential changemaker that's getting lost in today's telling of the story. Not all entrepreneurs are in the mold of Steve Murray or Fred Sachs. Many simply want to run their businesses and create a good life for themselves and their families.

But we can't lose sight of the importance of these key *New Builders* who take it upon themselves to lift their entire communities. One of the most important things we uncovered in researching and talking with *New Builders* around the country is the power of an individual visionary in a supportive community. It's easy to ignore individual small businesses because, by their nature, they are small. But together, they comprise a powerful group.

Perhaps this is what is most surprising to learn: just how impactful *New Builders* are in their communities. In a world where business success is too often defined by size and profit margins, these *New Builders* are pushing back and redefining – perhaps realigning – the metrics we use to judge success.

Endnotes

1. Interview with Steve Murray, 1996.
2. Ann Abel, "The 10 Coolest U.S. Cities to Visit in 2018," *Forbes,* February 26, 2018, www.forbes.com/sites/annabel/2018/02/26/the-10-coolest-u-s-cities-to-visit-in-2018/?sh=c29fcf663b55
3. Chad Umbl, "'Stevent' celebrates colorful life of Lancaster retailer, downtown icon Steve Murray," *Lancaster Online*, March 10, 2019, lancasteronline.com/news/local/stevent-celebrates-colorful-life-of-lancaster-retailer-downtown-icon-steve/article_a55a1b5a-42da-11e9-abcb-0f491caa422d.html
4. Ian Hathaway and Robert E. Litan, "Declining Business Dynamism in the United States: A Look at States and Metros," *Brookings,* May 5, 2014, www.brookings.edu/research/declining-business-dynamism-in-the-united-states-a-look-at-states-and-metros/
5. "Advocacy Releases 'Small Business GDP, 1998–2014,'" SBA, 2018, https://advocacy.sba.gov/2018/12/19/advocacy-releases-small-business-gdp-1998-2014/
6. Mona Chalabi, "What's the Most Common Street Name in America?" *FiveThirtyEight,* December 19, 2014, fivethirtyeight.com/features/whats-the-most-common-street-name-in-america/
7. "The Importance of Startups in Job Creation and Job Destruction," *The Kauffman Foundation*, 2010, www.kauffman.org/wp-content/uploads/2019/12/firm_formation_importance_of_startups.pdf

8. Andrew Ross Sorkin, "A Free Market Manifesto That Changed the World, Reconsidered," *The New York Times,* September 11, 2020, www.nytimes.com/2020/09/11/business/dealbook/milton-friedman-doctrine-social-responsibility-of-business.html

9. William Lazonick, "Profits Without Prosperity," *Harvard Business Review,* September 2014, hbr.org/2014/09/profits-without-prosperity

10. Derek Thompson, "A World without Work," *The Atlantic* 316, no. 1 (2015): 50–61, www.theatlantic.com/magazine/archive/2015/07/world-without-work/395294/

11. "Apple," Craft, retrieved January 21, 2021, https://craft.co/apple

12. Ufuk Akcigit and Sina T. Ates, "Ten Facts on Declining Business Dynamism and Lessons from Endogenous Growth Theory," 2019, static1.squarespace.com/static/57fa873e8419c230ca01eb5f/t/5cb32b49439f6700017544fc/1555245899346/AA_tenfacts.pdf

13. Interview with Larry Katz, June 2020.

14. Brad Feld, *Startup Communities: Building an Entrepreneurial Ecosystem in Your City,* 2nd ed. (Hoboken, NJ: Wiley, 2020); and Brad Feld and Ian Hathaway, *The Startup Community Way: Evolving an Entrepreneurial Ecosystem* (Hoboken, NJ: Wiley, 2020)

15. Clay Christensen, *The Innovator's Dilemma* (Boston: HarperBusiness, 2011).

16. Nathaniel Rich, "Silicon Valley's Start-Up Machine," *The New York Times,* May 2, 2013, www.nytimes.com/2013/05/05/magazine/y-combinator-silicon-valleys-start-up-machine.html

17. Pierre Azoulay, Benjamin F. Jones, J. Daniel Kim, and Javier Miranda, "Research: The Average Age of a Successful Startup Founder Is 45," *Harvard Business Review,* July 11, 2018, hbr.org/2018/07/research-the-average-age-of-a-successful-startup-founder-is-45

18. Wikipedia, "Otis Boykin," https://en.wikipedia.org/wiki/Otis_Boykin

19. Jonathan Gruber and Simon Johnson, *Jump-Starting America: How Breakthrough Science Can Revive Economic Growth and the American Dream* (PublicAffairs, 2019)

20. Robert D. Atkinson and Caleb Foote, "U.S. Funding for University Research Continues to Slide," *ITIF,* October 21, 2019, itif.org/publications/2019/10/21/us-funding-university-research-continues-slide

21. Cecilia Kang and Mike Isaac, "US and States Say Facebook Illegally Crushed Competition," *The New York Times,* December 9, 2020, www.nytimes.com/2020/12/09/technology/facebook-antitrust-monopoly.html

22. Interview with Joe Torsella, former PA Treasurer, Spring 2019

23. Thomas Friedman, "Where American Politics Can Still Work: From the Bottom Up," *The New York Times,* July 3, 2018, www.nytimes.com/2018/07/03/opinion/community-revitalization-lancaster.html

24. Nancy C. Lutkehaus, *Margaret Mead: The Making of an American Icon* (Princeton University Press, 2008)

CHAPTER THREE

The Definition of Success

W hen Isaac Collins looked at the kids gathered in the elementary school library, he saw himself. "I grew up a couple of miles away from here," he said. "These kids are me."[1]

The elementary school, the Academy for Integrated Arts, "wasn't in the best part of town," he said. But the hallways were decorated with art, and he was heartened by the stories he was hearing: of progress, of hope. A number of the students had made breakthroughs, especially through an innovative yoga program – one that Isaac helped found and fund – that was brought to the school. Instead of acting out in class, they were learning to calm themselves by taking a break for a few yoga poses. Although it might be counterintuitive to think of groups of elementary kids breaking out into yoga for a quick respite, the program was working. On field trips, the boys in particular liked to show off their poses. The tougher ones, of course, like the chair pose.

Most of the kids were minorities, primarily Black and Hispanic. All the kids had name tags, and the mats fanned out in a circle rather than in rows. The central idea was to teach the kids a way to regulate their emotions and a positive way to play.

A successful restaurateur, Isaac had started the Superhero Yoga nonprofit on the side with two friends, Janis King and Laurie Bomba, to bring half-hour yoga classes to schools in poor neighborhoods. And he loved it – he meditated and practiced yoga himself. But he struggled with what to tell the kids sometimes when he had opportunities to speak with them. He didn't like all the talk about saving people – especially saving Black people. In his mind it wasn't about that. It was about liberating people from a fundamentally wrong system. He wanted the kids to focus on accessing the resources they needed to succeed. He tried to inspire them to do that by telling his own story, as the son of two felons and who was now a successful businessman and community leader – the owner of three Yogurtini stores in the city (with a fourth in the works, despite the pandemic).

"Black people need to know that there's more than what they see around them," he said. "The narrative around the United States is that people of color can't get money, can't find success. It makes it hard for people to want to try."

Isaac has also represented his community by joining the Black Lives Matter protests, speaking out about his decision to the local media. "We're angry but deeper than that – we're scared," he told a reporter who visited his Yogurtini shop on Main Street south of the Plaza. "This is not a game to us. It's not a joke. It's spirit-crushing."[2]

Isaac embraced his role as a community leader. When he looked out at that room full of kids at Superhero Yoga, he knew what a lot of them were living with at home because he had lived with it, too. His parents were hustlers. "Scrappy as hell," as he described it. But for them, part of being scrappy was selling drugs to make ends meet. Both eventually turned their lives around after Isaac was born. Isaac's father became the second Black prison warden in Missouri, and the first without a college degree. His mother became a nurse.

Often, the message Isaac preached to kids was about taking themselves seriously. He'd done just that – writing a business plan at Missouri Western State University, where he attended college, and in so doing, winning a chance in 2012 to buy a Rocky Mountain Chocolate Factory store in partnership with Steve Craig. Craig had a real estate business, owning at one point 13 outlet centers in seven states, and had become a huge donor to Missouri Western.[3] One of the projects he settled on was helping business students at the school that bears his name become their own bosses.

With the help of Craig, Isaac bought the store for $104,000, paid off the debt, and sold it for $300,000. He used the money to get Yogurtini franchises started in Kansas City. He now employs 36 people across his businesses.

Isaac is a role model, a leader, and a successful businessman. Moreover, he loves what he does, creating a place where people gather, where they're served well, and where children delight in putting one of 65 toppings on their Yogurt. For kids, these are gummi worm, maraschino cherry, marshmallow bowls of heaven. He runs a "Books for Yo" program, where kids receive free yogurt for reading.

His work brings him a significant amount of joy. But there are headaches, too: bookkeeping and management, cash flow, and the seasonal ups and downs of running a business whose product is more popular during the summer months. But the good days far outnumber the bad ones, he tells us. "The key to my business is the key to every business. You need to have a good product, but ultimately it needs to be about more. So we are hyper-local in the area of each store. We invest in the community. We have a big emphasis on customer service, on keeping the stores clean, on providing friendly service like opening the door for our customers. We welcome them and treat them like we appreciate them."

Entrepreneurs like Isaac dream big. Big dreams don't necessarily mean size and scale, although Isaac certainly has growth in his sights. But impact is as important to entrepreneurs like Isaac: their role in their communities and their ability to impact the lives of others around them. *New Builders* dream of an idea, passion, or cause and then set out to create a business that reflects this ambition. Often, the role they will play in their community is an integral part of their dream.

Entrepreneurial Dreams

Most entrepreneurial dreams start in parts of the economy that are the most personal, places like restaurants, professional services businesses, and hair salons. At least one in five new businesses started in America are in the food and restaurant sectors or health, beautify, and fitness businesses. Food and restaurants were the most common business started in 2018. They accounted for 11 percent of all business starts, tied with "Business Services," a broad category covering everything from accounting and financial services to people who set up as "consultants" between more traditional jobs. General retail falls just behind at 10 percent of all new business starts, encompassing all sorts of Main Street shops and storefronts, as well as the maker spaces that are turning into mainstays in some communities.

Businesses like Isaac's aren't sexy, but they are found in the sectors of our economy that employ people at far greater rates than the high-flying companies of Silicon Valley fame. In many technology businesses, profitability is the result of how few people they employ relative to their size. For example, Facebook employed just 17,000 people to serve 2 billion users in 2017, compared to the *New York Times*, which, despite job cuts, employed more than 3,500 people to serve its 2.3 million digital subscribers that same year. Operational efficiency, as it is often described, means doing as much as possible with as few people as possible. And by their nature, most of today's high-tech companies are very good at generating revenue with relatively few employees. Not so with the service sector of our economy, especially smaller businesses.

Taken together, these small businesses are the employment and economic engines of our economy and critical infrastructure for our future economic well-being as a nation. Of the 5.6 million employer firms in the United States in 2016, 99.7 percent had fewer than 500 workers. Eighty-nine percent had fewer than 20 workers.[4] Outside health care and government, our main private industry employers pre-pandemic were in retail, leisure, and professional services: 62 million jobs out of 169 million. Companies like Isaac's are the absolute bulwark of the American economy, which means grassroots entrepreneurs like Isaac have to be at the center of our effort to revive the economy after the pandemic.

Owning a grassroots small business that steadily throws off enough profit to invest, or has an asset base that builds over time, remains a solid path to wealth creation – just not as common a path as it used to be. As entrepreneurship in America has declined, so have the fortunes of the middle class. Before 2010, the middle class owned more wealth than the top 1 percent. Not so since that time. As has been widely reported, the share of wealth held by the middle class has steadily declined, while the top 1 percent's share has steadily increased.[5]

The lack of access to entrepreneurial endeavors at least in part explains discrepancies in our society. More than 400 years of disproportionate treatment is a lot to overcome, and our country's long history of educational, economic, and societal inequality has had an enduring toll. The average White family in America has nearly *10 times* the wealth of the average Black or Latino family. Many Black families who have established themselves in the middle or upper-middle class are only one generation into that income and wealth class. Even for Black families who are climbing the education and income ladder, wealth lags. The average Black family where the head of household has a college education has less than one-third the wealth of a similarly situated White family. That same Black family lags in wealth even compared to a White family where the head of household only holds a high school degree. Net worth across income brackets also lags significantly behind for Black families. This is true for every decile of income bracket from top-earning Black families, who have one-fifth the wealth of their top decile White counterparts, to the lowest 20 percent of earners, where Black families have around one-quarter of the wealth of similarly situated White families.[6]

Most Black people have an idea for a business, Isaac told us. "Most of the people I know are trying to do something. If you're Black you have something else going on that you're trying to build – every Black person I know has a business idea, even if they don't have the means to make it happen." In the broader culture, entrepreneurship, once a hallmark of American lore, is deemphasized in almost every aspect of our lives. Little of the entrepreneurial economy's reality or power is reflected anymore in our business media, pop culture, or politics.

The Great Disappearance

Many, if not most, of the top TV shows of the 1970s and 1980s were centered on people who owned their own businesses – George

Jefferson, with his chain of dry cleaners, or Sam, the owner-bartender of *Cheers* – or the lives of people who worked at the local business, like Alice. Even the lone heroes of our earlier pop culture were often self-employed – like Marcus Welby, or Magnum PI. Who else would have the wherewithal to go off and solve a mystery or track down a killer, other than somebody who didn't have a boss to answer to?

Forty years later, after a long period in which much of the best pop culture explored the way that increasing corporatism and growing materialism was affecting American families – *The Wonder Years* or *King of Queens* – or went full-out into dystopia or science fiction, you have to look hard to find entrepreneurs in today's pop media. There's the animated *Bob's Burgers*; or *Atlanta*, in which a Princeton dropout manages the hip-hop career of his cousin; or the occasional self-employed lawyer who turns up as the main character of a TV series. But many protagonists of today's hit shows either don't seem to have a recognizable source of income or are part of the larger corporate machine.

Pop culture reflects a lot more than just the norms of economic life. And a lot of great culture in the past few decades has explored the realities of gender, race, and sexuality hidden under the mainstream narratives of the middle of the century. Entertainment and culture also have become fractured so that fewer TV or movie producers are trying to capture the experiences of a broad swath of Americans.

But perception follows reality. Heroes, whether they're comedic, dramatic, or tragic, matter. And, while the majority of working Americans are still entrepreneurs – people working in or for small businesses – or people who have an entrepreneurial venture on the side, very little of our culture today reflects that. Neither does our support system for entrepreneurs reflect the reality of who they are or what businesses they're starting.

Meanwhile, people do keep going into business – just fewer and fewer of them. And in many cases, they're motivated by a passion that is at least on par with their motivation for material success, if not ahead of it. Many of the *New Builders* we profile blend a strong drive for business success with something beyond just money, whether that's a love for the land of their ancestors such as the Cheff family who operate a guiding business in The Bob Marshall Wilderness (whom we'll meet in Chapter 11), or becoming the first certified chocolatier in Arkansas, like Carmen Portillo (whose story we'll recount in Chapter 9). Many grassroots entrepreneurs start their businesses with an ulterior motive – something about their community or the world they want to see happen – and build a business around it.

Innovation, invention, and big dreams are what drive entrepreneurs. But those dreams can only be realized with some key ingredients, the most important of which is pretty basic: money.

It's About Capital. Hard Stop.

That Isaac was able to garner the outside capital he needed to get his start in business sets him apart from most aspiring business owners. The majority of American entrepreneurs don't have access to any outside capital to start or grow their businesses. Eighty percent of entrepreneurs lack access to either a bank loan or to venture capital, according to the Kauffman Foundation. This "capital gap" is a significant drag on US entrepreneurship and leaves would-be entrepreneurs few options for funding their ventures. Almost 65 percent rely on personal and family savings for startup capital, and nearly 10 percent use personal credit cards for credit for their businesses. This has meaningful implications on who can access capital to start a business, especially when considered in the context of the racial wealth and economic gaps. It's also significant to the question of which businesses are able to survive, especially in times of crisis such as the Covid-19 economic recession.[8]

Back in 2010, Chris Cain, a longtime community development executive and advocate for entrepreneurs, directed a small business development center for the Small Business Association (SBA) in Richmond, Virginia. She taught classes and helped workshop business ideas. About 80 percent of the people who came to the free classes were women of color.

Many had inspiring stories: they had left abusive relationships or were trying to put food on the table for children. With a talent or an idea for a business, they wrote business plans to get themselves off the ground.

It was brutal, Cain says. "You'd get an amazing business plan written and then go to a traditional bank and not get funded. I had no way of being able to help my clients get access to capital. They would have to save money or borrow money from friends."[9] In Chapter 8 we'll talk more about just how meaningful this discrepancy in access to lending capital actually is. Black and brown entrepreneurs are disadvantaged at every step of the process. They seek smaller loans than their White counterparts, they are turned down at higher rates, they receive less favorable terms, and they are more likely to be approved for smaller loans amounts. All of this is perhaps why Black and brown founders are less likely than White business owners to even apply for a loan in the first place.

When entrepreneurs launch businesses despite a lack of startup capital, they start out behind. In 2019, pre-Covid, the JPMorgan Chase Institute found that in the typical community, 29 percent of small businesses were unprofitable, and 47 percent had two weeks or less of cash liquidity. Communities with a greater number of non-White residents and lower home values had a higher proportion of unprofitable businesses.[10]

The Covid-19 crisis laid bare how the United States was falling short in supporting this most critical segment of our economy and the foundation of our economic future. In fact, perception has traveled so far from reality that when the US Congress designed the Covid relief packages that were specifically meant to help small businesses keep employees, the legislation was written in such a way that it failed to include many independently owned restaurants and storefront businesses, which are, as a group, the economy's largest employers, and who should have been front and center to any relief package.

By the time the legislation was passed, many undercapitalized restaurants had already laid off employees. There was no sense in taking out a no-interest loan – remember, those loans needed to be repaid – if there was little likelihood of reopening at all. The question of rent, the single biggest fixed cost for many entrepreneurs, wasn't addressed. The legislation also favored companies that had existing relationships with banks or who were sophisticated enough to access other forms of capital. Is it any wonder that, while it provided a short-term benefit to some, the

$3.5 trillion CARES Act did too little to help small businesses in the long term? Many didn't survive.

As winter of 2020 loomed, the community of Akron, Ohio, tried to take matters into its own hands. It had given out more than $5 million in direct grants through the CARES Act. But the challenges of small businesses accessing relief under the aid packages loomed large for the region. More than 90 percent of the 13,262 employers in Akron in 2018 had fewer than 50 employees. But together they employed as many as 160,000 people.

"To permanently lose 20 to 30 percent of them would be catastrophic," said James Hardy, the deputy mayor for integrated development, referring to Akron's small business base. "Particularly when you consider that Akron had only recently 'recovered' from the Great Recession of 2008–2009. Meaning we had returned to pre-recession job numbers."[11]

Local leaders are better aware of the role of small businesses as employers. As Hardy put it: "[Losing those small businesses] would be a gut punch to thousands of local residents and entrepreneurs. One that could set them and their families back for a generation. Sixty percent of Akron residents live paycheck to paycheck; or worse.[12] We know from this and other research that Black and female workers and business owners will continue to be hit the hardest."

The city was spending $200,000 on a new app – the city's version is called Akronite – to encourage residents to shop locally. About 2,600 people had signed up so far to earn "blimpies" and redeem the rewards for cash, one-on-one, at small businesses.[i] Hardy expected the investment in the app to pay off in higher spending at local businesses. But the biggest benefit was that small business owners might think that somebody cares. "They're scared and frustrated," Hardy said.

So was he.

If the pandemic made clear how vulnerable and underappreciated America's entrepreneurs have become, the spotlight and the next few years offers an opportunity to change the narrative. If we're going to rebuild, we need to let go of a few mindsets. Too much focus has been

---

[i] Akron is the rubber capital of the world and the home of Goodyear, the maker of the Goodyear blimp.

put on determining which entrepreneurs have the best chance to grow their businesses into large companies. This winner-take-all attitude belies the fact that most entrepreneurs are building more modest businesses and working at a much more local, grassroots level. They are an army of sorts, leading a revolution that continues from a centuries-long tradition in America of embracing grassroots entrepreneurship and supporting local and community businesses. We need to create an environment in our country that will help a much broader set of entrepreneurs to thrive.

In the fall of 2020, even one of the country's staunchest advocates for big business, CNBC's Jim Cramer, took to the airwaves to plead for more federal aid to help small businesses. Darden Group, the parent company of Olive Garden, was thriving because it had access to capital and the resources to implement technology across its chains. There's nothing wrong with Darden Group, Cramer said. "But do I want to eat out at Olive Garden every time?"[13]

No. And most people don't want to walk down Main Street where every shop is a chain, either. As the pandemic rolled on, Milton Friedman's singular focus on profits and growth to the exclusion of other values seemed to have reached its natural conclusion: *Free to Choose* doesn't look so appealing if every choice is the same.

Luckily, while the United States is remembering the value of small business, the entrepreneurs of America are continuing to be what they always have been: the most determined group of people you could ever hope to meet.

Endnotes

1. Quotes from interviews with Isaac Collins, July 2020 and October 2020.
2. Tommy Felts, "I'm Black and a Plaza Business Owner in That Order; Why a Main Street Entrepreneur Joined KC's Protests," *Startland News,* June 2, 2020, www.startlandnews.com/2020/06/isaac-collins-kansas-city-protests/
3. Alex Flippin, "Who Is Steven Craig?" *News Press*, July 14, 2016, www .newspressnow.com/news/local_news/who-is-steven-craig/article_472e12e4-4a07-11e6-9370-5f0bc1379fa4.html
4. Small Business and Entrepreneurial Council, "Facts and Data on Small Business and Entrepreneurship," https://sbecouncil.org/about-us/facts-and-data/
5. Isabel V. Sawhill and Christopher Pulliam, "Six Facts about Wealth in the United States," *Brookings*, June 25, 2019, www.brookings.edu/blog/up-front/2019/06/25/six-facts-about-wealth-in-the-united-states/

6. Dion Rabouin, "10 Myths about the Racial Wealth Gap," *Axios*, July 23, 2020, www.axios.com/racial-wealth-gap-ten-myths-d14fe524-fec6-41fc-9976-0be71bc23aec.html

7. Ibid

8. Ewing Marion Kauffman Foundation, *Access to Capital for Entrepreneurs: Removing Barriers*, 2019, www.kauffman.org/wp-content/uploads/2019/12/CapitalReport_042519.pdf

9. Interview with Chris Cain, Summer 2020.

10. JPMorgan Chase & Co. Institute, *Place Matters, Small Business Financial Health In Urban Communities,* 2019, institute.jpmorganchase.com/content/dam/jpmc/jpmorgan-chase-and-co/institute/pdf/institute-place-matters.pdf

11. Series of email interviews with James Hardy, Fall 2020.

12. "ALICE in Adams County," *United Way* ALICE Report – Ohio, 2016, http://ouw.org/wp-content/uploads/2018/11/18UW_ALICE_Report_COUNTY_OH_8.29.18.pdf

13. Kevin Stankiewicz, "Olive Garden Parent Darden Is 'More Attractive' the Longer the Pandemic Drags, Jim Cramer Says," CNBC, September 24, 2020, www.cnbc.com/2020/09/24/jim-cramer-says-olive-garden-parent-darden-is-a-buy-during-pandemic.html

CHAPTER FOUR

More than Grit

In her *New York Times* bestselling book, *Grit: The Power of Passion and Perseverance*, psychologist and researcher Angela Duckworth described this key ingredient for success. *Grit,* in Duckworth's telling, is the "tendency to sustain interest in and effort toward very long-term goals." It is passion and persistence applied to long-term ideas without specific regard or concern for rewards along the way. It's an internal, self-generated, and self-motivated belief that one can and will be a success. That you will do whatever it takes to turn your vision into reality.

Entrepreneurs have a certain drive and motivation that sets them apart from others. Business owners, especially women, immigrants, and people of color, persevere against incredible challenges due to their passion and belief about what they are doing. It's almost universally not ego-driven, in the sense that entrepreneurial drive is not typically the result of true hubris (though hubris sometimes accompanies it). It's more of a raw sense of determination and belief in one's own abilities.

The kind of grit required to build a business is almost maniacal in its focus and obsessive in its pursuit. *New Builders* possess this self-assuredness and determination in spades. It's something we celebrate in American culture – that anyone can come from any circumstances to rise above and become successful – and that has particular meaning in the world of entrepreneurship, which places tremendous value on the idea of meritocracy.

Not surprisingly, *Grit* became an almost instant darling of the Silicon Valley entrepreneurial world. Angela Duckworth's TED talk on the subject is one of the most viewed of all time, perhaps because most people in Silicon Valley like to think of themselves as possessing traits that are somehow special and different. In some ways, they are special – they've likely won the genetic lottery (the vast majority of Silicon Valley founders are White males, as are the venture capitalists who back them), but we aim to show in this book that they're not different.

There are entrepreneurs all over the country working on businesses as varied as you can possibly imagine that have the grit and drive to succeed. People start businesses because they have an idea they're passionate about. Because they want to be their own boss and take control of their own destiny. For some, it's a potential way out of their circumstances and a path to a better life. For others, it comes from a passion seated deep within themselves, or an idea that they've been thinking about for their entire lives.

But *New Builders* face a different set of obstacles and challenges as they build their businesses than the mostly White, male entrepreneurs that came before them. Women shoulder a greater burden taking care of children as well as household chores and activities, leaving their attention and time stretched between their business and other obligations. Women and people of color are less likely to have banking and other relationships critical to funding their enterprises. They hold less wealth and have less equity in their homes – critical means to gain access to startup capital. As a country, we've slowly been dismantling the system of community banks and local financial institutions that are more likely to loan money based on relationships, replacing them with national scale banks or technology firms that in many cases lack meaningful local connections, even if they do have local branches.

We can see these disparities in our response to the Covid-19 crisis. Initial relief money authorized by Congress failed to reach many women- and minority-owned businesses. The story told by Sky Kelley, a Black woman who founded a business-to-business marketing platform for supply chain companies, Los Angeles–based Avisare, is typical. The company, with fewer than 15 employees, applied for an emergency

Economic Injury Disaster Loan (EIDL — part of the massive initial Covid relief package passed by Congress) from the SBA. Then, the loan application stalled. As the weeks went on, her recourse was to call the SBA help desk, sometimes multiple times a day. Unfortunately, the people operating the help desk were not particularly helpful and couldn't provide updates on her application. She couldn't figure out if something had gone awry, but the rules said small businesses would be disqualified if they reapplied.

"Three months, the only answer we could get was that it was in process," she explained to a Congressional panel organized by the Center for American Entrepreneurship. By the time the approval came through, she had already taken an Entrepreneur-in-Residence position at Nike. Now, she's splitting her time between her EIR role at Nike, and working on Avisare full time.[1]

The federal aid package, known as the Payroll Protection Program (PPP), passed as part of the early-pandemic CARES Act, required businesses to work through SBA-approved lenders, including big banks and Silicon Valley firms that quickly applied for and became lenders. But women- and minority-owned businesses were less likely to have relationships with either of those types of lenders. As Kelly experienced, there was no one she could call.

Adding insult to injury, the program's initial rollout failed to include community development finance institutions (CDFIs), one of the key avenues for low-income entrepreneurs to obtain loans. It also left much of the underwriting criteria up to the banks themselves, which often favored other customers. And the program design — based on W2 payroll and primarily benefiting businesses that were in a position to open up quickly — failed to address the kinds of businesses most likely to be started by the *New Builders* of the world.

Our failure to change the way we're funding, mentoring, and supporting entrepreneurs to match today's *New Builders* is one of the key reasons economic mobility has declined so sharply in the United States. We can change this trajectory, but it's critical that we act quickly and decisively to lower the barriers to starting businesses and even the playing field between large and small companies.

As the writer Hugh Prather aptly put it, "There is a time to let things happen and a time to make things happen." *New Builders* understand that most of their time needs to be spent doing the latter. A few, however, stand out among the rest for the sheer incredibility of their determination.

Relentless Pursuit

Jasmine Edwards has an easy style and a firm tone; a confidence that, once you get to know her better, maps perfectly to the substitute classroom teacher that she once was. Approachable and formidable at the same time, she comes across as someone likely to succeed.

Jasmine developed her love for business, as well as her scrappiness, at an early age. Among Jasmine's earliest memories of childhood were her visits to her grandmother in Cleveland, Ohio, where Jasmine grew up. Jasmine's grandmother was an artist, and Jasmine and her cousins canvassed their neighborhood selling her artwork. This was a practical endeavor – her family used the extra money they earned selling art to buy necessities. "My grandmother really inspired me to be an entrepreneur," Jasmine explains, "I've always had the desire."[2]

Like many entrepreneurs, particularly women entrepreneurs, her career hasn't been linear. Her business ventures varied – from marketing and communications to jewelry. Sometimes she would combine her business with her life, like when she sold jewelry at her community college at the same time she was teaching jewelry-making to kids. Often she combined multiple jobs and internships – all to gain experience and make ends meet. But from the beginning, Jasmine knew she had bigger plans. "I always had this feeling that my creativity and my ideas – the way that I could change the world - was bigger than the confines of the position that I was in at the time," she said.

Eventually, she worked her way through a master's program in entrepreneurship and applied technologies from the University of South Florida. Her friends scratched their heads at the mention of it at the time (she started the program in 2013) – back then, the idea of a master's in entrepreneurship was a novel concept. Few people in Jasmine's circle of friends realized entrepreneurship was a subject in which you could receive an advanced degree.

Along the way, she had worked as a substitute teacher and a human resources manager in charge of hiring substitute teachers at a public school district. A few years later, after her graduation, she sought out work as a substitute again. But this time around, she realized how broken and fragmented the market for substitute teachers was:

> *I just started to notice things, like how hard it is to find substitute jobs. I was finding myself driving around to different schools to put in 15 different applications and then managing call-backs and potential openings manually. They would literally just call me in the morning if they needed someone. Sometimes no one would call; other times, I'd get five calls for the same day. You never knew.*

Meanwhile, she also recognized how badly the schools, especially in poor districts, needed high-quality substitutes. From this lived experience, a business idea was born: i-Subz was to be the solution to the mess that was the substitute teacher market. It was part marketplace, part job board, but more complicated than that given the licensing requirements involved. i-Subz would bring efficiency to this market and cut out the surprisingly large amount of bureaucracy and paperwork required for a school to bring a sub into the classroom. As the concept began to germinate in Jasmine's mind, she knew she needed help turning the idea into a business.

Here's where her grit and determination really started to shine through.

Doing What It Takes

Almost no entrepreneur is successful on their own. The mythology we've created about the solo entrepreneur – embarking on their venture alone and succeeding through nothing but personal grit and determination – ultimately works to the detriment of America's entrepreneurial dynamism. By perpetuating the false narrative of the lone founder who succeeds through sheer force of will or personality, we may be playing into America's love of individualism and late infatuation with libertarianism, but it doesn't reflect the truth about how businesses actually become successful. It is simply not true that successful businesses can be started in a vacuum, without the support of a broader community of advisors and mentors. Not to mention the infrastructure of finance and education systems that have a role in almost all companies, no matter their size, focus, background, or trajectory.

Jasmine heard of a program that was set up to help women of color: digitalundivided. The founder, Kathryn Finney, an entrepreneur herself (she sold a women's blogging network she had founded in the 2000s), set out to create a platform that would help accelerate similarly situated entrepreneurs on their own journeys. Finney eventually built a web of support for women of color and a body of insight and research about these entrepreneurs, something we'll discuss in more detail in Chapter 14.

For Jasmine, who had only an idea and the beginning of a plan, but nothing that a traditional funder would support, digitalundivided was a ray of hope. But there was a catch – and a big one. The digitalundivided program was in Atlanta, almost 500 miles away from her home in Tampa, Florida. For Jasmine, living with her husband and their three children, it would be a herculean effort to make the program work for her, even though digitalundivided was designed for flexibility around jobs and family.

Jasmine recalled telling her husband: "Hey, if I apply and get in, I have to go do this thing. We've got to do whatever it is that we need to do."

Interestingly, she applied to the program with a different idea than i-Subz. She had incorporated i-Subz and had been working through the concept but felt it was too early for digitalundivided. She had another project that she had been thinking about as well – one around sustainable fashion – and decided to apply with that instead. When considering applications for their programs, accelerators typically evaluate the *entrepreneur* more than the idea. In fact, most are quite public about this focus on team. And for good reason, as many businesses change pursuits mid-program. Quite frequently, companies come into a program with one idea only to find themselves working on something completely different by the end. In some respects, this is one of the superpowers of accelerators. Through market feedback and mentor advice, they can quickly help entrepreneurs understand whether their business is likely to see early market traction (and thus have a chance at succeeding) or not.

Funding herself with a credit card – she left her job to participate in digitalundivided – and commuting every week to Atlanta from Tampa,

Jasmine embarked on an entrepreneurial journey of determination and grit that stands out even among the many such stories that accompany *New Builders*. In 2018, she essentially moved to Atlanta during the week, leaving her husband to care for the couple's three children, then ranging in age from five to just over one year old. "Romaine [Jasmine's husband] was all in," she told us. "He knew I had this passion from the time we met and understood this was the path I had to follow." But that was just the first step in Jasmine's commitment to her business.

Ghost Startups

Jasmine had an idea for a technology company. If it was successful, it had a large market: public school systems. And, it was solving a clearly demonstrated problem of matching substitute teachers to schools who need their services. Unlike grassroots entrepreneurs such as Steve Murray, Isaac Collins, or Danaris Mazara, she could seek funding from equity investors – people who take an ownership stake in a company in the hopes of high returns.

But access to capital in the United States varies significantly for entrepreneurs from different demographic groups. This is especially true for technology businesses funded by angel or venture investors. Women receive only a fraction of venture dollars (2.2 percent in 2018, according to *Fortune*) compared to male company founders. And startups led by Black women have raised even less, only about 0.06 percent of total venture dollars invested between 2009 and 2017, according to digitalundivided's ProjectDiane. Black women may be the fastest-growing segment of new business founders, but in the world of tech startups and venture capital, they might as well be invisible. Of the nearly 7,000 funded startups in 2017 tracked in the latest ProjectDiane report, fewer than 4 percent were led by a Black woman. When Black women do raise funding, it tends to be in significantly smaller amounts than other entrepreneurs. Only 34 Black women raised more than $1 million in funding in 2017, for example. And, excluding those 34 companies, the average amount raised by a startup led by a Black female founder was just $42,000. That compares with the average seed capital raised across all startups of over $1 million.[3]

These trends hold true, if they're a little less extreme, for *New Builders* accessing other forms of capital. As a community, people of color are underbanked in the United States and lack the relationships with capital institutions that can lead to loans or other forms of debt capital. Some 20 percent of Black Americans don't have a bank account, according to FDIC data. And our banking system does a poor job of funneling money to Black and brown entrepreneurs, who are turned down at higher rates than their White male counterparts and receive a far lower percentage of the capital they are trying to raise. And with the median wealth of Black and Hispanic families nearly 10 times lower than that of White families in America, funding from relatives for founders of color is significantly harder to come by.

While capital isn't the only ingredient to a successful enterprise, it is clearly a critical factor. Given the wealth discrepancies in America and the fact that most businesses are either self-funded or funded through a network of family and friends, this lack of funding has created what we term a *capital gap* when it comes to *New Builders*. This capital gap is a massive contributor to the discrepancies in opportunities for businesses founded by women and, in particular, for people of color.

Addressing this capital gap is absolutely critical if we are to continue to thrive as an entrepreneurial economy. The capital gap contributes to the phenomenon of what we termed *ghost startups* in Chapter 1 – businesses that never existed because a founder couldn't access the capital or resources necessary to get it off the ground. One of the key contributing factors to the decline in new business starts just after the Great Recession of 2008–2009 was the significant decrease in wealth, especially in the value of real estate, which is a critical source of stored value for founders looking to fund their businesses, caused by the recession.

To put this question of access to capital in perspective, consider: the median amount of venture money raised by a technology business started by a Black woman in 2017 was $0.

Jasmine Edwards understood these capital odds as she entered digitalundivided.

Sometimes It's the Journey That Counts

Jasmine had hoped to secure at least a small amount of seed capital to see her through. "But that's just not how it often works for Black women," she said later. Instead, having left her job to focus full time on her company, she maxed out her credit cards and ultimately moved her family back into her parent's house so they could make ends meet on her husband's salary.

"And by move into my parent's house, I mean move into a single bedroom in my parent's house. Me, my three kids, and my husband. It was tight," she said.

All while she worked on her company. To hear her describe it, it wasn't a sacrifice as much as it was a calling. "Either we're all in or we need to get out right now," was how she thought about it at the time.

She was all in.

"I had to do that. There were no other options if I wanted to move forward. It is a long way before you get funding … you have to be scrappy, you have to sacrifice, and you have to find a way to get where you are going."

The power of Jasmine's story isn't in its ending so much as the journey she took. It would be great to report that i-Subz has turned into a meaningful business, scaled quickly, and attracted large amounts of investment capital. But that's not what happened. Jasmine had more than 200 substitutes on the platform, had signed up three paying schools, and placed teachers who served more than 2,000 students. But she couldn't raise the seed funding needed to sustain the business through its early stages. Ultimately, she had to shut it down.

Jasmine took a job working for digitalundivided, helping other entrepreneurs turn their seeds of ideas into something more. Eventually, she tells us, she'll be back to try her next startup idea. And that is the very essence of the *New Builders*.

In entrepreneurial America, failure is partly a badge of honor and one of the things that has set the entire US economy – not just Silicon Valley – apart from the rest of the world. But what the data show is a much bigger failure – one that's not a badge of honor. In the United

States, our current systems are failing many of the most promising entrepreneurs of today. If you want to understand more about why, you need to follow the money. We'll do just that throughout the remainder of the book, going back to where we started: Danaris Mazara in Lawrence, Massachusetts.

Endnotes

1. Details of Sky Kelly's experiences are from public records as well as several emails between the authors and Sky in the fall of 2020.
2. Jasmine related her story to us in a series of interviews we conducted in the Spring and Summer of 2020.
3. "ProjectDiane2018," *digitalundivided*, 2018, http://www.projectdiane.com/

PART II

How We Got Here / What We're Up Against

"I have not failed. I've just found 10,000 ways that won't work."

Thomas Edison

CHAPTER FIVE

Opportunity When You Don't Expect It

S weet Grace Heavenly Cakes was born in 2008, as the Great Recession ripped through our country, particularly affecting working-class communities like the one in Lawrence, Massachusetts. Danaris Mazara can identify the exact minute the bakery was born, in fact. She was lying on her couch, staring at the drop-ceiling of her rented house, $37 worth of food stamps to her name.[i]

In fact, it wasn't even *her own* $37 in food stamps. Her mother had stopped by earlier in the day to offer her support. "I know you are going through a hard time," she said, handing them to her daughter.

Danaris's shift at Samsung started soon, but that job wasn't enough to pay for rent and food. Her husband, Andres, was out of work and sliding into depression. The closure of Haverhill Paperboard, a local manufacturer that had been operating for over 100 years, cost him and 173 others their jobs. They'd lost their house and declared bankruptcy

---

[i] Our interviews with Danaris, David Parker, and Desh Deshpande took place between Spring 2019 and Fall 2020. Some were in person, some were by phone, and as the pandemic hit, others were by Zoom. On the first visit with Danaris in person, she served as an informal tour guide to one of the Dominican streets of Lawrence, and insisted on buying lunch, a traditional and delicious Dominican fish stew.

as the Great Recession of 2008–2009 came barreling down on the new lives the couple, immigrants from the Dominican Republic, had built in Lawrence.

"What are you going to do with $37 in food stamps?" Danaris asked herself. "In a couple of days, you won't have anything to feed your family because that is not enough money to buy groceries."

Their baby daughter, Grace, was asleep nearby. She had been conceived after a string of miscarriages. Danaris desperately wanted to stay home to care for her newborn but the family couldn't afford to lose her income. This balancing act, baby, factory job, depressed husband, was not for her. She was sure this was not the life she was meant to be leading.

Danaris believes in God, and at that moment, a divinely inspired thought came into her head: make flan.

The funny thing is that Danaris didn't know how to make flan. In fact, she thought God was joking with her. But she had a niece famous for the custard topped with caramelized sugar, so she called her to ask for the recipe. It might not have been what her mother had in mind for her to spend the food stamps on, but Danaris believed she was responding to a calling, and spent the $37 on the ingredients she needed to start baking.

The first batch was ruined, burned beyond saving (or eating). She stood by the oven, crying. "I was like, God just told me to do this, and look." Then she reminded herself, firmly, not to give up.

She fared better with her next batch. "They came out so beautiful," she remembered. The tops were dark brown, and the bottoms a perfect buttery yellow. She cut the flan in pieces, put them in small containers, and took them to work at Samsung. To her surprise and amazement, they flew off the break table for $6 apiece.

She made flan every day for a month, turning that initial $37 in food stamps into over $500. It was 2009, and she had a business on her hands if she could only figure out what to do next. But she faced many challenges, not the least of which were her limited English and a husband who didn't – then – believe in her. She was like many *New Builders*, especially women, women of color, and immigrants: the odds were stacked high against her. And she had little in the way of a network to help. But, she had friends, as well as a gift for making more. And she had at least one critical piece of luck on her side, though it probably didn't feel lucky at the time: she lived in Lawrence, Massachusetts, a place *Boston Magazine* referred to as the "city of the damned."

> *Crime is soaring, schools are failing, government has lost control, and Lawrence, the most godforsaken place in Massachusetts, has never been in worse shape. The public school system is in receivership. Public-safety cuts have been drastic, and felony crimes have skyrocketed from 1,777 in 2009 to 2,597 during the first 11 months of 2011. Unemployment is as high as 18 percent, compared with the state average of less than 7 percent. With 76,000 people squeezed into 6.93 square miles, violent crime on the rise, and a public school system that's the worst in the state, the once-proud "Immigrant City" has become an object lesson in how to screw things up.*[1]

But the magazine was missing what was happening at the same time: the Hispanic community in Lawrence, especially the women, were starting businesses. By 2016, an estimated 40 to 60 percent of the businesses in the community were owned by Hispanics, with both Dominicans and Puerto Ricans having a big presence in the city. And these new businesses were seemingly in it together – building up by leaning on each other.[2]

Some patterns hold true across the years in American life. From the late 1800s, when the mills were the source of prosperity in this part of the country, the wealthy owners and managers have always lived in Andover while the workers lived in the mill towns of Lawrence and Lowell. From across the river in Andover, a couple named Jaishree and Desh Deshpande were watching what was happening in Lawrence. From their prosperous vantage point, they'd been increasingly troubled by Lawrence's disintegration. Out of Desh's experience as one of the most successful entrepreneurs of the telecom industry in the 1990s, the idea for a unique business accelerator was percolating. In 2010, they launched the organization that would become Entrepreneurship for All.

But Danaris didn't know about that – yet.

She had learned how to make flan expertly from her cousin, from YouTube tutorials, and from lots of experimentation. Years later, at her storefront bakery, she is still selling small containers of flan – paying homage to where things all started for her. By selling flan on the side, she was bringing in income to supplement her work at Samsung and the job Andres was able to get eventually at American Airlines.

It was a start, but still not enough to make ends meet. A friend of hers, Ruth Rojas, was working with a credit counseling company. Ruth's deep ties in the community meant she was a connector, and she offered to introduce Danaris to a woman who knew how to bake cakes. Generously, that friend-of-a-friend offered to teach Danaris what she knew. Three Saturdays in a row, she arrived at Danaris's house, equipment in tow, and they baked and made frosting. "When she did that, I immediately got it," Danaris said. "She was amazed at how fast I learned."

Realizing the potential for selling these higher-priced baked goods, and after taking a class on cake decorating, Danaris added cakes to her repertoire. She started selling cakes to everybody she met. And slowly, but methodically, by 2010, Danaris Mazara had become the cake-maker of choice for the Dominican community in the area surrounding Lawrence. And no wonder, since she sold each cake – which took her hours to make – for $20 each! She sold them constantly. "Everywhere I went, I offered to make cakes," she said. The work poured in, but the money she was making barely covered the ingredients, let alone her time. And she was essentially working two jobs. Three, if you included being the mother of a toddler.

She came home one day to hear her daughter string words together – almost a sentence – which elated Danaris. But when she mentioned it to her mom, her mother said bluntly, "She's been saying that for a while."

"I burst out crying…I cry for everything," Danaris said. "I was thinking, 'God, I am losing all the best years of my daughter's life.' I asked God for this baby, and she's going to end up raising herself."

With Andres's reluctant acquiescence, she took the most momentous decision of her journey so far: she would stay home, focus full-time on the business, and become a great businesswoman and a great mother. The business exploded – though she was working herself to the bone, sleeping a scant four or five hours a night.

Meanwhile, her husband wasn't happy. He'd gotten a job at American Airlines, an income that along with the money Danaris was bringing in allowed them to buy a house. But Andres was a traditional man. When he came home, he wanted to have dinner on the table. She'd spent the day baking, scrubbing frosting off the walls, and caring for their daughter. Then at night she would care for her husband.

Tension in their family rose.

In the midst of this, Danaris found out she was pregnant again. It was a joyous turn of events, but one that added to the stress she and her family were under. With a sense of dread and constant, overwhelming nausea, she quit her business.

If her entrepreneurial journey had ended there, we would likely have never met Danaris. Her story would have faded into the background like those of so many entrepreneurs – and an unknown number of *New Builders* – who start a business but aren't able to make it work.

Danaris wanted to back out. But her customers had different plans. On her first trip out of the house to buy diapers after her second daughter, Rebecca, was born, she ran into a former customer in the grocery store. "I need a cake for this Saturday," her customer pleaded.

It's hard for outsiders to understand the breadth and importance of parties in the Dominican Republic. The birthplace of merengue, one of the most joyful and seductive forms of dance, the island and its people have integrated festivals from all over the world – everywhere immigrants and travelers coming through its port came from. Festivals rooted in Catholic, Spanish, Cuban, and African traditions all have places on the Dominican calendar. Then there are the birthdays, weddings, funerals, and quinceañeras. And, of course, the baseball games. Dominicans don't need an excuse to throw a party – it's ingrained in the culture.

It took this interaction with her customer for Danaris to see the opportunity in providing cakes to Dominican factory workers. She started to recognize how much they would pay for a cake that would be the centerpiece of a party.

Danaris couldn't say no to her customer in the grocery store that day – she was a friend and a nurse who didn't have time to bake herself. So she agreed to help out. The next day, another customer called, and a month later, she was making 10 or 15 cakes every weekend. A few months after that, she hired her first employee.

Two young children, her marriage, and now her business, meant these were crazy years for Danaris. By 2014, she had hired two more women, which meant four people, all working in her small kitchen. Every day, she received customers in her living room. Every night and every weekend, they all baked. On one memorable day, Danaris looked into a mixing bowl to discover her baby daughter Rebecca's pacifier, like a giant piece of plastic fruit, embedded in the mix of sugar and butter. Her daughter had discovered a pacifier was better than a spoon to transfer the sugary treat to her mouth!

It was fun, but hard work. And the business was bursting at the seams in Danaris's home. Just when she was at her wit's end, another friend stepped into the story, telling her about Entrepreneurship for All, an organization that helped people like Danaris take their companies to the next level. They also offered some programming in Spanish. Taking part would mean going to a class, making a pitch, and then, if she was accepted, entering their accelerator program.

"I have to do something," Danaris thought, deciding to check it out.

She showed up at the first class, where people sat in a horseshoe-shaped curve of desks. It turned out the class was in English, which meant Danaris was struggling to learn Excel and the idea of business plans at the same time she was translating the class instruction from English into Spanish. At home she was still doing everything she had been doing – keeping her marriage together, mothering her two girls, managing her employees, and, of course, baking. Always baking.

When the classes ended and it was time to pitch her idea, Danaris got up in front of a room full of strangers and asked for their help to expand her budding bakery business. She needed a facility. She had it all in her head. But she was so tired that day that when she opened her mouth, nothing came out at first, not even the name of her business.

The pitch contest was being held at the facility of the local Lawrence Entrepreneurship for All program (EforAll, in short), and was over-flowing with local businesspeople, friends, and family members of the entrepreneurs who were presenting. In addition, there were a number of community leaders and local celebrities, like TV news personalities, as well as a few bankers and lawyers.

Danaris didn't win any of the prizes that night. But EforAll's executive director, David Parker, had been watching closely. He liked the cake samples. And he had noticed how hard Danaris worked during the class.

"I was so, so embarrassed," Danaris said. But David, a lean man with an intensely focused gaze and a deep voice, came up to her afterward. "Don't worry," he said, as Danaris remembered it later. "We're going to help you grow your business because we know, eventually, you'll have a really good business on your hands."

Parker was a former tech company executive whose new goal in life was teaching people who didn't have his advantages how to become successful entrepreneurs. And he in turn had been recruited and backed by Deshpande to expand EforAll.

The story of Desh, David, and EforAll builds on a long American tradition of philanthropic support by people who have seen the difference that a small leg up in the right direction can bring. They include philanthropic greats like Andrew Carnegie – whose mixed legacy also includes a history of worker exploitation – and Ewing Marion Kauffman, both major donors to entrepreneurial causes. Carnegie grew up reading as well as watching his father struggle for work. "I began to learn what poverty meant. ... It was burnt into my heart that my father, though neither abject, mean, nor vile ... had nevertheless to beg a brother of the earth to give him leave to toil," Carnegie wrote, referencing a Robert Burns' poem.[3] After he made his millions, he went on to create opportunities for others less advantaged. But true to his ethos, his donations were in the form of opportunity, not direct monetary support. He donated libraries and the resources they contained. Anyone with ingenuity and drive, in his thinking, could take advantage of the riches that lay inside.

Like Carnegie, *New Builders* and the people supporting them tend to believe that the problems of inequity can only be partially solved by money. Know-how and the opportunities that come from the right network are critical ingredients, and in some ways they are harder to come by than money alone. People who believe in entrepreneurship also believe in a combination of agency and environment. What successful entrepreneurs learn, viscerally and over and over again, is that you cannot change people. You can only create the right environments for people to make changes themselves and in their environments.

Entrepreneurship, for David, Desh, and Danaris, was a faster solution to the inequities they saw, such as the one between the residents of cities like Andover and Lawrence. It can take decades to give a person an education – but an entrepreneur can build a business in months.

It was a way to lift a community, to generate income and wealth for Danaris and her family, as well as a way for all of them to be part of a community they wouldn't otherwise have found. Out of those connections, long-lasting transformations can happen that reinforce dignity, build long-lasting bonds, and help people less advantaged rise up.

If you look back at American history, you realize that the belief in the power of entrepreneurship and community has been core to our identity from the beginning.

Endnotes

1. Jay Atkinson, "City of the Damned," *Boston Magazine,* February 28, 2018, www.bostonmagazine.com/news/2012/02/28/city-of-the-damned-lawrence-massachusetts/

2. Brian Latimer, "In Massachusetts Town, Growing Latino Presence Fosters Entrepreneurship," NBC News, November 28, 2016, www.nbcnews.com/news/latino/massachusetts-town-growing-latino-presence-fosters-entrepreneurship-n686896

3. Andrew Carnegie, "Autobiography of Andrew Carnegie," p. 13, *Project Gutenberg,* https://www.gutenberg.org/files/17976/17976-h/17976-h.htm

CHAPTER SIX

A Brief History
of Entrepreneurship
in the United States

In 1775, Daniel Boone led a small expedition through the Cumberland Gap in the Alleghenies, entering what would eventually become Kentucky. We think of him as an explorer, but he was also an entrepreneur. He worked for a business venture called the Transylvania Company that anticipated westward expansion and was trying to figure out how to make money from it. Most Americans at the time were farmers – or wanted to be – and as such, land was wealth. Discovering and colonizing new land, even when it meant taking the land from indigenous people, killing them in the process, was big business.

In fact, almost every early American figure was at least part entrepreneur. All of them have complicated stories. We think of George Washington as "the father of America," and in the next breath remember that his legacy is stained by his ownership of enslaved people. While Washington's political prowess and military ingenuity was what won America its independence, it may have been his entrepreneurial acumen that enabled the fledgling United States to survive the initial years after British rule (and, in particular, allowed the country to pay off its massive war debt). He was, among other things, an innovative farmer (he was the first person to breed horses with donkeys) and the owner of a large whiskey distillery.[i] That there are also troubling aspects to the lives of the men recognized as the founders of the country speaks to the challenge of fully embracing America's entrepreneurial past. And perhaps it explains why it is easier to gloss over some of the details and turn our history into something more akin to a myth.

Part Myth, Part History

This is the deep-seated truth to the mythology of the United States as a country of and for entrepreneurs. Our entrepreneurial past is ingrained in our present-day concept of the American dream. Many celebrated business leaders have been entrepreneurs – people who started and grew businesses. Many others whom we don't think of as entrepreneurs, were. Today's American entrepreneurs build on a lineage of daring and boldness established by the founders of the republic and the pioneers who pushed our country westward, and the innovators, industrialists, and technologists who changed the nature of business and work.

Across dozens of interviews, *New Builders* consistently told us that in America, people can accomplish the impossible and create something out of nothing. The American Dream remains, although it is under threat.

During the Colonial Era and the Western expansion, the presence of entrepreneurs as new states and territories were formed helped shape the country's legal system and institutions. Many of the inventions and the innovations of the Industrial Revolution, supported by those institutions, were born of entrepreneurs' brains. More recently, the

---

[i] Historian Edward Lengle, who is also the director of "The Papers of George Washington," leads an effort to preserve and analyze all of Washington's letters, writing, and documents. He wrote a book about Washington which he titled *First Entrepreneur*. While the notion that he was truly the nation's "first" entrepreneur might be a stretch – essentially all of the early settlers of what eventually became the United States were entrepreneurs – the title moniker does reflect the influence of entrepreneurship on Washington's thinking, actions, and policies.

entrepreneurs who have come to define the modern version of that term – the entrepreneurs of Silicon Valley – led a revolution in the creation and adoption of new technologies that have transformed almost every aspect of American life.

Understanding how and why entrepreneurship is entwined in our history provides an essential link to why today's *New Builders* are so important. Entrepreneurs created entire swaths of the American economy and played an outsized role in creating America itself. Across the history of the United States, if one were looking for a glimpse into the economy of the future, you would need to look no further than what that era's entrepreneurs were creating.

The Great Communicator might have articulated this best. In the spring of 1988, Ronald Reagan made a historic visit to the Soviet Union, shortly after Mikhail Gorbachev took power. In a speech to an audience of 600 computer science students at Moscow State University, he perfectly captured the role entrepreneurship plays as part of the American identity.

Historian Margaret O'Mara described the scene in her book, *The Code: Silicon Valley and the Remaking of America*

> [Reagan] rhapsodized about the glories of the American-made microchip. These miracles of high technology, the president told the crowd, as a giant statue of Vladimir Lenin loomed behind his podium, were the finest expression of what American-style democracy made possible. Freedom of thought and information allowed the surge of innovation that produced the computer chip and the PC ... .

The next revolution, Reagan explained that day in Moscow, would be technological. "Its effects are peaceful, but they will fundamentally alter our world, shatter old assumptions, and reshape our lives." And leading the way would be the young technologists who had worked up the courage "to put forth an idea, scoffed at by the experts, and watch it catch fire among the people. ... In this telling, Silicon Valley seemed just like the latest and greatest example of the American Revolution in action.[1]

Entrepreneurship, in Reagan's eyes, was the perfect example of American exceptionalism.

Entrepreneurial from the Beginning

When we started our research for this book, we looked for accounts of the history of entrepreneurship, expecting to find the kinds of weighty historical tomes ubiquitous in academia. But surprisingly few books have been written to detail the history and growth of entrepreneurship in America.[ii]

Tom Nicholas is one of a small but growing number of academics with serious research into subject matters that touch entrepreneurship. The William J. Abernathy Professor of Business Administration at Harvard Business School, he has been studying entrepreneurship for decades. As an academic discipline, entrepreneurship runs into fundamental challenges, according to Nicholas. By its nature, entrepreneurship is *idiosyncratic,* to use his term. Because there are so many paths to entrepreneurial success, it's tough to create a prescriptive narrative about what works and what doesn't. That stands in contrast to the more methodical, measurable way corporations work, making them easier to study. This explains why Harvard and other leading business schools have "typically been focused on big businesses and the strategy behind big business," versus focusing their academic efforts on entrepreneurship or management education (interestingly, Stanford and MIT are exceptions, which perhaps explains their entrepreneurial pedigrees).[2]

Surprisingly for a country that thinks of itself as so entrepreneurial, the history of entrepreneurship that has been written and recorded to date has tended to focus on individual entrepreneurs in a vacuum, not on telling their stories in the broader context of the entrepreneurial economy. Or, for that matter, the important and often outsized role entrepreneurs and small business people play in American society. When, in some cases, entrepreneurs go on to great success, we celebrate their actions in relation to the size of the business they created rather than the environment that allowed them to create it. Additionally, what's been largely left out, even from these accounts of individual

---

[ii] One notable exception is *An Entrepreneurial History of the United States* by Gerald Gunderson (Beard Books, 2005), which is one of the only works that attempts to provide a more complete exploration of the relationship between entrepreneurship and the growth of America. That work helped inform this chapter.

entrepreneurial heroism, are the experiences of women, people of color, and the many people who ran relatively small enterprises, but who played significant roles in our entrepreneurial past. Also left out of the historical narrative are the even greater number of people who "failed" but upon whose failure future successes were eventually built. The experiences of these entrepreneurs do exist within the written history of the United States – but they lie under the surface and as a result must be divined, like ghosts in the system. This is due in part to a system that defines success by virtue of scale and profit.

The Age of Exploration

Our country was discovered, founded, and expanded by entrepreneurs, some of whom made it into the history books and many others who didn't.[iii] But even a quick glance shows how important they've been, as the US economy has relied on the innovations, jobs, and explorations of entrepreneurs since before it was even a country. When the right kind of finance was available, entrepreneurs created entirely new business categories and economies. In fact, they played a crucial role in America's founding – by spearheading voyages to the world outside Europe and eventually landing in what would become the United States of America.

The explorers who defined the Age of Exploration – from the early fifteenth century to the middle of the seventeenth century – were the entrepreneurs of their time. This was the beginning of a modern European global presence – colonialism, mercantilism, and the establishment of colonies overseas.[3]

Prince Henry the Navigator, regarded as the founder of the Age of Exploration, took as his motto the decidedly entrepreneurial "a hunger

---

[iii] To be clear about our use of the word *discovery* – we mean this in the sense that it was discovered by Europeans; at the time that the first European set foot in the Americas, over a million people already lived here, as they had for generations. Additionally, prior to colonization, other explorers clearly found and set foot on New World soil. None of this, as well, is meant to gloss over the brutality and sheer lack of humanity that were the hallmarks of many explorers, particularly Columbus. His exploits were and are deeply troubling, although now are a permanent part of our history as a country.

to perform worthy deeds." The definition of *worthy*, then as now, was shaped by the norms and ethics of the time. The son of John I of Portugal and Philippa of Lancaster, Henry financed his explorations not with his own money. Rather he appropriated funding from the Order of Christ, the successor order to Portugal's Templar – the knights that became infamous during the Crusades. As doubts rose about the profit potential of his efforts to expand Portugal's reach to Africa, Henry landed on a horrific source of revenue: slavery. A religious man, he developed an elaborate rationale (with the unfortunate support of the church) that justified the slave trade because the slaves were being "converted" to Christianity.[4]

Prince Henry's exploits launched the model for other explorers. Present-day entrepreneurs will find many of the details of their stories familiar, from pitching ideas (and failing to sell them) to recruiting teams and crew, to dividing ownership in their ventures through profit sharing and bonuses. The business of exploration and discovery was exactly that – a business.

Christopher Columbus pitched his expedition to several potential backers who turned him down before he struck an agreement with the Spanish monarchs Ferdinand II of Aragon and Isabella I of Castile. Indeed, his "Enterprise of the Indies" business plan fell flat to many early backers, including those in Portugal and England. Ultimately, his contract with Spain included the stipulation of 10 percent profit sharing for everything he discovered (not to mention a noble title and right of governorship for any territories he encountered).[iv]

It's unclear exactly how Columbus recruited the 87 crew members who manned the *Nina, Pinta,* and *Santa Maria.* Contrary to popular belief, most were not convicts (Spain offered amnesty to convicts who went on the journey, but only four of the crew fit this description). The

---

[iv] Columbus's idea fell squarely on the backs of others that went before him, as many entrepreneurial endeavors often do. He was not the first to propose that Asia could be accessed by sea, sailing east from Europe. That notion likely dates back to Roman times and the relatively early notion that the Earth was round and not flat, although it took centuries for scientists to understand the truth of that "theory." And, of course, although Columbus didn't know it at the time, Leif Erikson had led a group of Vikings from Greenland into North America around the year 1000, likely exploring the area that is now Newfoundland and Canada.

details of their treatment are fuzzy, but we know that the crew's reported wages were modest. Like a modern-day entrepreneur, Columbus must have enticed his employees through some combination of the promise of adventure and the idea of the riches that awaited them if they were to find an eastern passage to Asia. The Spanish explorer Juan Ponce de León, who led the first known European expedition to "La Florida," was a "gentleman volunteer" on Columbus's second voyage, for example. Not surprisingly, this entrepreneurial drive continued from the earliest days of the first colonies.

The compact between the wealthy merchants and monarchs of Europe – investors – and the explorers of the day – entrepreneurs – sent many restless spirits overseas. Numerous explorers after Columbus continued to map what was designated as "America" by cartographers as early as 1507, named after the Italian explorer Amerigo Vespucci.[5] While the Spanish and Portuguese primarily explored the lands of current-day South and Central America, the French and English ventured farther north into what is now the northern part of the United States as well as into modern-day Canada.

Colonial Ingenuity

The English imprint on early America was entrepreneurial, too. The founder of the Colony of Virginia was The London Company, which was issued a charter by King James in 1606 to create a settlement of 100 square miles along the East Coast. The London Company was indeed that – a company in the conventional sense – and was backed by investors and existed to seek profit. The early settlers of Jamestown, arriving in 1607, were paid employees of the London Company; any profits they earned were paid back to the company and, ultimately, its shareholders.

Because of England's control over the New World's northern areas, aspiring colonists needed to obtain a charter from the Crown to establish themselves in the new land. It was not uncommon for England to pit aspiring settlers against one another to gain better economic terms for itself. With a charter in hand, aspiring entrepreneurs then needed to raise the necessary capital and recruit a team of settlers (managers in a sense) to embark on their mission.

The establishment of the colonies provided a certain amount of economic activity for the settlers. They needed to build the housing and other infrastructure required to survive, and many of the early colonies relied on agriculture and the export of raw materials, as well as precious metals and other local goods, back to England. Transporting these goods to Europe helped create the first American industry, shipping. Merchants in New England found the cost of shipping the raw materials from their region (timber and the like) to be too expensive to make up for their relatively cheaper cost in the Americas. However, they came to realize that if they consolidated shipping for their southern neighbors, who had the advantage of the cash crop of tobacco, they could more economically deliver their goods back to Europe. They eventually established a port for colonial America that aggregated goods from smaller shipments along the coasts to consolidate into larger shipments across the Atlantic. The return journey for goods coming from Europe followed suit, with these shipments going to a larger port to be broken up and distributed via smaller vessels across the colonies. As the colonial economies developed, they took advantage of America's abundant natural resources.[v] While goods had to be produced at a substantial discount to cover the cost of shipping them back to Europe, early American entrepreneurs embraced the challenge and in relatively short order, established markets for materials produced in the colonies, such as pig iron and potash.

With their developing economy, Americans began to feel more self-reliant and to realize that their interests were diverging from those of the English empire. For example, during the French and Indian War, many Americans were reluctant to help the British in their fight against the French, believing (in hindsight rightfully so) that the French were a counterbalance to English influence in the region. With an economy substantially large enough for America to fend for itself, pressure mounted to avoid the tax (literal and figurative) of remaining under British rule.

The Business of Revolution

The American effort in the War for Independence relied heavily on the ingenuity and cunning of entrepreneurs. Setting up supply lines for

---

[v] Resources, it should be noted, that were stolen from Native Americans.

fighting forces, for example, brought many entrepreneurs into action to solve the challenges of inland navigation and food and arms supply (the most famous, Jeremiah Wadsworth of Hartford, Connecticut, was the "quartermaster of the Revolution"). Robert Morris – one of the wealthiest merchants of America at the time – propped up the struggling finances of the war effort when he became Superintendent of Finance in 1781. It was Morris who came up with the idea to create a central bank for the United States – the Bank of North America – to provide a more reliable currency to the economy (in addition to backing part of the Continental Army debt with his own collateral). He also lobbied for and created the first federal tax – a 5 percent tariff – to be used to pay down the considerable debt the fledgling state was accumulating because of the war effort.

After the war and the signing of the Declaration of Independence, American entrepreneurs rebuilt the economy and helped set up the new government. Many of the men we refer to as Founding Fathers were small business owners and merchants. Self-determination was writ large across the Declaration of Independence and the US Constitution, both of which are, in many ways, credos to the entrepreneurial spirit. But there were, without question, many problems with the early American system. Men were writing the rules of the American economy, with women excluded from the decision-making and, as a result, also largely excluded from owning anything of value in the early economy. White men ruled the day, and the rights of others – especially women, Black, and Indigenous people – were left unconsidered. Many of the Founding Fathers in fact enslaved people. And the colonization of the United States and the push westward had devastating effects on enslaved people and the Indigenous people living in the Americas before Europeans showed up.

The slave-owning southern states and the plantations that fueled the southern economy were the first industries that developed into substantial businesses. By the time of the Civil War, an effective oligarchy of rich plantations had been created, primarily around cotton, and the wealthiest men in the country were cotton plantation owners. These southern business elites derived nearly the entirety of their wealth from cotton and the slave-based agrarian economy they created around it.[6]

We continue to struggle with the consequences of 400 years of systemic disenfranchisement of large swaths of our population stemming from these early actions in our country's history. Perhaps it is why it has been so easy for many to overlook the changes that are transforming our current entrepreneurial landscape and, especially, the rise of the *New Builders*. Then, as now, new forms of capital and finance were required to support America's burgeoning entrepreneurial economy.

The Revolution of Business

The abundant resources and lack of existing bureaucracy left plenty of room for innovation in the early United States. Entrepreneurial economies developed along with financing suited for them. Take, for instance, whaling – which foreshadows today's venture capital business.

Whaling expeditions were highly risky, expensive, capital intensive, and front-end-loaded with costs. As a result, a complex ecosystem developed to support the industry that used a multitiered structure to staff, provision, and fund what were often year-long (or longer) excursions in search of whales. "Agents" were intermediaries between the captain, crew, and the capital required to fund a journey. They were responsible for acquiring the whaling ship, arranging for the captain, recruiting the crew, and ensuring that the ship had the credit necessary to re-provision in far-flung ports across the globe. Owners were the funders of these business ventures. It was common for syndicates to form around whaling expeditions to allow owners (investors) to diversify their risk across multiple excursions. In cases where agents were also owners, they also often looked for outside capital to reduce their risk as well as allow them to invest in multiple projects simultaneously. Owners were commonly merchants or professionals whose primary business was in a different field. Their investment in the whaling industry was an exercise in profit-seeking and diversification from their primary vocation.

Some whaling ventures took a step further from the partnership structure described above to form corporations for the purpose of funding their ongoing operations. Captains were paid a "lay" or profit share of proceeds, as was much of the crew (obviously at lower rates than the captain). This payment form closely mimics the stock-based incentives common in today's startups. Similar to today's venture capital markets, the returns from these ventures followed a power curve with the majority of voyages failing to return capital and just a few returning a profit rate greater than 100 percent.[7] Interestingly, the success rate of agents also followed somewhat of a power curve, with the best agents significantly outperforming the average agent. Likewise, today, only the top tier of venture capital firms beat the returns of the S&P 500.[8]

By the late 1800s, whaling agents and owners were among the wealthiest Americans, and New Bedford, Massachusetts, became the whaling capital of the world. This was not because New Bedford was particularly well situated from a geographic standpoint, but rather, because of its role as the center for capital and expertise around whaling. It was, in many respects, the Silicon Valley of its time.[vi]

The Land of Opportunity. For Some.

The industrialization of America gave rise to the first Superstar Entrepreneurs. These men – Andrew Carnegie, John D. Rockefeller, Henry Ford, and others – were famous for their business prowess and inextricably linked to the companies they created.[vii] They challenged the conventional wisdom of the time and introduced tactics that would radically reduce the cost of goods, including in some cases by exploiting their workers. They changed the way that companies thought about management structures and even the potential size and scope of operations possible under one roof.

In many regards, Andrew Carnegie epitomizes the American Dream. An immigrant born in Scotland to a poor family, he moved to America as a boy with his parents in search of a better life. His first job was in a cotton mill as a young teenager. He became a telegraph messenger boy in the Pittsburgh Office of the Ohio Telegraph Co. Eventually moving into rail, he built a network of connections that

---

[vi] We researched background material on the history of whaling from a number of sources, but in particular relied on both Tom Nicholas and Jonas Peter Akins, *Whaling Ventures* (Boston: Harvard Business School, 2012), and Tom Nicholas, *VC, An American History* (Boston: Harvard University Press, 2019).

[vii] While we've highlighted a number of impressive women entrepreneurs of early America, all of the first "Superstar Entrepreneurs" were men. Even today, the vast majority of America's best-known businesspeople are men, a trend that we believe is beginning to change.

led him to a business opportunity in steel. At the Carnegie Steel Co. and its predecessor, Carnegie experimented with a vertically integrated supply chain and management practices that were well ahead of his time. He actively pursued investments in his supply chain to control the market for the raw materials that made up his product (for himself as well as for his competitors). He frequently looked for opportunities to cash out his partners and consolidate control of his business. He was a stickler for costs and forced his managers to run each operation inside of his company effectively as separate business units. He incentivized his managers with operating targets and bonuses based on their performance. He pioneered practices that would be followed for generations of business leaders after him. Carnegie also became a pioneering philanthropist.

Carnegie gave some of his best entrepreneurial advice to students at the Curry Commercial College of Pittsburgh in 1885. "And here is the prime condition of success, the great secret: concentrate your energy, thought, and capital exclusively upon the business in which you are engaged. Having begun in one time, resolve to fight it out on that line, to lead in it, adopt every improvement, have the best machinery, and know the most about it. ... 'Don't put all your eggs in one basket' is all wrong. I tell you, put all your eggs in one basket, and then watch that basket."[9]

Carnegie's libraries – he funded 2,509 around the world, most of them in the United States – were an expression of his deeply held belief in giving to people who were "industrious and ambitious; not those who need everything done for them, but those who, being most anxious and able to help themselves, deserve and will be benefited by help from others."[10] It was an immigrant's credo, one that became deeply embedded in the American entrepreneurial myth. His disdain for people with inherited wealth was rather less embedded. "I would as soon leave my son a curse as the almighty dollar," he famously said.

John D. Rockefeller's story exemplifies the, at times, uneasy relationship the United States has always had with its superstar entrepreneurs. Rockefeller's business reduced kerosene and oil prices significantly, allowing more consumers to access lighting and heating for their houses. Yet Standard Oil was also accused of depressing workers' wages in search of profit as well as manipulating market prices for its benefit.

Journalist Ida Tarbell, who was later a media entrepreneur herself as the co-founder of *The American Magazine*, helped precipitate the breakup of Standard Oil with a series of articles, later compiled into a book, that detailed how the company rigged railroad prices. America might allow its superstar entrepreneurs to get extremely wealthy – Rockefeller was probably the wealthiest person in American history – but they were still expected to play fair. And the history of Standard Oil points to America's uncomfortable relationship with businesses that become *too* successful. We celebrate successful entrepreneurs but at the same time believe in the idea that a business with too much power crosses the line.

Before the Civil War, the American system enabled slavery, and afterward, racism. In the South, the growth of the economy and banking sectors was inextricably tied to slavery and the slave trade. Commercial banks readily accepted enslaved people as collateral for loans – sometimes underwriting and collateralizing the sale of slaves. Unlike other assets, enslaved people had unique characteristics that the early southern banking system in the United States found desirable: they were readily convertible into cash (what Walter Johnson termed the "chattel principle" as he pointed out the grave contradiction and hypocrisy of slavery: specifically that slaves were at once considered commodities and at the same time were acknowledged, and even valued, for their specific human attributes). They were also considered mobile, transportable property. By 1860 more millionaires were living in the Lower Mississippi Valley than anywhere in the United States, based on the "value" of their slave holdings. It was estimated that year that the total value of enslaved people ($\sim$ 4 million people in total) in the southern states was $3.5 billion. In fact, they were the single largest financial asset in the United States at the time, worth more than the value of all manufacturing and railroads combined.[11]

Slavery ended with the Civil War. But the financial implications of the theft of 240 years of labor is profound for Black entrepreneurs today. "It's like there were two trains in the station, and one of them got a 240-year head start," says Demetric Duckett, associate director of capital innovation at Living Cities, a nonprofit developing new investment funds with the explicit aim of reshaping the system. "How fast do we need the second train to go to catch up?"[12]

The statistics make slavery's legacy on Black founders clear. Black founders own approximately 2.6 million businesses, representing

12.2 percent of American firms. However, the 19 million White-owned businesses are responsible for 88 percent of total sales and 86.5 percent of employment. In contrast, Black businesses are responsible for only 1.3 percent of total sales and 1.7 percent of employment. The result is that White founders have at least three times more wealth than Black founders.[13] All founders need funding for operations, sales and marketing, product/service development, and for making key hires. Black founders, however, often don't have the network of wealthy friends and family members, and lack access to venture capital funding for startup capital at anything approaching the rate of White founders.

Black founders also continue to deal with overt racism. As reported in the 2015 CB Insights Analysis, about 1 percent of venture capital investments end up in the hands of Black founders, despite the fact that Black founders represent 11 percent of the population. In addition, Black founders are often denied loans or receive a lesser loan amount than requested. More than 53 percent of loan applications by Black founders are denied. In contrast, approximately 25 percent of loans for White founders are denied.[14]

America survived and thrived in its first centuries because of its entrepreneurial spirit, which attracted the men and women who made up its early inhabitants. American forebears of all races were far away from home, and because of that they embodied – perhaps their circumstances required – an entrepreneurial spirit. That spirit is colorblind, even if society's reaction to it is not.

Starting Over versus Failing

As the new country established its legal infrastructure, some of those values found their way into its codes and regulations.

For instance, early on, forming a corporation required an act from a state legislature (a holdover from the British requirement that charters be only granted "by the Crown"). This made it hard to set up a company, especially for those without connections. Before the Civil War, a corporate charter was granted only by a special act of the legislature for purposes deemed to be in the public interest.[15] As a result, these charters were the purview of insurance companies, banks, and infrastructure-related businesses, such as canal companies and dock businesses. Early companies were basically public/private partnerships set up to further the public interest in some way. All other businesses existed as an informal arrangement – a legal gray zone.

In 1811, New York became the first state to establish a simple registration process for new businesses. This started to change the landscape for entrepreneurs. As a young nation and because of the way it came into being, America suffered less from the burden of an aristocratic society and the cronyism, favoritism, and hierarchy it entailed (whether we are still relatively free of the class infrastructure, however, is a matter of debate). To be clear, women and people of color continued to be left out of equal opportunities. But the door was open just slightly wider in the United States compared with its European and Asian counterparts. America was building an economic system that better allocated resources – through its budding free-market system – to those best positioned to capitalize on those opportunities.

Another great advantage Americans had as they started new ventures was the freedom to fail. The Bankruptcy Act of 1800, although limited to traders and focused on involuntary bankruptcy, was the first attempt by Congress to codify the notion of business failure into law. While the law was repealed three years later, it served as the basis for more extensive rules on bankruptcy that would emerge decades later through the Act of 1841 (the first to describe voluntary bankruptcy), the Act of 1867, and the Bankruptcy Code in 1898. Ultimately expanded with the Bankruptcy Act of 1938, the United States took early European models of debtor–creditor relations and modified them greatly to allow for greater risk-taking and expanded debtor powers.

The congressmen of the day knew how vital the work was. In a speech that a century later was called one of the greatest moments of American political oratory,[16] Senator Daniel Webster said,

> "I believe the interest of creditors would be greatly benefitted [by passing bankruptcy legislation] … and I am quite confident that the public good would be promoted. … I verily believe that the power of perpetuating debts against debtors, for no substantial good to the creditor himself, and the power of imprisonment for debt … have imposed more restraint on personal liberty than the law of debtor and creditor imposes in any other Christian and commercial country."[17]

Importantly, the United States abolished debtors' prisons in 1833 at the federal level, with most states following by 1850. This further decriminalized failure and separated America from Europe, which continued to imprison debtors for decades. When the country finally reached a consensus, the result was an acceptance of failure as a crucial part of risk-taking. Silicon Valley leaders sometimes take credit for a unique acceptance of failure, but in truth this has been a hallmark of American entrepreneurship for nearly 200 years.

America's nascent banking system also grew up in support of this budding entrepreneurial ecosystem. Commercial lending flourished in the American economy – especially after the advent in the late 1800s of the checking account, providing banks with a ready source of capital from which to feed their developing lending practices. Unlike in Europe, where commercial banks held onto their banking monopoly, the late 1800s also saw the emergence in the United States of investment banks. These banks could not take deposits or issue notes but instead acted as intermediaries that helped fuel the financing of railroads, mining, and other capital-intensive industries taking hold across America, particularly in the industrial North and the new frontier of the West.

With the National Banking Acts of 1863 and 1864, the federal government created a national system for chartering banks. The National Banking Act also encouraged the development of a national currency, backed by the US Treasury and, through a series of taxes and other incentives, led to the retirement of individual bank-issued currency. While the process of retiring bank-issued notes and the adoption of a centralized US currency took some time, its importance in enabling the national scale businesses that followed in the late nineteenth and early twentieth centuries was critical. Commerce was transformed from hyper-local (since individually issued banknotes could only be exchanged or deposited at their issuing bank) to national. Money could "travel" farther and was accepted widely. By nationalizing money and standing behind our currency, not to mention by providing a national framework for the banking system (to this day banks continue to be formed under either the national system or the state system, but the creation of a national system created greater uniformity among the state systems), the country laid the groundwork for the free flow of commerce at a time when recognition of available natural resources was beginning to emerge, and America's identity as a land of freedom and opportunity had begun to draw immigrants.

Collaboration Thrives

At the same time that the East Coast was developing into a financial and industrial powerhouse, the West was being settled by entrepreneurs. Connections to the resources of the cities and the civilization of Europe were even more tenuous for people in the interior of the early United States. Importantly, these pioneers were obliged to cooperate rather than compete. This is a strong thread that runs throughout the history of American entrepreneurship, though one we tend to overlook as we celebrate entrepreneurial success more as individual achievements rather than collaborative efforts. But in the early West, personality conflicts had to be overlooked for the greater good. "One might have a knack for basic blacksmithing. Another could build and operate a small gristmill," Jeff Guinn wrote in *The Last Gunfight*, which takes on many of the myths of the American West, repainting it as a place where a hard-edged community spirit grew and thrived. Western communities thrived on cooperation and collective action. And contrary to the myth of the lone gun-toting cowboy hero, most major cow towns and mining communities of the West had gun laws prohibiting guns inside city limits.[18]

The stories of entrepreneurs in American history are woven inextricably with their communities. Black entrepreneurs often were part of enclaves, some targeted in racial massacres as they grew more successful. Entrepreneurs of color and women entrepreneurs and inventors, meanwhile, proliferated around the turn of the century, a time of scientific innovation and discovery that also led to great advances in public health, philanthropy, and – probably not coincidentally – women's right to vote.

During the late 1800s, patents obtained by women grew at three times the corresponding rate of patents granted to men.[19] We celebrate an inventor's flash of insight, but it takes an entrepreneurial mind to recognize that there is a market for an invention in their community. In particular, women in the West and in rural areas patented devices to reduce housework. Their patent rates were exceeded only by women in the large cities of the northeast. As US expansion moved west, entrepreneurs were an important factor in settling the land, and women-invented devices that made life on the frontier easier played an important role in westward expansion. These inventions, and the women behind them, are an underappreciated and under-recognized part of American history.

At least a tenth of urban businesspeople in the mid-nineteenth century were women, and by the early 1900s, there were tens of thousands of women-owned businesses. But because many of them were not formalized, historians and economists have overlooked their effect on the overall economy. Certain undocumented trades such as midwifery or laundering services were almost entirely the purview of women. These activities were not only important, they were a significant part of the economy and the service sector.

As with women, the stories of Black entrepreneurs lie just under the surface of our history. For example, Garret Morgan, a Black inventor and the son of slaves, came up with the design for the three-light traffic light, which he patented in 1923 (before his invention traffic lights consisted of two lights). Also, both notable and in common use today is the light bulb filament, which was invented by the Black inventor Lewis Latimer in 1881. There is a rich history of invention and innovation among Black entrepreneurs.

For both women and people of color, entrepreneurship represented a way (in many cases, the *only* way) to participate in the American economy. We don't have a precise accounting of the number of early Black and female entrepreneurs, but we do know that they have had a significant impact on the American economy throughout our history.

The entrepreneurs of the late nineteenth and early twentieth century had something no one before them had: a sense of possibility offered by the size and growing infrastructure of the United States. Aided by railroads, and later, the interstate highway system, entrepreneurs could sell goods, services, and products to a national market. It was during this period that America saw some of the innovations that would come to dominate business and commerce. Henry Ford famously introduced the assembly line in 1913. The first grocery store opened in 1930 (prior to that, shoppers had to visit individual merchants to buy produce, meat, cheese, and so on). McDonald's pioneered the national fast-food model starting in 1955. And, of course, the information and computer age was birthed as the twentieth century progressed with Hewlett Packard's founding in 1939 and eventually with firms such as Microsoft (1975) and Apple (1976).

The Dawn of the Internet Age

Firms such as National Cash Register and IBM began producing early computers in the mid-twentieth century. Technology adoption accelerated in the latter quarter of the century as the "home" computer was developed and nonprogrammers were able to access and use these devices. Prices dropped and adoption spread rapidly. Ultimately, by the end of the century, a project that had begun as a government-sponsored idea to stitch disparate computers together in what was termed in the first paper on the subject (by JCR Licklider of MIT in 1962) as a "galactic network" became what we now know as the World Wide Web.[20] The adoption of the Web as an underpinning for new businesses was a fundamental change that in turn spawned both business and social changes that we continue to wrestle with today.[viii]

In many respects, technology has taken over our perception of what is entrepreneurial, a development that we believe is significantly detrimental to our broader understanding of business creation and economic development. Technology receives outsized attention in relation to the actual number of new business starts that are technology businesses. This partly reflects the power of technological innovations at work and the way those innovations have propelled the size of some companies. But they comprise less of our economy than many would give them credit for. *Forbes,* for instance, reported only 184 technologies businesses in its "Global 2000" index.[21]

[viii] You can argue that the development of the internet eclipses the impact of such other critical technology developments like trains, electricity, or the telephone – all important and each significantly impactful, but in ways that fall well short of the impact the internet has had on both the breadth and pace of innovation, according to Seth. All of them may shrink in comparison to the importance of the development and introduction of the birth control pill, accomplished by the nonprofit entrepreneur Margaret Sanger, according to Elizabeth.

Venture Capital Is Born

Just as earlier waves of innovation were powered by particular forms of finance that grew up around them, the growth of the technology sector was propelled by the venture capital industry.

The American Research and Development Corporation was founded in Massachusetts in 1946 by the "father of venture capital," George Doriot. However, the venture industry started in earnest at the dawn of the technology era in the 1960s and 1970s. The first "venture startup" is typically considered to have been Fairchild Semiconductor, a firm that produced the first commercial integrated circuit (the building block for all computing infrastructure), funded in 1957.

Brand-name firms that are still actively investing started during this era, such as Kleiner, Perkins, Caufield & Byers, Sequoia Capital, Mayfield Fund, and New Enterprise Associates. Venture capitalists raised or pooled money and invested it into entrepreneurs in exchange for a portion of the business. The money wasn't a loan to be paid back at a set rate; it was shared ownership with unbounded upside potential.

Wealthy individuals and families, along with pension funds and other institutional investors, saw a way to invest through venture capital in the innovations emerging from Silicon Valley, and to some extent, in early-stage companies in other sectors of the economy. However, it was during the "dot-com" bubble of the late 1990s and early 2000s that the venture industry exploded – both in size and in the consciousness of the American public. Venture capital proved to be enduring and cyclical. In 2020, investment funds flowing into venture capital firms reached the same peak they had in the 2000s.

At the time of this writing, of the five most valuable companies in the world, three are technology businesses (the others are the Saudi state oil company, ARAMCO, and the Chinese oil and gas company PetroChina). At the end of 2019, 7 of the 10 most valuable companies by market capitalization were technology businesses (notably, 5 of those 7 were started in the last 25 years).

The Silicon Valley Version of Entrepreneurship

In the post–World War II era, a hive of scientific minds, independent labs, and defense contractors had sprung up around Stanford University, which was the Western newcomer to the ranks of America's elite universities of the East Coast.

It was in Northern California, in 1957, that eight young men dramatically nicknamed *The Traitorous Eight* wanted to leave a lab, Shockley, to continue their work on a groundbreaking new area, semiconductors. The company they formed was Fairchild Semiconductor (mentioned above as the first venture startup), which in turn spawned the initial generation of Silicon Valley companies innovating around the silicon chip. Those companies – manufacturers of the silicon-based computer chips that eventually would form the basis for the US computing industry – ultimately gave rise to the moniker *Silicon Valley*.

Often not appreciated was the role the federal government played in the early days of Silicon Valley. Without government research dollars, early Silicon Valley companies (and many of the more recent ones) would not have existed. Research and development made up 10 percent of the entire US federal budget for the first half of the 1960s, and it was flowing freely in the form of contracts to companies in Silicon Valley and elsewhere. Much of the early research into what we now know as the internet was either funded by the US government or conducted by researchers working for the government.

When Silicon Valley wrote the myth of its founding, according to historian Margaret O'Mara, whose work is the source of this short retelling of Silicon Valley history, it left out some crucial points, perhaps the most important being the government's role in funding the breakthrough innovations that led to the high-tech industry. She argues that the most valuable lesson to be drawn from the history of Silicon Valley is that the government poured money in without exerting too much control. Technology was commercialized "at a furious pace," creating the incentives of wealth and winning in the interests of fulfilling a national mission.

The role of government – of collective action – was forgotten in favor of a more romantic, politically expedient story of lone risk-takers: entrepreneurs and the venture capitalists who backed them. The tech entrepreneurs took over the role that had been filled two centuries before by frontiersman and founders. "Mistrust Authority – Promote Decentralization," read one plank of the "hacker ethic" journalist Steven Levy used in 1984 to describe the remarkable new subculture of hardware and software geeks who had helped make the computer personal. "Authority" meant Big Blue (IBM, the nemesis of the early startup technology industry), big business, and big government. It was the perfect message for the times.

After more than 10 years of unrelentingly dismal business news – plant shutdowns, blue-collar jobs vanishing overseas, fumbling corporate leaders, and the pummeling of American brands by foreign competitors – high-tech companies presented a bright, promising contrast, O'Mara wrote. America loved this new brand of brash CEO, like Jerry Sanders of Advanced Micro Devices (AMD), who bought a Rolls Royce one week and a top-of-the-line Mercedes the next. And, of course, there were Steve Jobs of Apple and Bill Gates of Microsoft, who came to exemplify a new sort of corporate leader. Labeled as an *entrepreneur,* they were young, nonconformist, and rich.

The Silicon Valley version of entrepreneurship was a convenient story for pretty much everybody. It pulled on the threads of the bootstrap myth and the strains of individualism that Americans seem to love. It eventually crowded out the older idea that change could come from just about anywhere, from a Black immigrant in San Francisco to a woman in a frontier town in the early West. We also lost track of the fact that many great companies were built by older people. The founders of McDonald's, Coca-Cola, and Kentucky Fried Chicken, for instance, were all over 50 when they launched their empires. Journalist Vera Wang did not begin designing clothes professionally until the age of 39.[22]

Additionally, we have neglected one of the fundamental lessons from our past: entrepreneurs are part and parcel of their communities. From the Main Street businessman in Pennsylvania, to those making fortunes from the publicly financed railroads and internet infrastructure, to the people of color building a community in Tulsa, entrepreneurs form the fabric of our communities and provide the stability, resilience, and vibrancy that makes our cities and towns come alive.

By the end of the twentieth century, software-based companies, the ones that had evolved out of the groundbreaking semiconductor and chip industries of the middle of the century, pretty much owned the idea of change in America – and around the world. Governments looked to technology not only for innovation but for growth in jobs. The entrepreneurs of Silicon Valley were by far the loudest voices in the American business firmament, embodying a new, narrow version of the American dream: not only could you create change and build a business – but you could do it incredibly quickly.

With its roots in the patriarchal science elite of the 1950s and 1960s, this high-tech world has been unrelentingly White and male. The most successful entrepreneurs "all seem to be White male nerds who've dropped out of Harvard or Stanford and they absolutely have no social life," said John Doerr, one of Silicon Valley's leading venture capitalists, in 2008. "So when I see that pattern coming in, it was very easy to decide to invest."[23]

Given the popularity of Ray Kurzweil's *The Singularity* in Silicon Valley circles, it's fitting that entrepreneurship and technology businesses themselves have reached something of a singularity. Gone is the broader definition of entrepreneurship as a person – any person – pursuing their passion and building a business and a life for themselves, no matter what industry they've chosen. Instead, when we speak of entrepreneurship in 2020 we are generally referring to businesses being created in or around technology, and usually by White, Ivy League–educated men.

This is a huge mistake.

By allowing ourselves to narrow the definition of entrepreneurship, we've put blinders on to the real work that is being accomplished across America by our next generation of entrepreneurs, the *New Builders*. And by ignoring them, we're failing to understand the obstacles today's economy throws in their paths. The result has been a significant decline in entrepreneurship in the United States, and critically, a less dynamic, less robust, and less egalitarian economy.

Endnotes

1. Margaret O'Mara, *The Code: Silicon Valley and the Remaking of America* (Penguin Press, 2019)
2. Interview with Tom Nicholas, June 2019.
3. Peter C. Mancall, "The Age of Discovery," *Reviews in American History*, Volume 26 (University of Western Ohio, 1998)
4. P.E. Russell, *Prince Henry "the Navigator": A Life* (New Haven, CT: Yale University Press, 2001)
5. Erin Allen, "How Did America Get Its Name?," *Library of Congress*, July 4, 2016, https://blogs.loc.gov/loc/2016/07/how-did-america-get-its-name/
6. Sven Beckert, *Empire of Cotton: A Global History* (Vintage, 2015)

7. Tom Nicholas and Jonas Peter Akins, "Whaling Ventures" (Boston: Harvard Business School, 2012)

8. "We Have Met the Enemy...And He Is Us," *Kauffman Foundation*, 2012, https://www.slideshare.net/kloeckner/kauffman-foundationventurecapital

9. Andrew Carnegie, "The Road to Business Success: A Talk to Young Men," An Address to Students at Curry Commercial College, Pittsburg, June 23, 1885, www.historytools.davidjvoelker.com/sources/carnegie.html

10. Andrew Carnegie, "The Best Fields for Philanthropy," *The North American Review* 149, no. 397 (1889): 682–698, www.jstor.org/stable/25101907?seq=1#metadata_info_tab_contents

11. Sharon Ann Murphy, "Banking on Slavery in the Antebellum South," Presentation at Yale University Economic History Workshop, May 15, 2017, New Haven, CT, https://economics.yale.edu/sites/default/files/banks_and_slavery_yale.pdf

12. Interview with Demetric Duckett, October 2020; Demetric also referred us to a recent study that shows a current wealth gap of 228 years, https://ips-dc.org/report-ever-growing-gap/

13. William Darity et al., What We Get Wrong About Closing the Racial Wealth Gap, *Samuel DeBois Cook Center on Social Equity, Insight Center for Community Economic Development*, 2018, https://socialequity.duke.edu/wp-content/uploads/2019/10/what-we-get-wrong.pdf

14. Jonathan Sherry, "A Data-Driven Look at Diversity in Venture Capital and Startups," *CB Insights*, June 15, 2015, https://www.cbinsights.com/research/team-blog/venture-capital-diversity-data/

15. David McBride, "General Corporation Laws: History and Economics," https://scholarship.law.duke.edu/cgi/viewcontent.cgi?article=1605&context=lcp

16. David A. Skeel Jr., *Debt's Dominion: A History of Bankruptcy Law in America* (Princeton University Press, 2003)

17. Ibid

18. Jeff Guinn, *The Last Gunfight* (New York: Simon & Schuster, 2012)

19. B. Zorina Khan, "'Not for Ornament': Patenting Activity by Nineteenth-Century Women Inventors," *The Journal of Interdisciplinary History 31, no. 2* (2000): 159–195, www.jstor.org/stable/207141?seq=1

20. Mark Ollig, "Licklider's Vision: An 'Intergalactic' Computer Network," *Bits and Bytes Online*, October 24, 2011, https://bitscolumn.blogspot.com/2011/10/lickliders-vision-intergalactic.html

21. Jonathan Ponciano, "The Largest Technology Companies in 2019: Apple Reigns as Smartphones Slip and Cloud Services Thrive," *Forbes*, May 15, 2019, www.forbes.com/sites/jonathanponciano/2019/05/15/worlds-largest-tech-companies-2019/

22. Remy Blemenfeld, "Too Old to Become an Entrepreneur? Surprise Yourself with This New Research," *Forbes*, January 26, 2020, www.forbes.com/sites/remyblumenfeld/2020/01/26/too-old-to-become-an-entrepreneur-surprise-yourself-with-this-new-research/?sh=3f83d0b27f48

23. Sam Colt, "John Doerr: The greatest tech entrepreneurs are white, male nerds," *Business Insider*, March 4, 2015, www.businessinsider.com/john-doerr-the-greatest-tech-entrepreneurs-are-white-male-nerds-2015-3

CHAPTER SEVEN

The Elephants
in the Room

To stroll the Main Street in scenic Nantucket, Massachusetts, is to take a walk back in time. Uneven cobblestone pavers, a throwback to the town's early days in the 1600s as a whaling and commerce capital, bounce cars up and down as they make their way up the main business drag. Church spires peek out above the tops of the two- and three-story buildings that line the street. Here and there, you catch glimpses of the town's historic waterfront.

Benches welcome those looking for a quick rest or a more extended stop to watch the tourists amble up and down the street, pausing to peer into shop windows in the slow, unhurried manner of people on vacation and with nowhere in particular to go. A monument to June Bartlett – the patriarch of the island's oldest farm – stands on the street's west side. The latest generation of Bartletts still sells produce and flowers from the back of a truck during the summers, something their family has done since the 1930s. Nantucket's Main Street has been a Historic District since 1955, and the style and type of buildings have been tightly controlled ever since (in fact, since 1971, the entire island has been a Historic District – something that at once brings the island its charm, but has also led to some of the nation's highest home prices).

Nantucket values its history and the role of entrepreneurs and small businesses in a way others talk about but few can turn into action.

In 2006, the town took the extraordinary step of eliminating chain stores from its downtown business district, enacting what is termed a *Formula Business Overlay District*. As described at the Town Meeting where the new regulation was passed:

> [t]he purpose and intent of the Formula Business Overlay District (FBOD) is to address the adverse impact of nationwide, standardized businesses on Nantucket's historic downtown area. The proliferation of formula businesses will have a negative impact on the island's economy, historical relevance, and unique character. These uses are therefore prohibited in order to maintain a unique retail and dining experience. Formula businesses frustrate this goal by detracting from the overall historic island experience and threatening its tourist economy.[1]

The FBOD places limitations on what types of businesses can operate in downtown Nantucket. New businesses along Main Street and across downtown are prohibited from opening if they are part of a chain (defined as a group of stores with 15 or more locations that have shared characteristics such as the same logo, interior design, menu, etc.). In enacting the ban, Nantucket joined a handful of other wealthy tourist towns, including Carmel, California; Bristol, Rhode Island; Ogunquit, Maine; and Port Townsend, Washington, in banning chain stores.[2]

It was a bold move, one that came, perhaps surprisingly, in response to the appearance of a Ralph Lauren store along the cobblestone way. It served as a wake-up call to island dwellers who worried that, unchecked, chain stores would turn their Nantucket into the equivalent of a bland corporate mall. Walk down Main Street in almost any US city, or for that matter pretty much any mall or even strip-mall, and you're bound to see the same shops, the same offerings, the same merchandise. Mixed in, perhaps, will be a handful of local shops. These local businesses are increasingly being squeezed out by stores that are a part of larger enterprises. Nantucket had other ideas.

"I wasn't sure it would work," recalled Wendy Hudson, owner of Nantucket Book Partners, and the driving force behind the initiative.

Wendy has the look of someone who might own a bookstore: thoughtful, probing, inquisitive, and with a friendly intensity. Owning a business wasn't her plan. During her childhood, she sailed with her grandparents around the sound between Cape Cod and Martha's Vineyard. Occasionally, they ventured farther out to Nantucket. In college, she spent summers on the island working for Bartlett's Farm. During one of those summers, she met her husband, Randy, with whom she started the local Nantucket brewery, Cisco Brewers in 1995 (a "nanobrewery" as they described it – feeling at the time that it was too small to even be considered a microbrewery). After she and Randy moved to the island permanently, she started working at the local bookshop, Nantucket Bookworks. Her timing was fortuitous. Within a few years, the shop owners agreed not only to sell her the shop but also to stay involved and help transition the critical business relationships. By the late 1990s, she was the owner of the local bookstore and a part-owner of what by then had become a thriving and well-known brewery (the nanobrewery having, by then, graduated into the microbrewery category).

Nantucket was lucky to have Wendy, who got the idea for the District from a meeting of the independent booksellers trade group, the American Booksellers Association, and who worked closely with Andrew Vorce, Nantucket's director of planning, to craft the idea. She had the vision to think about implementing something as audacious as the District, as well as the local knowledge and respect to champion a potentially controversial idea. The law was modeled on one enacted in 2005 in Port Townsend, Washington. She was pushing into new waters, but the way was not completely uncharted. "We wanted to preserve the character of our downtown core business district," explained Wendy. "And we knew others had already done the same."

Convincing others in the town, she thought, might prove challenging. She assumed that landlords and others with short-term profit motives would be against the idea, including potentially the town Select Board, whose budget relies in part on sales taxes and other merchant fees.

There was also the question of the legality of such a ban. Yes, others in the country had attempted something similar, but would any of this stand up to legal scrutiny? And specifically, what Massachusetts law covered a concept such as this? And finally, the town's Select Board – not necessarily a group that looks for controversy – would have to approve of the change. These were daunting obstacles to overcome, and there were many potential pitfalls, any one of which could easily lead to a dead-end for Wendy's vision.

However, much to Wendy's surprise, local opposition to the project turned out to be short-lived, as she was able to frame the idea in terms of the future health and prosperity of the local business corridor. Ultimately, local real estate agents and large downtown property owners did not oppose the concept, recognizing that preserving the old town's downtown flavor and character was in their long-term best interests. The Select Board quickly came around as well, wanting to serve the wishes of the community, which was increasingly behind such a ban. Ultimately, the biggest hurdle turned out to be the legal framework through which such a regulatory change could be enacted. It took several years to work through the specifics of enacting the FBOD, but in April 2006, the town adopted the new zoning restriction. Preserving the character of downtown had become law.

Dozens of cities and towns across the United States have enacted similar ordinances to limit or ban chain stores' proliferation in their downtown areas. Some are considering similar ideas in the wake of concerns about small business vibrancy due to the Covid-19 economic crisis (Cambridge, Massachusetts, is the latest example of this, as they consider enacting an ordinance to preserve the historic character of Harvard Square). By no means does eliminating chain stores from certain downtown areas offer *the* solution against the mall-ization of cities. Still, it does offer one potential tool for towns to consider as they push to maintain their character in balance with economic vibrancy. We have witnessed communities fighting and seen ways to strengthen and support this quiet but powerful movement. To understand what they're up against, we need to understand the roots of today's economy and how it works.

Go Big or Go Home

To put it simply, today's business climate favors size rather than speciality. On Wall Street, the saying is: "Go big or go home." Even before the economic crisis brought on by Covid-19, American entrepreneurs were under increasing pressure from the consolidation of the US business landscape. The advantages of size are squeezing out America's smaller businesses in favor of larger ones.

American companies opened roughly 50 percent more new branches in 2011 than they did in 1978 – meaning that chain businesses are growing much more rapidly than they have in the past. According to the Cleveland Federal Reserve, this trend has resulted in roughly 40 percent of new business establishments being new locations for existing businesses, rather than the opening of new storefronts. That's double what it was in the late 1970s when 80 percent of "new establishments" were startups. Now that number is down to 60 percent.[3]

This is arguably a boon to consumers – you can now get the same Starbucks latte in over 14,000 locations in the United States alone (almost 30,000 globally). But the commodification and concentration of business present impediments to *New Builders,* as well as our economic vibrancy as a whole. We risk destroying the soul of Main Streets for the perceived benefit of ease and convenience.[i]

"Our argument to the town was a character argument," Nantucket's Wendy Hudson explained. "We felt like we were risking what made our downtown special and unique if we let the chain stores take over. That the town broadly supported this effort showed that they understood the value small businesses bring to our community, and that local businesses with local ownership are a part of the community in ways that larger stores simply can't be."

One of the reasons the takeover of Main Street by chain stores is so insidious is the economics of larger chain operations vs. smaller businesses. Beyond the obvious economies of scale offered to companies buying massive quantities of goods and services, many chain stores make a significant portion of their revenue and profit from their online operations. Because of that, some retail locations – especially in high traffic, high rent areas – can be operated as marketing "loss leaders" for these chains. Big companies use these storefronts to drive traffic to their online operations and don't rely on any single location's profitability. This

---

[i] We are certainly not arguing that large companies can't be good community citizens, and Starbucks is a good example of a large business that has a strong culture of community service. But part of the reason it is often referenced as a stand-out example is because it is more the exception than the rule in terms of meaningful community involvement.

perverts the economics of Main Street, pushing out more mom-and-pop retailers that don't have the budgets for sophisticated websites or national brand reach. They need to operate their storefronts to make a profit. Chain stores are proliferating on Main Streets; so are big banks and real estate firms – all businesses with very different economics than a local shop. With retail landlords looking to maximize rents and profits, the result is that fewer individual businesses can survive in the downtown corridors of many towns across America. Instead, businesses are slowly being replaced by operations that benefit from economies of scale, have significantly different cost structures compared to a single local business, or view a downtown location as an acceptable expense to support larger retail ambitions.

The Covid-19 crisis appears to be accelerating consolidation in the retail sector and consumers' move to online shopping. Not surprisingly, as the economy shut down in the early days of the Covid crisis, consumer spending at retail outlets fell sharply and was consolidated around essential goods and services. However, sales at so-called "big-box" retailers (all chain stores) fared the best, as consumers stocked up on essential items and presumably felt safer with the wider aisles and larger formats of the big-box environment. Online shopping, unsurprisingly, increased – the only segment in the retail sector to see a growth in sales in the early months of the crisis. While industry-wide data are not yet widely available, individual store data suggest that the largest online retailers – especially Amazon and Walmart – fared quite well. Walmart alone saw a 10 percent overall increase in revenue in the early days of Covid, driven by a 74 percent increase in online sales.

It's important to note here that the retail of today will not look like the retail of tomorrow. One of the hallmarks of *New Builders* is that, like generations of entrepreneurs before them, they are at the forefront of change. Today's entrepreneurs are reinventing "retail" into "experiences."[ii] But those transformations are less likely to succeed in today's uneven economic landscape.

Big businesses have emerged as dominant players in the retail landscape in the past few decades. Their increasing power lately is part of a bigger story: Americans' long on-again, off-again love affair with size.

[ii] Such as the independent bookshops that curated "mystery" book boxes to survive the pandemic, or local restaurants that put together ready-to-cook, family-style meals.

Where Did Our Love Affair with Size Come From?

Early in our country's history, the expansive geography of the United States and our relatively primitive infrastructure prevented businesses from operating in far-flung places. Instead, the early American business landscape consisted mostly of small vendors and local farms and shops, as Matt Stoller's book *Goliath: The 100-Year War Between Monopoly Power and Democracy*, from which much of this history is drawn, tells us.[4]

As the country emerged from the Civil War, early businesses remained relatively small and local. The exceptions were industries that benefited from either regulatory oversight or massive economies of scale. Railroads benefited from both (along with a serious amount of political corruption) and were among the first of America's large businesses. Until the 1880s, most industries were regulated at the state level through restrictive corporate chartering (meaning the ability to incorporate a business). Aspiring business owners had to apply to the legislature for permission to operate. Naturally, this restricted the number of firms and favored the more well connected, creating a merchant "class" of people who had the political clout necessary to obtain a business license.

A key provision in state charters restricted corporations from buying stock in another business. This limited their ability to consolidate market power. Even if a single person owned multiple companies, those companies were effectively run independently (with separate charters and separate boards of directors). It was John D. Rockefeller – the "Superstar Entrepreneur" – who figured out a work around to this restriction. He invented the corporate "trust" that allowed a single board to control multiple entities within and across state lines. This legal end-run to state charter laws effectively created the monopoly era of the late 1800s and early 1900s and led to the consolidation of power in several key industries, including oil, steel, and rail. The age of big business in America began in earnest.

Eventually, "big business" spread from its roots in transportation and extraction to include other heavy industries. Spurred on by relatively lax oversight and minimal antitrust enforcement, mergers proliferated and helped create large, vertically integrated conglomerates in the chemical, auto, and banking industries. This trend also included the food industry (the giants of the day were companies such as National Dairy Products, Standard Brands, and General Foods). A critical but often overlooked Supreme Court decision in 1911 allowed retail stores to sell below their cost as a method for driving their competitors out of business. It was this ruling that effectively created the chain store movement. Companies with capital could use this short-term pricing tactic, along with their strong balance sheets, to drive competitors out of business. A leader among these new chain stores was the Great Atlantic & Pacific Tea Company – A&P. As a testament to how effective this price undercutting strategy was, A&P grew revenue from $31 million in 1914 to $440 million just 10 years later. The number of A&P stores grew by nearly 30 times during this same period. By 1930, A&P's sales topped $1 billion, making it the largest retailer in the world.[5] Other chains such as Safeway, Kroger, and Walgreens expanded rapidly during this time as well. The age of chains had begun, much to the chagrin of some ("I would rather have thieves and gangsters than chain stores in Louisiana," declared senator Huey Long in 1934).[6]

The early twentieth century was an ebb and flow of action either in support of or against these large conglomerates. The "trust-busters" emerged and took their fight both to the halls of Congress as well as to the courts. Many large trusts, such as Standard Oil, were broken up. Others were allowed to continue to operate essentially unchanged. The banking sector saw massive consolidation leading up to the market crash of 1929 and the Great Depression, but thereafter was subject to increasing regulatory oversight. This included the Emergency Banking Act of 1933, which effectively ended a run on banks that had threatened to topple the entire US banking system, as well as the more famous Glass–Steagall Act (also passed in 1933), which separated retail banks from investment banks (severing bank depositor accounts from the riskier and more speculative investments these investment banks were making in the stock market).

There is a paradox to our love affair with big. We turn people like Andrew Carnegie, John Rockefeller, and Jeff Bezos into celebrities. But we have a history of also trying to regulate or break up businesses if they get too big and too powerful. Interestingly, there is a compelling argument that breaking apart large, monopoly businesses such as American Tobacco (1904), Standard Oil (1911), and Alcoa (1945), or in more recent times AT&T (1994) and Microsoft (2001),[iii] creates a healthier and more dynamic economy. While Rockefeller fought the Standard Oil breakup for years in court, it ultimately benefited him personally as well as consumers more broadly. The companies comprising Standard Oil, once broken up, grew more quickly and ultimately became worth much more on their own than they had been when Standard Oil was operating as a single business. And they did so by serving more consumers at more consumer-favorable prices.

You might think the current rise in power of big business took hold in the 1980s under the policies of Ronald Reagan. But in fact these changes can be traced back to the 1970s. The genesis was the focus on consumers and the consumer advocacy movement, which in turn had their roots in the post – Vietnam War era of the mid-1970s. This push came from the left side of the political spectrum, although it likely wasn't the intention of those original consumer advocates to support the increasing consolidation of business and the rise in power of larger brands. Ralph Nader's influence in the Carter Administration laid the groundwork for this change in our business mindset. Through the 1960s and 1970s, the Federal Trade Commission, and government regulators more generally, had been focused on small businesses, which in this time were meaningfully starting to see the effects on their business from chain stores and mass merchandisers. Under Carter, this focus shifted to an emphasis on consumer protections and – perhaps understandably, given the rising inflation of the time – lowering consumer prices. Liberals also did away with the "fair trade" laws that allowed manufacturers to set retail prices. Now larger chains with more purchasing power and better balance sheets could further undercut prices. Before these changes in fair trade laws, retailers had primarily differentiated themselves through service, since they were generally required to sell the same goods for essentially the same prices as their competitors. Under the new laws, pricing wars erupted. The consumer shopping experience started to

---

[iii] Microsoft reached a settlement with the government and ultimately wasn't fully broken up, but was forced to significantly change its business practices as a result of the government's action. More recently, the government has been threatening action against Facebook and Google in an attempt to quell their increasing market dominance.

Downtown Staunton, Virginia, is an old agricultural and railroad hub. (photo credit: Lisa Helfert)

The old factories of Lawrence, Massachusetts, sit on the Merrimack River. (photo credit: Scott Suchman)

The East Side of Oklahoma City has been a redlined district for generations. (photo credit: Scott Suchman)

Danaris Mazara, surrounded by her work. (photo credit: Scott Suchman)

Sweet Grace Heavenly Cakes on Essex Street in Lawrence, Massachusetts. (photo credit: Scott Suchman)

Flan, where it all started for Danaris and Sweet Grace. (photo credit: Scott Suchman)

Danaris and her daughters Grace (left) and Rebecca decorate cupcakes. (photo credit: Scott Suchman)

Two generations of immigrants: Danaris Mazara walks with Frank Carvalho. (photo credit: Scott Suchman)

Fred Sachs experiments with new varieties of wheat on Grapewood Farm. (photo credit: Cathy Sachs)

Jasmine Edwards launched her company to help Title I schools find substitutes. (photo credit: All Photos Considered Photography)

Kirsten Quigley founded Lunchskins from her kitchen table.

Seth Goldman co-founded Honest Tea and went on to be executive chairman of Beyond Meat. (photo credit: Eric Elofson)

Isaac Collins taking a quick snack break. (photo credit: Scott Suchman)

Isaac Collins working behind the scenes. (photo credit: Scott Suchman)

Outside Yogurtini on a February evening. (photo credit: Scott Suchman)

Yogurtini fan mail. (photo credit: Scott Suchman)

The Cheff family. (photo credit: Philip Vaughan)

Mark Cheff maintains the family's herd, bred from racehorses and Tennessee walkers. (Photo credit: Donald Zanoff)

Claire Cheff on horseback in the Bob Marshall Wilderness. (photo credit: Mark Cheff)

Jahleel Pettiford showing off one of his T-shirt designs in Staunton, Virginia. (photo credit: Lisa Helfert)

Molly Rose Murphy of Queen City Music Studios and Chris Cain, director of the Staunton Creative Community Fund. (photo credit: Lisa Helfert)

Joe Harman in front of the Frederick House, the Inn he started in Staunton, Virginia. (photo credit: Lisa Helfert)

The Makerspace in downtown Staunton, Virginia. It is one of thousands of similar spaces popping up all over the country. (photo credit: Lisa Helfert)

As the need for PPE became acute, members of the Makerspace jumped into action to make masks. (photo credit: Lisa Helfert)

Outside the EastPoint Development on the east side of Oklahoma City. (photo credit: Scott Suchman)

Sandino Thompson, Jill Castilla, and Jonathan Dodson. (photo credit: Scott Suchman)

Some of the business owners now occupying EastPoint. (photo credit: Scott Suchman)

Jill Castilla and Jonathan Dodson review plans for Phase II of the EastPoint Development. (photo credit: Scott Suchman)

The authors with Booker T. Wilkins ("T") outside his barber shop in Alexandria, Virginia. (photo credit: Lisa Helfert)

The cash register in T's barber shop. The register only rings transactions up to $5 so to charge for his $20 haircuts, T rings up four separate transactions. (photo credit: Lisa Helfert)

David Parker left a career as a tech executive to become head of EforAll. (photo credit: Scott Suchman)

Desh Deshpande, founder of Entrepreneurship for All, became a telecomm entrepreneur in the early 1990s. (photo credit: Emil Kuruvilla)

John Hamilton of the New Hampshire Community Loan Fund. (photo courtesy of The New Hampshire Community Loan Fund)

Carmen Portillo creating chocolate treats. (photo credit: Allie Atkisson Imaging)

Afternoon lights strikes downtown Staunton, Virginia (photo credit: Lisa Helfert)

The Bob Marshall Wilderness of Montana encompasses two million acres of preserved land. (photo credit: Elizabeth MacBride)

shift to lower prices, but at the expense of customer experience. Stores became larger, and sales volume per store rose sharply.

This period marked a permanent shift in the regulatory and oversight emphasis across both Democratic and Republican administrations. Under this more lax view of antitrust and competition, corporations embarked on a merger craze. Unlike mergers of prior decades, where businesses purchased other companies unrelated to their core business, due to restrictions on ownership and a regulatory fear that consolidation within an industry would be blocked at the federal level, the merger wave that started in the 1980s saw businesses buying direct competitors in an effort to consolidate market power. Monopoly power was on the ascension. Under the guise of supporting consumer buying power, politicians and regulators in both parties appeared happy to be along for the ride. We've watched this consolidation trend continue in America throughout the end of the twentieth and into the twenty-first century. And it's touched all aspects of the US economy. Just one notable example is the news industry, where, since 2004, over 2,000 newspapers have disappeared.[7]

Consumers, meanwhile, participated actively in these changes, flocking to superstores like Bed Bath & Beyond, clicking on Facebook's addictive posts, and happily settling down to watch Disney movies in front of TVs produced at the lowest cost in manufacturing plants located far outside the United States. America's love affair with the short-term rewards of big business thrives, with far-reaching consequences for our economy.

And along with their grasp on consumers, these large businesses are exerting an increasing dominance over public policy and debate with devastating consequences for small businesses.

Big and Politically Powerful

Politicians of both parties love to talk about small businesses. Ronald Reagan proclaimed that "[e]ntrepreneurs and their small enterprises are responsible for almost all the economic growth in the United States."[8] Later he put it even more succinctly: "Small business is America." Bill Clinton echoed Reagan when he said that "virtually all of the new jobs come from small businesses." President Obama had praise for small business, declaring that "small businesses are the backbone of our nation's economy."[9] Both the Republican and Democratic party platforms from 2016 had high praise for America's small businesses. The Republican platform proclaimed that the twentieth century became known as the American Century because of the "ability of individuals to invent and create . . . . Back then, they were called risk-takers, dreamers, and small business owners. Today they are the entrepreneurs, independent contractors, and small businessmen and women of our new economy."[10] Not to be outdone in their praise, the Democrats declared the "critical importance of small business as engines of opportunity for women, people of color, tribes, and people in rural America." The 2020 Democratic platform expanded on this praise of small business when it said, "Democrats know that small businesses are among the best job creators in our country."[11] The Republican Party opted not to put out a party platform in 2020, but we imagine that they would have referenced small businesses if they had. During his time as president, Donald Trump said of small businesses, "Small business owners embody the American pioneering spirit and remind us that determination can turn aspiration into achievement."[12]

In truth, however, most politicians are completely out of touch with small businesses. A real challenge for US Congressional staff is finding small businesses to appear in perfunctory roles at the occasional roundtable discussion or congressional event. It's not that small companies don't exist in their districts – small businesses are everywhere – it's that small business owners lack the kind of access and close relationships that larger companies have with congressional members from their districts. And along with that lack of access comes less sway over laws and decision-making. Small businesses are quite literally losing their voice, despite the rhetoric of politicians. Business media, meanwhile, serves large institutions. Mainstream media, as befits their liberal perspective, sees people as consumers rather than producers.

The power of big business accelerated after the Supreme Court's 2010 ruling in *Citizens United v. FEC*, which eliminated many restrictions on corporate money's role in US elections. More broadly, the regulatory safeguards put in place over decades starting in the 1900s and accelerating through FDR's New Deal have been under attack under the guise that regulations are bad for business and bad for the overall economy. In reality, most Americans are strongly in favor of a reasonable regulatory framework.[13] Over 90 percent of consumers, regardless of political party affiliation, support the regulation of financial institutions.[14] Three-quarters of Americans believe there should be more government regulation about what companies can do with private and personal information.[15] American's views toward regulation are favorable whether we're talking about environmental regulation, factory farming, campaign finance, or just about any other area of American life.[16] This attitude stands in stark contrast to the role that regulatory frameworks are often portrayed.

A robust regulatory environment protects small businesses and entrepreneurs by leveling the playing field with larger firms and preventing anti-competitive behaviors and practices. Regulations can also directly benefit smaller enterprises by giving them access to more favorable lending rates or economic development dollars. The continued dismantling of the regulatory framework – something that accelerated dramatically under the Trump administration – poses a threat to individuals and small businesses alike.

Ellinor Ostrom, the first woman to win the Nobel Prize for Economics, is best known for her ideas in this area. Interestingly, her work showed that the "Tragedy of the Commons" (the tendency for groups to act in their own best interest at the expense of the greater good) actually doesn't occur in smaller, closer knit communities. Perhaps it is paradoxical, given that support of bigger businesses and less regulation often go hand in hand, but in fact Ostrom's work suggests that in an economy with a more vibrant small business sector, less overall regulation is needed. Importantly, Ostrom's work was informed by life experience more than theoretical ponderings. Living through the Great Depression, she witnessed the way her community banded together to survive. This informed her ideas, but also her approach to her subject – preferring to be in the field and in the trenches rather than observing from afar. This makes her theories all the more meaningful; she observed them first hand, almost in the style of an anthropologist versus a traditional economist. Her real-world observation that the Tragedy of the Commons is naturally overcome through the shared efforts of these smaller communities is something we found over and over again as we met with *New Builders*.

Shifting government treatment to favor larger businesses is true on both the national and local levels. As municipalities vie to keep their economies vibrant, they play right into the hands of larger businesses. "If I had a headline tomorrow that said, '1,000 Call Center Jobs Move to Community X,' I would have everyone in town high-fiving me," Karl R. LaPan, former chair of the National Business Incubation Association, recently told *Inc.* magazine. "If my headline said, 'Five Three-Person Businesses Started Last Year,' it would end up on the back page."[17]

The 2018 fight for Amazon's second headquarters was just the latest high-profile case of cities vying against each other for the benefit of large business. It's not that companies shouldn't look to government for reasonable accommodations and incentives (although we can debate in this context what constitutes "reasonable"). It's that what gets lost in the frantic push to lure large corporations and the jobs that come with them is the role that smaller businesses play in supporting these same communities – that, and small businesses' need for similar incentives and government help.

These factors combined powerfully to change the corporate view of their respective responsibilities. Businesses have shifted their focus to profits and stock price accretion at the expense of reinvesting in their operations, creating jobs, and supporting their communities. At the same time, these businesses are learning to consolidate their powers by leveraging political relationships to garner favorable legislation and decreased oversight. Large companies typically act to consolidate their market power and increase their stock price – often at the expense of investments in longer-term growth. This is a type of Tragedy of the Commons behavior that Ostrom suggests can be thwarted by a more vibrant small business community. Consider what happens to a town when the local factory or plant is taken over by a larger corporation, with roots elsewhere and motives that skew to profit maximization. That they shift jobs to lower-cost regions or countries is to be expected – under the Milton Friedman doctrine, it's effectively in their nature. From the perspective of the new owners of the plant, these moves make logical sense. By shifting ownership outside a community there is less vested interest, or even understanding, of the community cost of such a move. *New Builders* are finding opportunity in this landscape in part because community connections and ties are one of their strengths.

We saw the connection between government policy and big business behavior clearly with the Tax Cuts and Jobs Act (TCJA) of 2017. The TCJA enacted meaningful changes to the corporate tax code. First, it changed corporate tax from a sliding scale that topped out at 35 percent to a single fixed rate of 21 percent. Additionally, it changed the way that taxes on foreign profits were calculated. Before the TCJA, foreign gains were taxed when the money was repatriated back to the United States. This tax system caused many companies to keep substantial sums of capital outside US borders to avoid paying US taxes on foreign profits, resulting in these funds not being invested in the United States. An estimated $2.8 trillion of corporate profits accumulated in overseas accounts.[18] Under the TCJA, corporations were only taxed on income derived from operations in the United States, leaving foreign earned money to be taxed under whatever tax regime was in place where the money was earned. An essential feature of the law was a "tax holiday" that allowed corporations to bring money that was earned before 2018 back into the United States at significantly reduced rates (15.5 percent for "liquid assets" such as cash, and 8 percent on other assets).

Proponents of the tax law argued that the US corporate tax system was both too complicated and too expensive compared to other economies. They believed that corporations would use the tax savings to invest in US-based infrastructure and research and development (R&D) spending that would pay long-term benefits to the economy. In truth, effective US corporate tax rates (the rates actually paid by the average company, not the theoretical rates of the tax code) compared favorably with many other developed nations prior to the act. And in fact the United States collected a smaller percentage of its GDP in corporate taxes than most other countries. After the Act, the US corporate tax rate became lower than all other leading world economies, with the exception of the UK.[19]

Not surprisingly, once the TCJA was passed, the behavior of corporations ran counter to what had been promised, but very much in keeping with the "consolidate power and increase stock price at all costs" mentality that has been on display for much of the past decades. Stock buy-backs – companies using cash from their balance sheets to purchase their stock in the open market for the purpose of retiring that stock and increasing their earnings per share – hit an all-time high in 2018, with over $800 billion spent on such efforts. That was an increase of over 50 percent from the prior year and represented the most extensive annual stock buy-back total ever recorded (the previous record was 2007, just before the Great Recession of 2008–2009). Contrast that to more traditional R&D investing that increased at a much more modest 8.8 percent that same year.[20] When given the choice of where to invest the additional dollars generated from paying lower taxes, companies chose to invest in boosting their stock price, not in their businesses' future development or in their communities.

Perhaps that's because many companies lack the opportunities to invest that money wisely. Just because you have a lot of excess cash lying around doesn't mean you know where best to invest it. In fact, several studies have suggested that most companies fail to invest optimally in R&D.[21] If this fact surprises you, consider how important the role of small business is in driving the economy, given that larger companies often lack the wherewithal to invest intelligently. Policies that invest money back into the economy via small business loans or other forms of support for the entrepreneurial economy could have yielded a much larger return. While stock buy-backs are, on the whole, not especially productive for the economy, for an individual business – especially when viewed through the short-term lens of stock price – repurchasing stock may indeed be the rational choice. But contrast that with the option of government spending on R&D, which has historically been quite effective, having quite literally launched entire industries (the internet is just one example). By taking money out of government coffers to be used for corporate stock buy-backs, the TCJA may very well have actually exacerbated inequality trends.[22]

Fortunately, there are signs that this "profit-at-all-costs" mentality is changing – something that appears to be true across the political spectrum. Our grassroots entrepreneurs and *New Builders* are poised to grow in number and strength, as more people realize that a world dominated exclusively by big businesses isn't one in which we want to live.

Signs of Change?

In August 2019, CEOs from 181 publicly traded companies, the self-described "Business Roundtable," signed a joint statement proclaiming new principles of governance, purportedly signaling an end to Milton Friedman's doctrine of shareholder primacy. But KKS Advisors, supported by the Ford Foundation, found these companies have been just as ruthless as nonsignatory companies since their CEOs made this public statement meant to signal a change in operating philosophy.[23] Meanwhile, the Brookings Institute found profits at 13 big retail companies rose a combined $16.9 billion, or 39 percent, in 2020 through the early part of the pandemic. The average pay for front-line workers was up only $1.11 an hour, or 10 percent. And by the second wave of the virus in the fall of 2020, big retailers had abandoned hazard pay for retail workers.[24]

The difficulty of actually enacting change, even as profits washed over many large companies during the most widespread and devastating economic crisis since the Great Depression, shows how deeply ingrained the culture of shareholder primacy is, built on centuries of law and institutions designed to keep capital in the hands of people who already have it.

Change in labor markets is more likely to come from *New Builders*. Our children's generation, shaped by the social upheaval of the past few years and the pandemic, may value health, dignity, security, and time with family and friends, more than their predecessors. We have the choice now to create more competitive economies and an equal playing field between big and small companies, which will spur the growth and innovation we need.

When an area has a rising number of chain stores, the rate of new startups drops, according to Brookings economist Robert Litan.[25] This is a powerful example of how big businesses can grow to a point where they suck all the oxygen out of an economy and starve smaller enterprises out of the market. Driven by the increasing power of online giants such as Amazon and the consolidation of retail spending in chain stores in general, this is true across the retail industry. For example, in the grocery sector, sales from the 20 largest food retailers account for two-thirds of US grocery store sales.[26] That same group comprised less than half of US grocery store sales 20 years ago. This is exactly what communities like Nantucket are trying to avoid when they decide to self-regulate to limit the growth of chain stores. They have the ability (one could say privilege) to be more directive about the scarce resource that is Main Street.

Viewed through this wide lens, Wendy Hudson from Nantucket Bookworks is a David who won against the Goliaths. In fact, *New Builders* win surprisingly often. But *New Builders* are hindered by America's informal caste system and the many obstacles that society throws in their way.

Who Can Fight Back?

We don't subscribe to the "big is bad" theory of business. The convenience and choice offered to consumers from the emergence of larger chains and online platforms have many positive effects. And the reach of online brands such as Amazon to far-flung locations across America has, in many ways, benefited people living in rural and isolated areas. But this convenience has come at a cost. And that cost has been in many ways the vibrancy of our communities, the richness of our experiences, the connection we have with the merchants we purchase from, and the opportunities that starting and owning a small business afford many people in our economy. The result is an economy that is less dynamic, is more concentrated, and offers less mobility for those at the bottom rungs of economic status.

Nantucket was well-resourced enough to say no to chain stores. But consider another neighborhood, once just as distinct and vibrant. In Alexandria, Virginia, Booker T. Wilkins has owned a barbershop on Queen Street for 50 years. To stand in his shop is to quickly and intimately become aware that one can't replicate the rich surroundings of a locally owned business: red-and-white checkered floor, a framed letter from the mayor congratulating the shop on 50 years in business, and an ancient cash register, white receipt curling from the top. "T," as Booker is known, keeps that old register even though it only rings transactions up to $5. It is a reminder of the character and charm that so many small businesses bring to our communities (to charge for his $20 haircuts, T rings up four $5 charges). He still draws a loyal clientele, but the once-thriving Black neighborhood that surrounds his shop – one featured in the movie *Remember the Titans*, about the integration of Alexandria's high school – has steadily shrunk around T's barbershop to only about two blocks.

Small businesses are places for people to connect. Outside on the street, a small group of men is hanging out on metal folding chairs, having just emerged from the Sunday prayer meeting T holds inside. Wilkins lost two of his children to cancer, many years ago. In the time after, when he was struggling with depression, a deacon came in for a haircut. "He sat in this chair," Wilkins said, pointing to one. "He said, 'Hold on for today, Brother Wilkins. Every day after this one will be better.'"

T is politically aware and a leader in the Black community. But his voice has often gone unheard – such as when the city government has over the years used eminent domain to uproot Black communities to make way for development. He feared the same tactic would eventually be turned on the remaining Black-owned businesses, as Alexandria competes with other cities to land the lucrative big chain stores that add to its tax base.

T was named after Booker T. Washington and reads the leader's biography about three times a year. Washington is a sometimes controversial figure in Black history because he advocated for economic security and self-determination before civil liberties. Wilkins loves his personal story. Washington walked 500 miles to attend a school for free Blacks and founded the National Negro Business League and what became Tuskegee University. "I feel like I can do anything," T said, "because he did so much."

One hundred years later, T copes with some of the same obstacles as the man he is named for. Black *New Builders* in the United States face present-day racism and systemic barriers born of our country's troubled history, a tremendous loss of economic power, dynamism, and innovation. The barriers women of all races face are different but likewise pernicious. It takes a different lens to see them.

Endnotes

1. ISLR (2006), "Formula Business Restriction – Nantucket, MA," https://ilsr .org/rule/formula-business-restrictions/2315-2/
2. Stacey Stowe, "Nantucket Votes to Ban Chain Stores from Downtown," *The New York Times* (April 12), www.nytimes.com/2006/04/12/realestate/ commercial/nantucket-votes-to-ban-chain-stores-from-downtown.html

3. Leigh Buchanan, "American Entrepreneurship Is Actually Vanishing. Here's Why," *Inc.,* May 2015, www.inc.com/magazine/201505/leigh-buchanan/the-vanishing-startups-in-decline.html

4. Matt Stoller, *Goliath: The 100-Year War between Monopoly Power and Democracy* (New York: Simon & Schuster, 2019)

5. Ibid., p. 44

6. Ibid., p. 161

7. Douglas A. McIntyre, "Over 2000 American Newspapers Have Closed in Past 15 Years," 24/7 Wall St, July 23, 2019, 247wallst.com/media/2019/07/23/over-2000-american-newspapers-have-closed-in-past-15-years/

8. Ronald Reagan, www.brainyquote.com/quotes/ronald_reagan_183751

9. Barack Obama, www.azquotes.com/author/11023-Barack_Obama/tag/small-business

10. "Republican Platform 2016," https://prod-cdn-static.gop.com/media/documents/DRAFT_12_FINAL%5B1%5D-ben_1468872234.pdf

11. "2020 Democratic Party Platform," www.demconvention.com/wp-content/uploads/2020/08/2020-07-31-Democratic-Party-Platform-For-Distribution.pdf

12. "President Donald J. Trump Recognizes the Importance of Small Businesses During 2018 Small Business Week," Whitehouse.gov, 2018, www.whitehouse.gov/briefings-statements/president-donald-j-trump-recognizes-importance-small-businesses-2018-small-business-week/

13. "The War on Regulation," *Coalition for Sensible Safeguards*, 2018, https://sensiblesafeguards.org/waronregs/

14. "Polling Memo: Voters Support Strong Consumer Financial Protections and Tough Regulation of Wall Street," *AFR*, 2020, https://ourfinancialsecurity.org/2020/09/voters-support-strong-2020/

15. "How American See Digital Privacy Issues Amid the COVID-19 Outbreak," Pew Research Center, 2020, www.pewresearch.org/fact-tank/2020/05/04/how-americans-see-digital-privacy-issues-amid-the-covid-19-outbreak/

16. "Polling," Coalition for Sensible Safeguards, 2020, https://sensiblesafeguards.org/polling/

17. Buchanan, "American Entrepreneurship Is Actually Vanishing. Here's Why."

18. Austin Herrick, "Estimates of TCJA Repatriation of Foreign Earnings on Investment and GDP," Penn Wharton Budget Model, August 29, 2018, https://budgetmodel.wharton.upenn.edu/issues/2018/8/29/estimates-of-tcja-repatriation-of-foreign-earnings-on-investment-and-gdp

19. "Key Elements of the US Tax System," Urban Institute and Brookings Institution Tax Policy Center, 2020, www.taxpolicycenter.org/briefing-book/how-do-us-corporate-income-tax-rates-and-revenues-compare-other-countries

20. Fred Economic Data, "Gross Private Domestic Investment: Domestic Business," https://fred.stlouisfed.org/series/W987RC1Q027SBEA

21. Anne Marie Knott, "Why That Tax Cut and Jobs Act (TCJA) Led to Buybacks Rather Than Investment," *Forbes,* February 21, 2019, www.forbes.com/sites/annemarieknott/2019/02/21/why-the-tax-cuts-and-jobs-act-tcja-led-to-buybacks-rather-than-investment/#c5a988e37fbc

22. William Lazonick, Mustafa Erdem Sakinç, and Matt Hopkins, "Why Stock Buybacks Are Dangerous for the Economy," *Harvard Business Review,* January 7, 2020, https://hbr.org/2020/01/why-stock-buybacks-are-dangerous-for-the-economy

23. Peter S. Goodman, "Stakeholder Capitalism Gets A Report Card. It's Not Good," *The New York Times*, September 22, 2020, https://www.nytimes.com/2020/09/22/business/business-roudtable-stakeholder-capitalism.html

24. Molly Kinder, Laura Stateler, and Julia Du, "The COVID-19 hazard continues, but hazard pay does not: Why America's essential workers need a raise," *Brookings Institution*, October 29, 2020, https://www.brookings.edu/research/the-covid-19-hazard-continues-but-the-hazard-pay-does-not-why-americas-frontline-workers-need-a-raise/

25. Buchanan, "American Entrepreneurship Is Actually Vanishing. Here's Why."

26. "Retail Trends," *USDA*, 2020, www.ers.usda.gov/topics/food-markets-prices/retailing-wholesaling/retail-trends/

CHAPTER EIGHT

Where's the Money?

In 2008, Kirsten Quigley was a stay-at-home mom of four kids, ranging in age from preschool to fourth grade, when her oldest son brought home information from school about ways to be environmentally friendly. This led their family to discover more research on schools and environmentalism. One of the most shocking statistics they uncovered was that 20 million plastic sandwich bags are sent to landfills every day from kids' lunchboxes. A lifelong environmentalist and not one to shrink from a challenge, Kirsten set out to inspire children to be more environmentally conscious. Determined to encourage kids to become change-makers and drive them into action – specifically to show people that many small, simple choices every day can have a significant impact on our planet – she and several friends founded 3greenmoms to try to address what they saw was a large and impactful market opportunity. Plastic is a big contributor to greenhouse gas emissions and climate change. The extraction of fossil fuels to make plastic, emissions during the manufacturing process, and the eventual disposal of plastic, either into a landfill or through incineration, all have a significant impact on our planet.

"The kitchen table is to women entrepreneurs as the garage is to men: the legendary birthplace of some of the best ideas," she joked.

The trio of mothers realized that their kids' schools' environmental efforts, to the extent they even had them, were focused on messages around recycling and sustainability. All laudable goals, but too abstract to appeal to kids. Ideas around "going green" clearly weren't resonating with their kids or their classmates. For sure, the kids could remember to recycle, but most were already doing that, and the impact was minimal.

"I was looking at how I could raise a generation that thinks green and to how we could make green more mainstream," Kirsten told us. And as she and her friends thought about the daily lunches they prepared for their kids an idea for a product popped into their minds: what about, they thought, reusable sandwich bags?

Kirsten is direct but careful, and quietly relentless. Building a company when you're a woman entrepreneur requires navigating a business world constructed by men, toggling between fulfilling the roles expected of you and by you. In Kirsten's case, that meant being a good wife and mother, and the less defined role of being a female entrepreneur and business leader. But Kirsten has been able to successfully inhabit these multiple roles. Her two business partners left in 2014, but she persisted. Twelve years later, Lunchskins — as the company is now referred to — is thriving, with sales in the millions of dollars. And the idea of reusable packaging is gaining real steam, especially now that more and more municipalities are banning the use of single-use plastics. Perhaps a bit ahead of the mainstream market when she started, Kirsten and Lunchskins are right in the thick of one of the most important trends in changing consumer behavior. Lunchskins paper bags are a big seller, in Whole Foods, Target, The Container Store, and 3,500 other stores – and Ziploc itself has followed Lunchskins with the introduction of its own reusable paper bags.

"I'm extremely proud of what we've built. It's authentic, and we walk the walk, when it comes to our mission. That's been really important to us," Kirsten said.

But sometimes, a nagging doubt enters her mind. "Maybe I've stunted the company's growth," she says. "Maybe we could have grown faster." Among women, even tremendously successful entrepreneurs, self-doubt is a near-constant refrain, reinforced by hundreds or thousands of books and courses that offer to teach women how they need to adapt to men's leadership styles and career tracks impossible to combine with family lives. The problem isn't women. It is a system that in subtle and unsubtle ways confines them to particular economic paths and then tells them their discomfort at being confined is a sign that they need to change. The struggle women entrepreneurs face accessing capital is a critical element of an unjust system. Access to capital, whether from friends and family, through a home equity loan, or from a bank loan, is the sine qua non of entrepreneurship. Access to advice, mentorship, and networks is closely tied to capital and in many ways related.

On the surface, Kirsten should have had access to everything she needed. She grew up upper-middle class and had big personal and professional networks. She and her partners started 3greenmoms with a relatively modest amount of capital, less than $10,000 as she remembers it, but were able to fund that amount themselves. And in the early days (and for many years after), Kirsten was able to forgo paying herself because of her family circumstances. That is to say that compared to many – in fact, most – entrepreneurs starting businesses, she and her co-founders had key advantages.

But even seemingly well-connected entrepreneurs struggle to get the attention and capital they need to start and scale their businesses. It wasn't until she was able to establish a relationship with a local community bank that she built the foundation for access to the capital and other banking services that she needed to scale her company into a bigger wholesale operation. And Kirsten struggled for years to build the mentor relationships that are the hallmarks of many successful businesses.

Women-Owned Businesses Are Our Single Biggest Potential Source of Economic Growth

Entrepreneurship, and the economic power that comes from entrepreneurship, is the latest frontier in a long journey toward equal rights for women. In 1982, feminist economist Charlotte Perkins Gilman published the novella *The Yellow Wall-Paper*, a horrifying depiction of how the medical and legal systems worked together to institutionalize or otherwise isolate ambitious women simply by spousal fiat.[1] Laws establishing women's right to practice professions of their choosing were passed in the late 1800s and the efforts to put legal protections into practice have continued since. In 1963, the Equal Pay Act passed, requiring equal wages for women and men doing equal work. It was the first federal law prohibiting sex discrimination.

Female entrepreneurs today, especially in the sciences, are aware of their place in the history of this struggle. Women of color are double barrier-smashers. And women have made more headway as entrepreneurs than in the corporate world. The number of women CEOs among the Fortune 500 is anemic – around 5 percent. While this represents progress from 10 years ago (when 3 percent were female) and 25 years ago (when not a single Fortune 500 company was led by a woman), it pales in comparison to the progress women are making starting businesses.[2]

Since 1997 there have been an average of 608 net new women-owned firms launched each and every day – and the rate in 2019 and 2020 was 887 per day. The number of women-owned firms is increasing at a rate 1.5 times the national average, meaning women are starting new businesses at a much higher rate than their male counterparts.[3] But researchers looking into the overall problem of why entrepreneurship in the United States is declining have noticed a problem: women-owned businesses are also more likely to be small, stay small, and also to fail.[4]

For women-owned businesses, the average number of employees decreased from 0.8 in 2014 to 0.7 in 2019, while the average number of employees for all privately held businesses and among all public and private firms similarly declined from 2.0 in 2014 to 1.8 in 2019 and from 4.1 in 2014 to 3.8 in 2019, respectively. As online platforms have made it easy and affordable to source freelancers, companies have hired fewer permanent employees. In addition, the use of technology, including artificial intelligence and automation, has reduced the need for employees.[5]

But even accounting for these changes in the overall economy, women-owned businesses often remain small. The revenue disparity between women-owned and all privately held businesses has increased since 1997. For every dollar that a privately held company generated, women-owned businesses generated 37 cents in 1997 and 30 cents in 2019. In 2019, women-owned businesses averaged earnings of $142,900 compared to $474,900 for all privately held businesses and $1.4 million for all firms (including publicly traded companies).[6] Leveling the playing field so that more women can succeed as entrepreneurs requires recognizing the complexity of the patterns that keep them from achieving this success. Researchers are picking up signs just under the surface that while things are changing, some important things – capital and networks – are staying the same, or at best changing much more slowly.

A Different Flavor of Iced Tea

A decade before Kirsten devised Lunchskins at her kitchen table, Seth Goldman also recognized a trend well ahead of its taking hold in popular culture. Sugary drinks were barely on the health radar in 1998 when he started his company, Honest Tea, with the idea of selling a lower-sugar and healthier alternative to soda. Consumption of soda more than doubled in the United States from 1977 through 2002.[7] This coincided with an increase in obesity of similar magnitude. But the public discourse around the hazards of sugary beverages, which included not just soda but also juices and other flavored beverages, was only just starting to take shape.[8]

Seth and his co-founder, Barry Nalebuff, his professor at Yale School of Management, had talked about the need for lower-calorie drinks when Seth was a student. But it wasn't until a handful of years later that he came back to the idea and reached out to his former professor for help. The timing was fortuitous – Nalebuff had just written a case study about the Tata Tea company in India. Together they outlined an idea for brewing tea that had less sugar than the drinks that were then ubiquitously available in shopping markets and convenience stores around the country.[i]

---

[i] The recounting of Seth Goldman's story is drawn from interviews Elizabeth conducted in 2015 in preparation for an article for CNBC.com, as well as her time with him at an Aspen Institute retreat, the Socrates Program, in 2017, and follow-up interview in Fall 2020. We also drew on the book Seth wrote with Barry, *Mission in a Bottle*.

Meanwhile, Goldman, the son of a father who was a professor at Wellesley, a mother who taught at Boston University, and both of whom received PhDs from Harvard, was lucky. His father had invested on behalf of his two children many years before. The elder Goldman cashed in Seth's stock and gave the money to him, enabling Seth to work for a year, full-time, on the business. In 1998 Barry and Seth started brewing tea in Seth's kitchen in Bethesda, Maryland.

That year they landed their first account in Fresh Fields Markets (which was eventually bought by Whole Foods Markets as part of their rapid, national expansion in the 2000s). It was a struggle to find the right balance between low sugar and taste. In fact, in the early days of the business, some of the products they introduced had so little sugar, they were rejected by consumers.

One thing Seth and Barry had in abundance was money. They raised $500,000 from friends and family shortly after starting the business. It was work, of course; from almost day one, Seth spent about half his time on fundraising and sales. His hit rate, as he remembered it, was less than 1 in 10. Nevertheless, they were always able to find capital when they needed it. And that capital fueled the success of the business.

Honest Tea grew, and grew rapidly, introducing new flavors and transitioning to fully organic. In just their fifth year of operations, the company generated more than $5 million in sales.[9] By its tenth year, 2008, the Coca-Cola Company purchased 40 percent of the business for a reported $43 million.[10] Three years later, with the business on track to record $75 million in sales, Coca-Cola purchased the rest of the business and Honest Tea became a wholly owned subsidiary of Coke.

Honest Tea saw the kind of success that many entrepreneurs dream about. From its beginnings, the company charted a course in a new and emerging market – practically creating that market along their road to success. They were scrappy and the lore of the business includes stories of their founders driving samples from store to store to find buyers. Ultimately they found investment, scale, and success doing something they were passionate about and which they believed was good for the world. And in the end, it was a financial success for themselves and their investors.

And for Seth Goldman, as we'll see, it was just the beginning.

The Nexus of Capital, Network, and Culture

In 1986, Scholastic Publishing launched a phenomenally successful series for preteen girls called *The Baby-sitters Club*. It follows the adventures of girls as they establish a babysitting service in their neighborhood. The series, which ran from 1986 through 2000, eventually sold more than 176 million copies[11] and spawned a television series.

It showed girls building a business – but a certain kind of business. Scholastic's mindset about what professions and businesses women filled was perhaps aptly revealed in an interview its editorial director, David Levithan, gave to *The New York Times*: "This whole generation of girls who had grown up reading *The Baby-sitters Club* were now teachers, librarians, or mothers," Mr. Levithan said. "And at any opportunity they had, they let us know they wanted them back. We couldn't go to a convention without having women come up to us and say, 'You've got to bring these books back.'"[12]

Our systems and networks were built primarily to support White men and build on their ideas – the images that people see of entrepreneurs are men, and perhaps just as importantly, the images we see of women entrepreneurs show them at the helm of particular kinds of businesses that tend to remain small.

And this is to say nothing of Silicon Valley and access to the larger sums of venture capital or that fuel the tech economy in the United States. Women receive only a fraction of venture dollars (2.2 percent in 2018 according to *Fortune*) compared to male company founders.[13] These discrepancies reach down into all areas of our support system for entrepreneurs. *New Builders* who are women lack access to capital at the scale their White, male counterparts enjoy. Not surprisingly given these discrepancies, women also struggle to find mentors and access the business networks that help White men turn their ideas into companies and grow them. And when they do find mentors, those relationships tend to be less effective and produce less benefit for women than they do for men.[14]

The obvious question is why, in an age where there's a rising commitment among many White men to share the power, *and* a new imperative to grow the economy, is it still so difficult for promising women to find mentors, who are often the key to unlocking capital and other resources? A growing number of women entrepreneurs push themselves to develop relationships with men in business settings but meet with silence, rejection, and sometimes outright misogyny.

To get to the heart of that question, we asked one of the world's experts at communicating across cultural divides, the peacebuilder John Paul Lederach. He told us he believes that in most cases men's difficulty in offering help comes down to a level of comfort. Because many men feel more comfortable with each other, and many don't have the skills to develop close relationships with women (or anyone who is outside their "norm") in business settings, "The safer option will always be to stay with what is known, closer to the place where men in leadership positions feel more comfortable reading cues and controlling process and outcome. Ultimately, feeling insecure means not feeling in control, and in an environment where feeling out of control designates weakness. So my guess to your question, the default will revert to avoiding whatever feels insecure and beyond control."[15]

In the business world, as in other parts of American society, the desire by men to be part of an "inner circle" is often enhanced by taking part in that circle's "othering" of women and people of color. In the worst cases – there are, unfortunately, many examples of the worst cases – people with power dehumanize people without power, in racial, misogynist, and homophobic terms. Perhaps protected somewhat by her social standing and skin color, Kirsten was lucky not to encounter overt prejudice, despite struggling to find supporters and mentors.

Grassroots Growth

Entrepreneurs by nature don't spend much time dwelling on obstacles; they'd never be able to build businesses if they did. In the beginning, Kirsten and her co-founders set out, idea in hand, to find a replacement for the ubiquitous plastic sandwich bag. It needed to be food-safe, of course, and durable so it could be cleaned – ideally in a dishwasher – and reused. Their search ultimately led them only a few hours' drive away from their home base in Bethesda, Maryland, and an initial manufacturer that was able to service them for their first product even at the nascent scale of a business that was just getting started. Lunchskins was born.

"I wanted to meet people where they were with a solution that was easy, convenient, and affordable," she explained of her early thinking. "The last feeling I wanted to give people was guilt."[16]

In the early days of the company, Kirsten enlisted the help of her kids and her friends to fulfill orders. They carried packages to the post office, "standing in line with an armful of packages like everybody else waiting."

Kirsten and her early partners had enough tech-savvy to build their own website and the self-confidence to walk into specialty stores and small groceries to pitch their product themselves.

There have been plenty of breaks for the business. In March 2010, Lunchskins was featured in *Oprah* magazine and in May 2014 on the Katie Couric Show. "It literally broke our servers," Kirsten said. But there were also many setbacks. Kirsten eventually split from her partners and now is the sole owner of the company. In particular, she struggled over the years to access the mentor relationships that she knew would help her scale and grow the company.

Some people she reached out to didn't respond or turned down her requests to connect. In part, her challenge to develop these mentor relationships came from her own reluctance to put herself out there. In fact, she says it's one of her biggest mistakes. "I wish I'd come out of my shell sooner and opened up, been vulnerable, and invited people in," she says.

As confident as she was on the surface, she was plagued with something that is familiar even to the most successful women (and more men than we probably realize): imposter syndrome. She didn't want someone to look deeply at Lunchskins because she was afraid they'd tell her how wrong her systems were. It was a challenging time for Kirsten, but ultimately, she found support through joining a broader community of entrepreneurs and learning that she was not alone in her struggles. "I learned that there were a lot of people out there running businesses who were scared, like me, of failing or letting their teams down or letting their families down. Having a place to share insecurities and experiences helped me regain my footing and my confidence," she told us, describing that time in both her company's history and her personal journey as a CEO.

Kirsten remains sanguine about her journey and the slow build that not being able to access greater amounts of capital required. "There is a benefit to what being small, nimble, and scrappy forced us to do. To be focused. To not stretch our product lines too quickly but own the space we were in."

Kirsten is typical of successful entrepreneurs. She recognized a problem that was right in front of her but for which no one had found a solution. It was a winning idea, and the paper and reusable bags she makes have replaced more than 2.5 billion plastic bags. Their motto is making "a life less plastic" easy, affordable, and accessible to everyone. Their impact has been impressive, but the financing that could have allowed her to grow faster wasn't available to her, despite her success. And the result is that, now 12 years into Lunchskins, sales, while impressive, are still relatively modest given the market potential and demand.

We celebrate scrappiness and grit as qualities of entrepreneurs, but that celebration shouldn't disguise a central question: Where's the money?

Capital Matters

Our inability to adapt our systems of finance to include *New Builders* is a critical reason that entrepreneurship in the United States is flagging. In their book *Where the Jobs Are: Entrepreneurship and the Soul of the American Economy*, John Dearie and Courtney Geduldig interviewed more than 200 founders about the challenges of building businesses. Their subjects cited five: insufficient access to capital; difficulty finding people with the right skills; immigration policies that keep talent out; onerous taxes and regulations; and economic uncertainty. Those go a long way toward explaining why companies struggle to scale. But they offer only a partial explanation for why fewer companies start in the first place.

After the financial crisis and Great Recession of 2008–2009, access to startup capital became increasingly difficult, especially for women, immigrants, and people of color. And the home equity loans that many entrepreneurs historically relied on to get their businesses afloat became more challenging, if not impossible, to obtain. This tightening of credit continues to make it harder for entrepreneurs to start successful businesses.

Because so many businesses rely on personal capital to start their ventures, the increasing discrepancy between the capital class and everyone else is creating substantial barriers to entry to those wanting to start a new business. Those at the top of the wealth scale have a greater propensity to start businesses than those at the bottom, according to data compiled by Erik Hurst of the University of Chicago and Annamaria Lusardi of Dartmouth College.[17] The fact that so many people from lower ends of the income scale, disproportionately women and people of color, are starting businesses despite this constraint suggests a large pent-up entrepreneurial demand unmet by our financing infrastructure. Even an increase in home equity value has been shown to be positively correlated with starting new businesses.[18]

Clearly, the lack of capital access is a drag on entrepreneurial activity. One study by researchers Casey J. Frid, David M. Wyman, and Bentley Coffey explored the relationship between wealth and entrepreneurship (their paper was aptly titled: *Effects of Wealth Inequality on Entrepreneurship*).[19] The conclusion was stark: "Entrepreneurial success is concentrated at the top of the wealth distribution, despite notable evidence of capability for those at the lower end of the wealth distribution."

People lower on the wealth scale find it harder to sustain their businesses through the initial phases – what Frid, Whyman, and Coffey refer to as the *gestation period*. The study found "strong evidence of higher dropout rates among low-wealth and moderately wealthy nascent entrepreneurs." Simply put, entrepreneurs with fewer personal resources weren't able to stick it out and survive through the tumultuous early days of starting a new venture. If they were able to survive that gestation period, the study suggested that rates of success evened out. These trends are also borne out in the world of high-tech and tech-enabled entrepreneurship. One study found that firms coming out of business accelerator programs (programs set up to help early companies work on their ideas and accelerate their growth) grew their top line by 30 percent more in the following two years than companies that failed to raise capital. Additionally, they employed 50 percent more people than their peers who were not externally funded.[20]

The research on entrepreneurship, by definition, focuses on entrepreneurs who have already started businesses. That is to say that they leave out the millions of potential entrepreneurs who, for lack of resources, don't even try to set a course for their entrepreneurial dream. This is the real tragedy of the funding gap – the unknown numbers of entrepreneurs who never get their start.

"We have much less ability to understand what's happening six months before you start a business, or when you decide not to start a business even though you wanted to," said Samee Desai, former director of knowledge creation and research in entrepreneurship at the Ewing Marion Kauffman Foundation. "I'm worried that we don't really understand enough about the people who never get to start.... When we look at a statistic such as three out of every thousand people are new entrepreneurs, what about the people who could, or want to, but don't? How many are there, and why?"[21]

Banks

After five years, Lunchskins hit a rough patch. They had decided to open a physical office and focus more intently on scaling the business. "Building and marketing a consumer product requires a lot of collaboration between teams," Kirsten recounted. "Innovation and design, operations, sales, marketing. Being together streamlined our ability to collaborate together." With wholesale orders coming in – Target alone had 1,700 locations carrying their products – they'd found an overseas manufacturer that could help them scale at a lower cost. But Kirsten needed access to more capital to expand.

In Nike founder Phil Knight's biography of his entrepreneurial journey, *Shoe Dog*, he recounts the benefits of being able to walk across the street to talk face-to-face with a banker and ask for credit – something he did a number of times by his telling, as Nike struggled to get off the ground in its early days. Kirsten needed the same kind of help. She had struggled for years inside the labyrinth of a large national bank. Eventually, she woke up to the reality that trying to navigate this banking maze was never going to give her access to the services she wanted. It was then Kirsten made a fortunate move.

Eagle Bank wasn't literally across the street from Kirsten, but it was close enough.[22] A Washington, DC – area bank with 21 branches, Eagle provided Kirsten the capital she needed to place that crucial overseas order. And more importantly, Kirsten had access to bankers who would take the time to understand the business she was building and what credit and other services she needed to grow. We heard stories like this regularly from *New Builders* as we traveled (and later, after the pandemic hit, Zoomed) across the country meeting with them. Accessing capital is a critical part of being able to start and grow a business, but finding someone who could help them look at their business and spend the time that was needed to come up with creative solutions to their financing and business needs was what set these relationships apart.

Just as some of the systems were starting to fall into place, sales plateaued. Kirsten's partner left and she became the sole leader of the company. "It was an opportunity to take a hard look at what we were doing. We were no longer the only kid on the block. There were a lot of copycats doing Lunchskins-like stuff." Until then, the company had focused only on reusable bags. At this point, Kirsten looked deep into her environmentalist's heart and decided that she could justify introducing a paper sandwich bag. It wasn't reusable, but it was a step in the right direction.

> As well as we knew our customers, we weren't really listening very well to the nuances. Not all of them were green in all aspects of their lives, and many still wanted the convenience of throwing their stuff out. They'd tell us: Hey, my kids recycle, it's the gateway into being green. This gave birth to our recyclable but sealable paper food storage line as an alternative to plastic. We essentially launched a new company with a different line of sustainable products (different manufacturing partners, different distribution channels, different marketing).

Lunchskins might never have made the leap from promising startup to growing enterprise without the help of this community bank. As Kristen put it: "Eagle Bank really supports women and supports entrepreneurs. They have taken some chances on us and given us a healthy line of credit. We just couldn't have sourced our production overseas as an anonymous small business with a big national bank."

Banks like Eagle are crucial for entrepreneurs – especially so for *New Builders*. But these banks are becoming increasingly rare.

The Slow Decline of Community Banks

Only about 20 percent of entrepreneurs are able to take advantage of various banking and government loan programs, and the increasing consolidation of the banking sector has made it harder for minority, female, and rural business founders to access capital. Between 1994 and 2014, the number of community banks declined from 10,329 to 6,094. These banks are often the initial source of capital for businesses and disproportionately serve the rural United States (community banks are four times more likely to be located in rural areas). New community banks are essentially at a standstill with only six new community banks opening between 2011 and 2017, compared with over 1,000 such banks opening in the seven years before that.[23]

At the same time, large banks have become larger. During the same 20-year period between 1994 and 2014 that saw such a stark decline in the community banking system, large banks actually grew – from 73 to 120. Larger banks emerged from the Great Recession of 2008–2009 in far better shape than their small counterparts. Federal aid restored their balance sheets and increased regulation created greater barriers for smaller banks. "Big is beautiful" morphed into "too big to fail."[24]

Fed by the decline in the community banking system, the overall banking system has been shrinking, as measured by the number of banks. In fact, the total number of banks in the United States in 2018 – just under 5,700 – was the lowest in over a century.[25]

With some exceptions, big banks are remarkably unfriendly toward *New Builders*. In 2016, less than half – 40 percent – of businesses owned by people of color received the full amount of capital they sought in their loan applications.[26] This compares to 68 percent of nonminority-owned businesses. SBA loans to women-owned businesses accounted for only 18 percent of the total number of SBA 7(a) and 504 loans approved. Entrepreneurs are remarkably resilient – but at a certain point, throwing yourself and your loan application against the brick walls of a $2 trillion international bank only to be met by email silence starts to feel hopeless.

"While [minority-owned businesses] are equally likely to apply for funding, they are more likely to experience less positive outcomes than businesses owned by Whites," noted researcher Alicia Robb. "They are more likely than White-owned businesses to have been denied credit, they are less likely to receive most or all of the funding requested, and they are more likely to be financially constrained. They are also more likely to be discouraged and to not apply for funding when needed because they feared their applications would be denied."[27]

We believe larger banks can offer similar services. After all, most large national banks have local offices and local bankers. In fact, we believe that large banks need to do so if we are to help support the number of entrepreneurs that are needed to keep our economy thriving. There are some large banks that are making meaningful investments in historically underbanked communities. But we need to recognize that the consolidation of the banking system, along with the increasing complexity required to support *New Builders* is, in its current configuration, not working. Too few *New Builders* have access to capital and those that do often are unable to obtain the full amount of investment they're looking for. This is making it harder for *New Builders* as a group to get their businesses off the ground and is harming the growth and vibrancy of our grassroots entrepreneurial economy.

More than Just Capital

In 2017, as Lunchskins launched the recyclable paper sandwich bags that would propel its next growth, Seth Goldman was two years into his latest venture. The sale of Honest Tea to Coca-Cola had made Seth wealthy – and expanded the company's impact. Seth had demonstrated that the public wanted lower-sugar drinks, and by the early 2000s, the entire drink category had moved in that direction. In 2012, Seth had invested in a small Los Angeles startup, Beyond Meat, making a new kind of meatless meat, made of pea protein, among other things.[28]

Beyond Meat's first product was a failure, but in 2015, Seth joined as executive chairman to help drive the company's growth toward an IPO. Ultimately, he helped guide the company's growth during a critical time when they developed the Beyond Burger – a product that became the first plant-based protein product to be carried in the meat section of grocery stores. The Beyond Burger also opened doors for Beyond Meat to launch with national restaurant chains, including fast-food outlets, and helped the brand expand overseas. By 2019, Beyond Meat burgers could be purchased in TGI Friday's and Dunkin' Donuts, among many other locations.[29]

Seth was going through the same process Kirsten did as she moved her product toward paper. They both had recognized that achieving their ultimate aim, influencing consumer taste, required meeting consumers in the middle. When Beyond Meat went public, Seth owned 2 percent of the company. At the time of its IPO, the company was valued at $3.8 billion.[30,31] Its value has more than doubled since then.

If you looked at Honest Tea and Lunchskins, you'd be struck by similarities between the two. Both Kirsten and Seth are from upper-middle-class to upper-class families with all the advantages that economic status brings. And as a result, both could afford to go without a salary while they worked on their companies. Both businesses were at the very front end of what ultimately became important and systemic trends in American culture, and each helped define changes in that culture.

But Honest Tea took a much faster trajectory and ultimately achieved financial and market success much greater than Lunchskins has been able to obtain, despite the similarities in their founding stories. Was it simply a better idea? Was the execution of that idea far superior? Or were other factors at play?

It's hard to take two businesses in different markets and started at different, if overlapping, times and compare them directly. The course of Honest Tea took many twists and turns, as Seth and his co-founder Barry Nalebuff write about extensively in their book *Mission in a Bottle*.[32] But it's clear that Seth wouldn't have become the entrepreneur he is without Barry's mentorship. Crucially, that mentorship led to the push to raise meaningful initial capital – $500,000 – compared with Kirsten's and her partners, who invested $10,000 of their own funds. Kirsten turned to family for a loan when they needed to scale manufacturing and operations as they expanded their distribution into mass market and grocery stores. Seth was able to raise capital from outside investors.

We can't know how much easier it was for Seth and Barry to develop a relationship because they were both men, or whether it was easier for Seth to sell Honest Tea because he fit the more stereotypical image of an entrepreneur as he walked in the door of chains like Whole Foods.

We view Kirsten's journey as a true entrepreneurial success story in its own right, and one whose ultimate success is ongoing and enduring. But Honest Tea was nearly 100× larger than Lunchskins at the same time in its history. Its success created a platform that enabled Seth to go on to even larger ventures.

What could happen if more people with power were willing to put in the effort to build mentoring relationships across divides, which in turn would likely lead to unlocking capital for nontraditional founders? What if women didn't have extra barriers to overcome? The impact could be tremendous.

In the book *The Trillion Dollar Coach*, Eric Schmidt, long-time CEO of Google, recounts how the legendary business coach Bill Campbell (successful entrepreneur and founder of BEA Systems) "played an instrumental role in the growth of several prominent companies, such as Google, Apple, and Intuit, fostering deep relationships with Silicon Valley visionaries."[33] The companies Bill Campbell worked with are worth well in excess of a trillion dollars, thus the title of the book. These companies employ hundreds of thousands of people and have created wealth not just for their founders but for thousands of other stakeholders. They've spawned more new businesses than can be counted. By any measure, the impact that Bill Campbell had on the US economy and our entrepreneurial ecosystem has been massive.

Our systems of financing – particularly venture capital financing but also bank and other financial institutions – is much too concentrated on a small number of founders in a relatively narrow portion of the economy, population, and country. Similarly, access to mentorship and coaching – the kind of advice that helped steer companies like Google to the incredible success it ultimately became, but also the kind of advice that could help a small business thrive versus just survive – is sorely lacking across much of our entrepreneurial economy. In Chapter 14 we'll dive deeper into some new models that are supporting *New Builders*. By then, it should be clear through the many stories of *New Builders* and their businesses that all businesses, not just high-flying Silicon Valley companies, which not coincidentally tend to be founded by men, benefit from the support structures and systems that are so common in the Valley and similar markets around the United States but lacking everywhere else.

Endnotes

1. Charlotte Perkins Gilman, "The Yellow Wall-Paper," *The New England Magazine,* 1892

2. The Data on Women Leaders," *Pew Research Center,* September 13, 2018, https://www.pewsocialtrends.org/fact-sheet/the-data-on-women-leaders/

3. Jessica Wu, "Women-Owned Firms Springing Up All Over," *American Express,* 2015, https://www.americanexpress.com/en-us/business/trends-and-insights/articles/women-owned-firms-springing/

4. "The 2019 State of Women-Owned Business Report," *American Express,* 2019, https://s1.q4cdn.com/692158879/files/doc_library/file/2019-state-of-women-owned-businesses-report.pdf

5. Samara Joy Nielsen and Barry M. Popkin, "Changes in Beverage Intake Between 1997 and 2001," *American Journal of Preventive Medicine* 27, no. 3 (2004): 205–210, https://www.sciencedirect.com/science/article/abs/pii/S0749379704001229#aep-abstract-sec-id8

6. "The 2019 State of Women-Owned Business Report."

7. Richard Bernstein (2009), Fighting for the Right to Drink Soda," *New York Times* (October 7), www.nytimes.com/2009/10/08/us/08iht-letter.html

8. Ibid

9. "Our Story," https://www.honesttea.com/our-story

10. Andrea Walker, "Drink Maker Finds Coke Its Cup of Tea," *Baltimore Sun,* April 16 2008, www.baltimoresun.com/news/environment/sns-honest-tea-coke-green-story.html

11. "The Baby-sitters Club," https://kids.scholastic.com/kid/books/baby-sitters-club/

12. Ibid

13. Emma Henchliffe, "Funding for Female Founders Stalled at 2.2% of VC Dollars in 2018," *Fortune,* January 28, 2019, https://fortune.com/2019/01/28/funding-female-founders-2018/

14. Kimberly Weisul, "Why Mentoring Helps Men More Than Women," CBS News, March 25, 2011, www.cbsnews.com/news/why-mentoring-helps-men-more-than-women/

15. Interview with John Paul Lederach, Fall 2020.

16. All quotes from an interview with Kirsten Quigley, July 2020.

17. Eric Hurst and Annamaria Lusardi, "Liquidity Constraints and Entrepreneurship. Household Wealth, Parental Wealth, and the Transition In and Out of Entrepreneurship," paper presented at Conference on Savings and Entrepreneurship, Hudson Institute in Washington, DC, April 2004, https://www.dartmouth.edu/~alusardi/Papers/Liquidity_dec06.pdf

18. "Access to Capital for Entrepreneurs: Removing Barriers," *Kauffman Foundation,* 2009, https://www.kauffman.org/wp-content/uploads/2019/12/CapitalReport_042519.pdf

19. Casey J. Frid, David M. Wyman, and Bentley Coffey, *Effects of Wealth Inequality on Entrepreneurship* (Springer Link, 2016), https://link.springer.com/article/10.1007/s11187-016-9742-9

20. Benjamin L. Hallen, Christopher Bingham, and Susan Cohen, "Do Accelerators Accelerate? A Study of Venture Accelerators as a Path to Success," 2014, www.researchgate.net/publication/276895878_Do_Accelerators_Accelerate_A_Study_of_Venture_Accelerators_as_a_Path_to_Success

21. Interview with Samee Desai, Fall 2020.

22. https://www.eaglebankcorp.com

23. Marshall Lux and Robert Greene (2015), working paper, "The State And Fate Of Community Banking," *Harvard Kennedy School Mossavar-Rhamani Center For Business And Government.*

24. Ibid

25. Search on FindBankSuite, FDIC, accessed summer 2020.

26. "2016 Small Business Credit Survey: Report on Minority-Owned Firms," FED Small Business, 2016, https://www.fedsmallbusiness.org/survey/2017/report-on-minority-owned-firms

27. Interview with Alicia Robb, Spring 2020.

28. Margaret Ng (2012), "20 Years of Research Lead to Soy Chicken Strips That Taste Like, Have Texture of Meat," *Missourian*, August 21,2012, https://www.columbiamissourian.com/news/years-of-research-lead-to-soy-chicken-strips-that-taste/article_f01af65e-d93f-52fd-84cc-36281bc7bdb2.html

29. Kaitlyn McInnis, "Major Fast Food Chains Selling Beyond Meat and Impossible Burgers," *Askmen*, November 20, 2019, https://www.askmen.com/food_booze/food/major-fast-food-chains-selling-beyond-meat-and-impossible-burgers.html

30. Hamza Shaban and Thomas Heath, "Beyond Meat, a Plant-Based Food Company, Suggest 163 Percent after IPO," *The Washington Post,* May 2, 2019, www.washingtonpost.com/business/2019/05/02/beyond-meat-plant-based-food-company-readies-ipo/

31. Deena Shanker, "Beyond Meat Just Had the Best IPO of 2019 as Value Soars to $3.8 Billion," *Yahoo!finance*, 2019, finance.yahoo.com/news/beyond-meat-inc-may-just-201250023.html

32. "Mission in a Bottle: The Story of Honest Tea," http://missioninabottle.net/

33. Eric Schmidt, Jonathan Rosenberg, *Trillion Dollar Coach: The Leadership Playbook of Silicon Valley's Bill Campbell* (New York: Harper Business, 2019)

CHAPTER NINE

Failure, a Hallmark of Builders New and Old

In a long career as a writer and entrepreneur, Elizabeth was part of the early team at Wealthfront, a Silicon Valley company that was the first online financial advisor. Her role was running the company's personal finance and investing blog to develop trust with clients. Wealthfront is now a successful and fast-growing company, managing more than $20 billion for hundreds of thousands of people in the United States.

But it took Wealthfront a while before it settled on a product that met the needs of its market. In Silicon Valley, course changes are known as *pivots*. At one point in the journey, CEO Andy Rachleff emphasized the necessity of pivots so often – "Everybody pivots," he said – that one of the engineers created a faux cover of the book *Everybody Poops* with the word *poops* crossed out to read *pivots*. Well-capitalized companies often change direction in pursuit of a new product or idea that they believe has greater potential. It's important that people don't see those course changes as failures, so Silicon Valley has come up with the *pivot* name for them.

Seth's business of venture capital is in many respects defined by failure. Even the best venture capitalists invest in more companies that fail than succeed. Across the venture landscape, over 65 percent of all investment rounds fail to return even the capital invested, let alone a profit.[1]

Everybody poops, everybody pivots, and everybody fails. But, in Silicon Valley and across the country, entrepreneurs have a unique relationship with failure. They don't love it, but they accept it and have found ways to redefine it and make it part of a process that leads to progress. It is, in some respects, what has set America apart from other countries where failure is seen as a mark against one's character. Here, changing course, rapidly if necessary, is a badge of courage – a challenge that spurs one on.

Even the most successful entrepreneurs fail. For many, that failure drives them. It forms the platform from which their later success is built. And, for the best entrepreneurs, those failures serve as a reminder that success can be fleeting and that it always needs to be worked hard for. Sometimes things simply don't work in the way you planned them out in advance in your mind. Entrepreneurs feel the same kinds of desperation and fear that everyone does, especially when they're in precarious financial situations.

But to many entrepreneurs, artists, and scientists, a lack of success is only a failure if you stop trying. Thomas Edison famously said, "I have not failed. I've just found 10,000 ways that won't work."[2] Michael Jordan – arguably history's best basketball player – redefined success as a process born from a series of failures:

> I've missed more than 9,000 shots in my career, I've lost almost 300 games. Twenty-six times I've been trusted to take the game-winning shot and missed. I've failed over and over and over again in my life. And that is why I succeed.[3]

America historically has had a somewhat unique tolerance of failure, which in turn has helped create an environment that enables entrepreneurs to take the risks necessary to start a business. If your first idea isn't successful, perhaps the next one might be. Lately, though, second chances have started to look like a privilege reserved for the wealthy.

"Here is one kind of failure story," the writer Kate Losse wrote in an op-ed in the *New York Times* about the unfairness of failure.[4] Losse wrote about the culture of Silicon Valley from the rare vantage point of a woman who was an early employee of Facebook in a book titled *The Boy Kings: A Journey Into the Heart of the Social Network:*

> In 2011, Bradford Shellhammer, a 38-year-old e-commerce entrepreneur, helped found a company called Fab, which took in $325 million in funding and eventually zoomed to a billion-dollar valuation – only to be sold [in 2015] for what Bloomberg called a "paltry sum." That didn't stop his next online shopping start-up, Bezar, from raising $2.25 million in its first round of funding that same year. Failure in some circles isn't an obstacle. It's a right of passage.

Beyond the inner circle of Silicon Valley, the consequences for failure have become too high. Losse writes in her op-ed:

> But there's another, less buoyant, kind of failure narrative. It takes hundreds of thousands of dollars just to field one start-up team, money that people like Shellhammer – which is to say, White men with social ties to angel and venture capital – can get relatively easily. "They can raise $100,000 with an email," Jhamar Youngblood, an African-American entrepreneur, told us. He is working on his third start-up, a messaging application called Blastchat, after he was unable to raise money for his first two.
>
> "What counts as failure is subjective," he said. "For people like me, failure is not being able to raise $100,000, and then when I go to angel investors seeking funding, they ask me if I've raised any money. It's like I've already failed because of the color of my skin and not having my own networks to provide resources."

One of the hallmarks of *New Builders* is that they are ferociously resilient. In fact, to have just survived in our economy, *New Builders*, who as a group experience setbacks in our society almost from the day they're born, are more likely to develop the grit and resistance to failure that goes hand-in-hand with being entrepreneurial. In part, this resilience likely comes from doing something they are passionate about, something they love.[5]

In Little Rock, Arkansas, we met *New Builder* Carmen Portillo, who fell in love with fine chocolate and a mistake at almost the same time. The man didn't last (the "mistake"). But her passion for chocolate became the foundation of a business, Cocoa Belle Chocolates, that has sustained her through two recessions and saw her become the first certified chocolatier in the state of Arkansas.

At 19, she had moved to Morton, England, for school. She ended up staying there, first in pursuit of her mistaken relationship, and then as she recovered from the breakup with the help of her newly discovered chocolate obsession.

"I'd never known that chocolate like that existed. I mean, you have here in Arkansas, Werther's Candies or maybe you see Godiva. But it wasn't anything as exquisite – as beautiful – as those you can see and taste there in Wimbledon. Everything about the chocolate-making process drew me in."

Ultimately she ended up back in the States. And like many entrepreneurs, her story took a detour. Being the daughter of a single mother, she felt like she needed to do the "responsible" thing. After graduating from college she landed her first job in a CPA firm. It made her miserable.[i]

Determined to chart a different course for her life, in 2007, after attending confectionary school to perfect her craft, Carmen became Arkansas's first certified chocolatier, opening a 300-square-foot market stand. In its first iteration, Cocoa Belle failed. Carmen underestimated the importance of the buying power of the middle class, especially in what turned into the Great Recession of 2008–2009. "Particularly the demographic of people that are here in my state," she said. "When gas is $4 a gallon, they're not going to spend $20 on nine pieces of chocolate."

She kept afloat with a few wholesale clients among hotels and businesses, and a few years later relaunched a retail business. Almost two decades later, she still loves chocolate enough to create an entire dress out of it for a local fundraiser, though she had to keep running the model back and forth out of a giant freezer to keep it from melting. She's had to figure out how to manage people – one of the hardest parts of running a small business – and over the past months, has struggled to keep the business going in the face of the pandemic. When Covid-19 hit, she lost a wedding, a shareholders meeting, and a hotel opening the same week. "That was a lot of revenue. That was thousands of dollars for us," she said. But she's holding out hope and holding on.

---

[i] The most commonly cited reason for starting a business according to The Small Business Trends Alliance is to "Be Your Own Boss," which was cited as a reason they started their business by 55 percent of respondents in the Alliance's 2020 survey. But the second most common motivation is: "Wanted to Pursue Your Passions" – with 39 percent of respondents to the survey indicating this as a factor in wanting to start a business.

"The day I don't love it, is the day I quit doing it," she says.

One of the reasons *New Builders* like Carmen are so critical to our future is that they remain resilient. That they are so resilient is important, because it turns out that our capacity to tolerate failure, a key element of entrepreneurship, is declining broadly.

Are We Starting to Fail at Failing?

For years, the Global Entrepreneurship Monitor has been asking entrepreneurs around the world about their fear of failure and whether that fear is contributing to a lack of desire to start a new business. As they frame it, it's the percentage of adults who indicate that there are "good opportunities, but [they] would not start a business for fear of failure." Over the past 20 years in the United States this measure of fear of failure has increased by nearly 65 percent, from about one in five respondents in 2001 to more than one in three in 2019.[6] While this is just one measure of our relationship with failure, it's striking to see just how much American attitudes toward failure have changed in such a short period of time. That this change in our view of failure also coincides with a sharp decline in entrepreneurial activity is disconcerting. While correlation is not causation, and we were unable to find definitive research on this question, it seems clear to us that these trends are related. Our increasing fear of failure is making us less dynamic and less entrepreneurial.

Look no further than the "participation" trophies handed out for the sheer act of showing up, or to the forced specialization of talent at early ages. We no longer let our kids explore, try new things, fail at some, and learn what they're truly passionate about. At the earliest signs of failure, they're pulled out of an activity, told it's not them but some external factor that created their lack of success, and are moved on to the next one, in search of some kind of greatness. Children in today's America are constantly reminded of how special they are, which over time creates the need for that feedback loop. We seem to have forgotten as a culture just how important it is to allow ourselves to try new things, even if we're not initially great at them. In that attempt, we may find a new passion. Or we may fail and learn something about ourselves in the process.

At the same time that resilience is declining in the overall population, the practical consequences of failure, which earlier (and perhaps wiser) generations sought to mitigate, are rising. We still celebrate failure and hold it up as an example, from Edison to Jobs. But a middle-class American whose business closes incurs a much higher cost than a generation ago. The economic realities today are harsher than they have been for decades, as we have slowly chipped away at the social safety net that was put in place in the mid-twentieth century. Consider a 2018 report by the Federal Reserve: 40 percent of Americans wouldn't be able to cover an unexpected $400 expense.[7] The median amount of savings of American households is just $12,000 (to give you a sense of how skewed this is to the top end of the wealth scale, the *average* savings across American households is nearly $200,000; as the joke goes, if Jeff Bezos, the founder of Amazon, walks into a bar of 50 people who earn minimum wage, *on average* they're all billionaires).[8] And the majority of these meager savings are tied up in 401(k) and other retirement plans. The net result of this is that the cost of failure for the average American in terms of real and personal economic concerns is significant.

At the same time it's becoming harder to fail, we are also narrowing the definition of success. Arguably, that's one of the reasons we aren't recognizing the value of *New Builders*.

In our consumer economy, we define success by what people own. Today, it's primarily fast-growth high-tech founders who are broadly recognized as successful entrepreneurs. Someone like Carmen Portillo, building a life that enables her to do what she loves and whose business is smaller in scale and reach, is seen as less successful. One of the themes that we heard over and over again as we interviewed *New Builders* and others working in the new economy is how much big business has taken over not just our business landscape but also our mindshare. This seems to dovetail with the takeover of the concept of entrepreneurship by Silicon Valley and technology startups in search of eye-catching headlines about growth and valuation. While there are plenty of these stories to celebrate, what seems to have gotten lost in this mantra of "bigger is better" is the value and worth of small businesses. That small businesses – a successful Yogurtini franchise or an Arkansas chocolatier – are successful in their own rights. And the larger question for our economy is how much growth we would see if we fully supported resilient people like Carmen and other *New Builders*.

Redefining Failure

We have seen examples of failure and those of resilience throughout this book and will continue to see plenty more as we meet more *New Builders*. Jasmine Edwards was unable to get her business, i-Subz, to a place where she could either sustain its operations or raise the capital required to keep her substitute teacher placement platform afloat – even after taking on substantial credit card debt and moving her family in with her parents. Isaac Collins wondered openly with us whether he could survive the Covid-19 crisis with his three Yogurtini businesses intact; Carmen Portillo told us in frank terms how much the pandemic has hurt her business; Danaris Mazara's career as an entrepreneur was launched in a moment of personal failure. Often stories of failure – some small, some life-changing – came up in our conversations with *New Builders*.

We can't continue to be a nation of entrepreneurs without re-embracing failure and redefining success. Leonardo da Vinci carried the Mona Lisa around until he died, repainting and reconfiguring the lines, in one extreme example. Every version was a failure in some sense because it was less than his vision, but the end result was a masterpiece.

We've long celebrated people who have overcome past failures only to later find great success with a new idea, venture, or project. Albert Einstein famously didn't speak until he was four years old (not technically American at that time in his life, although we tend to claim him). He also failed his entrance exam to the Swiss Federal Polytechnic school when he was 16. Later, after graduating from college, he worked as an insurance salesman but failed at that as well. One of the best selling authors in history, J.K. Rowling was a single mother living on welfare when she wrote the first Harry Potter book. It took her seven years to write *Harry Potter and the Sorcerer's Stone,* and once she completed it, it was rejected by 12 major publishers.

And of course, failure is all around us in science. Drug discovery companies regularly test compounds that end up having no clinical effect. Some 80 percent of drugs entering phase II trials fail.[9] Failure is built into the scientific process and is effectively a part of the scientific method, where researchers create what is known as a "null hypothesis," which assumes the predicted effect won't be observed. But, of course, researchers know that even an experiment that fails to reach the expected outcome provides important experimental results.

America institutionalized failure, building processes of innovation that incorporated it, and the capacity to recover from it, into our laws. The view of failure as part of the journey has created an environment of experimentation and innovation in the United States that has been one of the best in the world.

Institutionalized Failure, in a Good Way

Maybe our embrace of failure started because of the early challenges of settling the "new land." Or perhaps because there was an entrepreneurial spirit that pervaded the early days of the union. The Europeans who initially settled in what became the United States self-selected for the grit, determination, and resilience that would later be required to embrace failure as a critical tool toward an overall more successful society – one that embraced risk-taking and individuality along with cunning and cleverness.

Through the twentieth century, into the 1970s, America made it steadily easier to fail. The Bankruptcy Act of 1898 was the first law in the United States that allowed companies the option of being protected from creditors. During the Great Depression, this legislation was expanded through the Bankruptcy Acts of 1933 and 1934. That same year a critical Supreme Court decision in *Local Loan v. Hunt* interpreted bankruptcy law in the United States to offer debtors "a new opportunity in life and a clear field for future effort, unhampered by the pressure and discouragement of preexisting debt." More recently, the Bankruptcy Reform Act of 1978 created today's modern bankruptcy system. That 1978 act introduced the concept known as Chapter 11, making it easier for both consumers and businesses to file for bankruptcy protection.

Our laws around bankruptcy and business failure are generally more advanced than those of most other countries, which often fail to differentiate between business and personal bankruptcy and many of which have lengthy workout periods (5 to 10 or more years) before debts can be discharged. All of this has served to encourage risk-taking and innovation in the United States, whereas in other parts of the world the financial and reputational repercussions of failing at business are simply too steep for many to take the risks associated with starting meaningful entrepreneurial ventures.

Henry Ford helped change American transportation. But prior to inventing the assembly line, Ford had a string of failures. His first company went bankrupt. His second also failed after a dispute with his business partners. Colonel Harland Sanders, founder of Kentucky Fried Chicken (KFC), failed repeatedly throughout his life. Finally, in 1952, already in his 60s, he set out to sell his now-famous recipe for fried chicken. At the time he had $105 from a Social Security check to his name. Over 1,000 restaurants rejected him before one took him up on his offer.

Failure in entrepreneurial and business circles in the United States remains a constant. In 2009, the *Harvard Business Review* published an article titled "Why You Need to Fail" about exactly that: the benefits of failing.[10] Around 20 percent of all businesses fail in their first two years after opening, according to the Bureau of Labor Statistics.[11] Nearly half fail by their fifth anniversary. From there, things level off some, although, by their tenth anniversary, the BLS data suggests that only about 35 percent of businesses that started a decade before are still operating. All of this is to say that failure is a natural part of the entrepreneurial process and of business life. As we've already highlighted, it's also an important part of a dynamic entrepreneurial ecosystem.

The culture of Silicon Valley sets a high bar for success – extraordinarily fast growth – and turned the failure to reach that growth into a badge of courage, effectively removing even the reputational risk of failure, as if the person who failed had found something worthy of reaching for, even if they happen to have come up short. In more recent years, entrepreneurs such as Bill Gates failed at his first venture before starting Microsoft. Apple, one of the most successful companies on the planet, nearly failed several times and its founder, Steve Jobs, failed at multiple businesses.

Silicon Valley specializes in very fast innovations and in doing so has had to institutionalize, and even lionize, failure. The world of venture-backed companies – only about 1 percent of all startups – is marked by speed, which requires a lot of failure. Venture capitalists need to move on quickly from ventures that aren't working, so they let them fail. Entrepreneurs need to move rapidly from one idea to another to keep their companies growing.

This perhaps runs counter to our vision of the seemingly ubiquitous, fast-success models of Silicon Valley. But those stories are mostly illusions, like fish tales from expeditions that nobody else was on. The truth of both success and failure in the tech startup world is significantly different than what you might expect – and contributes to the myth of Silicon Valley.

Failure is the reality of life and business, and especially in the life of venture-backed companies. While the venture industry reports that approximately 25 percent to 30 percent of venture-backed businesses fail, other more comprehensive studies suggest that rate is much higher. Harvard researcher Shikhar Ghosh estimates that rate is actually several times that.[12] His research suggests that 75 percent of venture-backed companies ultimately fail. The incestuous nature of the venture world makes it hard to measure this statistic because what constitutes "failure" is often obscured by companies buying other companies for their employees (known as "acquihire" in the industry – an acquisition for purposes of hiring staff). These companies didn't succeed, but they didn't exactly fail, either.

We took a look at what percentage of venture investments returned the full original investment upon exit. This analysis looked at investment rounds, not companies, meaning each time a company received an investment (the data set available didn't enable us to break this out on a company basis). But cutting the data by investment round showed that 65 percent of venture investments returned less than the original investment amount.[13] Any way you cut the data, even in the rarified ranks of institutionally backed companies, failure is the norm.

The idea that failure shouldn't be a mark against one's worth as a human – but rather, is seen as part of the process of innovation and creativity – has historically set the United States apart from other countries. It has been a hallmark of the US innovation economy for generations. We celebrate failure because we understand that it is only through repeated attempts that innovation is successful. But if this key attribute of our national identity slips away, so does the global edge of our entrepreneurial economy. Recognizing this is the first step in starting to reshape our relationship with failure and to bring back our acceptance and understanding of its importance as a key driver of our economy – especially our grassroots entrepreneurial economy.

There are signs that America's comfort with and acceptance of failure are starting to wane. Consider the language used regularly by former President Trump (ironic given the number of times he and his companies have filed for bankruptcy, but that's a subject for a different book) stigmatizing "losers" and "failures." Beyond the populist former president, there is a growing national narrative around failure that is disconcerting when considered in the context of the importance of embracing failure in fueling our entrepreneurial economy. From an early age, we appear to be setting the next generation of Americans up to not differentiate between success and failure, or to equate size with success. We increasingly reward simply showing up and participating. This may make us feel like we're being egalitarian, but it's causing us to rear generations of children who don't understand the difference between the work required to improve and the rewards that come from that effort, and the act of simply putting in the time. Through this, we're losing not only some of the grit and resilience that comes from healthy competition and the feedback that comes from it, but also losing the edge comes from embracing the importance of failure.

Teaching Resilience

Over and over we witnessed resilience on the part of the entrepreneurs we met in researching *The New Builders* – but in today's America, they may be the exception rather than the rule.

Resilience plays a particularly important role in entrepreneurial success and has been studied most extensively as it relates to entrepreneurial failure. Related to the concept of *grit*, resilience is the "capacity to overcome difficulties."[14] It describes the ability of people to cope with stress and to adjust to misfortune and to cope with change.

The seminal study on individual resilience was conducted by psychologist Emmy Werner.[15] In her study, Dr. Werner followed the lives of 700 children from Garden Island, Hawaii, for decades. Thirty percent of her subjects grew up in challenging environments (poverty, abuse, some form of neglect, etc.). About one-third of these children developed into competent, self-confident adults. Werner believed that these children had specific character traits that helped overcome or mitigate the negative consequences of their childhood traumas. These were broadly defined into three categories: (1) individual factors (self-confidence, optimism, etc.); (2) family factors (trust and support); and (3) community factors (teachers, attentive neighbors, etc.).

It's interesting to consider how factors such as these translate into entrepreneurial resilience and the ability to overcome adversity and obstacles in a business environment. One study that sticks out in the research was conducted by Huibert de Vries and M. Shields in 2005. In it, they describe entrepreneurial resilience as a collection of behavioral characteristics: flexibility, motivation, perseverance, and optimism. Importantly they describe entrepreneurial resilience as the outcome of experience versus being an inborn personality trait. In some entrepreneurial circles, entrepreneurs are sometimes described as born and not made. The research by De Vries and Shields suggests otherwise.[16]

While the term can apply to systems (communities, the economy as a whole, etc.), in entrepreneurial circles, resilience typically is talked about in an individual context, although perhaps given our belief that we've overindexed to individualism in how we talk about entrepreneurs and entrepreneurship, we should extend the notion of individual resilience to include the support systems that surround a business owner. All the evidence we've looked at suggests that resilience can be taught, with a combination of honest assessments of successes and failures, a safety net so that the consequences for a setback aren't devastating, and a redefinition of failure as part of the process of innovation. When an organization or community does this well, as Silicon Valley has for decades, people have a reservoir of encouragement upon which to draw that enables them to persevere.

When Danaris Mazara looks back at her time participating in the Entrepreneurship for All accelerator, she highlights a specific aspect of the program for helping her succeed. Naturally a persistent person, she still needed someone to remind her to believe in herself. This was the real take away from EforAll: that she mattered. "What they did for me, I think they do with everybody," she said. "Some people don't believe in themselves, but they still have really good potential. [EforAll] made that the basis of their organization."

Sometimes, of course, resilience is forced on people. As the pandemic was rolling over the country, EforAll founder Desh Deshpande was thinking about how the post-pandemic environment might affect people's willingness to fail. Sometimes, he thought, people who have already lost a lot – a job, for instance – realize that what had been for them a fear of failure has turned into something new, something born out of different and challenging circumstances: a willingness to try. "They're not that afraid of losing what they have because they've already lost most of it. So now they're saying, okay, what else can I do?"

Endnotes

1. Seth Levine, "Venture Outcomes Are Even More Skewed Than You Think," *VC Adventure,* August 12, 2014, www.sethlevine.com/archives/2014/08/venture-outcomes-are-even-more-skewed-than-you-think.html
2. Thomas A. Edison, Dagobert D. Runes, ed., *Diary and Sundry Observations of Thomas A. Edison* (Abbey Publishing, 1968)
3. Peter Bregman, "Why You Need to Fail," *Harvard Business Review,* July 6, 2009, hbr.org/2009/07/why-you-need-to-fail.html
4. Kate Losse, "The Art of Failing Upward," *The New York Times,* March 5, 2016, www.nytimes.com/2016/03/06/opinion/sunday/the-art-of-failing-upward.html?ref=opinion
5. Wayne C. Booth, *For the Love of It: Amateuring and Its Rivals* (Chicago: University of Chicago Press, 1999)
6. Readers can access the GEM data for various countries and time periods here: https://gemconsortium.org/data/key-aps
7. Board of Governors of the Federal Reserve System, *Report on the Economic Well-Being of U.S. Households in 2018* (2019), www.federalreserve.gov/publications/files/2018-report-economic-well-being-us-households-201905.pdf
8. Mark Kiczalis, "How Much Does the Average American Have in Savings?" *MagnifyMoney,* November 13, 2019, www.magnifymoney.com/blog/news/average-american-savings/
9. Joseph Loscalzo, MD, PhD, "A Celebration of Failure," *Circulation,* March 4, 2014, www.ahajournals.org/doi/10.1161/CIRCULATIONAHA.114.009220?url_ver=Z39.88-2003&rfr_id=ori%3Arid%3Acrossref.org&rfr_dat=cr_pub%3Dpubmed&
10. Bregman, "Why You Need to Fail"

11. Michael T. Deane, "Top 6 Reasons New Businesses Fail," *Investopedia*, 2020, www.investopedia.com/financial-edge/1010/top-6-reasons-new-businesses-fail.aspx# (In this instance, the BLS is measuring businesses that are no longer operating, regardless of the reason they shut down.)

12. Shikhar Ghosh, "The Venture Capital Secret: 3 Out of 4 Start-Ups Fail," *Harvard Business School,* September 19, 2012, www.hbs.edu/news/Pages/item.aspx?num=487

13. Levine, "Venture Outcomes Are Even More Skewed Than You Think"

14. "Resilience," www.google.com

15. Emmy E. Werner, "Resilience in Development," *Sage Journals,* June 1, 1995, https://journals.sagepub.com/doi/abs/10.1111/1467-8721.ep10772327?journalCode=cdpa&

16. Herb De Vries and Michelle Shields, "Entrepreneurial Resilience: An Analysis of the Resilience Factors in SME Owner-Managers," *University of Central Arkansas working paper,* 2005

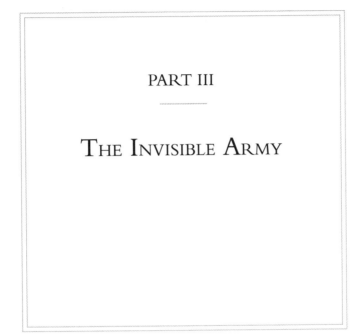

PART III

THE INVISIBLE ARMY

"Never doubt that a small group of thoughtful, committed citizens can change the world; indeed, it's the only thing that ever has."

Margaret Mead

CHAPTER TEN

Unlikely Heroes

In the United States, immigrants have historically been able to navigate paths to success and influence in a society that imagines itself open but remains closed in surprising ways. This success has led immigrants in the United States to start businesses at twice the rate of native-born Americans. The career of Desh Deshpande, one of three unlikely heroes in the story of Danaris Mazara and Sweet Grace Heavenly Cakes, is an example of the power and impact that immigrants have on our society.

In the late twentieth century, when the United States was the undisputed beacon for talented people from around the world, his success grew out of a combination of talent, persistence, and timing. Born in India, the son of a labor commissioner (a highly prized civil service job), he was studious and focused, receiving an undergraduate degree in electrical engineering from a local university. His aptitude for math and science served as a launching pad for Desh, who looked outside of India for greater opportunities. This led him to Canada for graduate school. Like many young, ambitious people, he had a plan. He was going to be an academic.

But fate and opportunity disrupt even the best laid plans, and in the late 1970s, after he had completed his PhD, academia lost its luster for Desh. Recognizing that his student was looking for a different path, a professor at Queens University in Kingston, Ontario, suggested he join a small startup in Toronto. Working for a successful business had a different kind of allure for Desh, and the experience gave him a taste for entrepreneurship and sparked his interest in starting a business, especially after the company he was working for was successfully acquired by Motorola.

This was the mid-1980s, and the internet was just coming to life, giving Desh a window of opportunity. But the first venture he founded didn't go well at all. He was newly married, and he and his wife had their first baby, who came with both joy and the challenges of a newborn. Adding to the stress of a young family, he had no income as his startup was just getting off the ground. He and his cofounder fought over the direction of the company, eventually leading Desh to quit the firm they had founded together.

Sometimes success can only come after failure and the learning, perseverance, and grit that come from setting out on a course that is ultimately unsuccessful. Buoyed by his initial setback, and with a strong belief in his understanding of the market he wanted to target, Desh tried again. His second business was Cascade Communications, an early pioneer in internet routing technology – how packets of information move around the networks that power the internet. Seven years later it was sold to Ascend Communications for nearly $4 billion, making Desh a rich man and a defining entrepreneur of the early internet era.

Not one to rest on his laurels, the following year he started Sycamore Networks, another network routing business. Sycamore saw remarkable early success, and in less than two years it went public at a valuation of nearly $20 billion. Desh owned over 20 percent of the company at the time of the IPO, making him one of the wealthiest self-made entrepreneurs at the time, and providing the financial platform from which he would give back to his entrepreneurial roots for decades to come.

Desh went on to become a trustee of the Massachusetts Institute of Technology (MIT), a founder of several other businesses, and an active philanthropist. Along the way, he also played a role in the Obama Administration's efforts to jumpstart entrepreneurship. "Since innovation cannot be mandated, you have to create a nurturing environment with freedom of thought," he told us. "But such environments become clubby ... innovators get into impressing each other as opposed to making an impact.... Let's say if a professor and his graduate students have an idea for curing cancer. If you go talk to them two months from now, they'll have 10 more ideas. The value you add in that innovation process is to help them pick which idea they should really pursue."

Perhaps most importantly, he had a vision to give back to his entrepreneurial roots and to create long-term impact by establishing organizations both here in the United States and in his native India that would help foster and support entrepreneurs from different backgrounds and circumstances. In the United States, the result of that vision was Entrepreneurship for All – the national organization that served as a launchpad for Danaris and Sweet Grace Heavenly Cakes. EforAll entrepreneurs are people like Danaris, who are often overlooked in our society but who, Desh understood, can be the backbone of economic growth and resurgence in their communities. Almost all of the entrepreneurs that EforAll works with don't have access to the kind of networks that lift up aspiring entrepreneurs working in other industries and other markets. Many of these entrepreneurs are *New Builders.*

EforAll does most of its work at the grassroots level and in the less flashy cities and towns across the country where their help is most needed – cities like Lawrence, Massachusetts, where there is plenty of grit but often not enough opportunity. There are many important lessons to be learned from EforAll about how to help entrepreneurs who don't come from privileged lives in America. For many of the people EforAll helps, the program offers a lifeline, as it did for Danaris. Through a community of like-minded entrepreneurs, all with the same overall goal of starting or growing a business, and by offering confidence, support, and mentorship, EforAll helps overlooked and underappreciated entrepreneurs succeed. If the issue in the elite halls of innovation is keeping budding entrepreneurs in touch with the real world, the issue for entrepreneurs who are mired in the big problems of the real world is putting them back in touch with confidence and hope that has been worn away over the years by their environments and circumstances.

In Desh's view, the world comprises people who see a problem and get excited about solving it, and people who see a problem and complain. The difference between a vibrant community and an impoverished community is the number of people who are solving problems rather than complaining about them.

"You can see in places like MIT and Harvard, that they don't have enough problems to solve," Desh told us. "They're constantly trying to convince you this app is going to save your life. The side effect of that excitement is that obvious problems don't hang around in those communities [very] long. … Then you go to communities like lower Lawrence. People get deadlocked. They try a little bit, but cannot succeed. Then they feel victimized and helpless."

By encouraging problem solvers, Desh believes, you can create vibrant, entrepreneurial ecosystems.

"Converting people into problem solvers is the essence of [EforAll]. It's not a top-down process," he said. "You cannot do a proclamation, you cannot do a policy in Washington. You have to somehow work hard on identifying five people and making them successful. And then 5 becomes 20, becomes a hundred, a thousand, and at some point, it becomes a critical mass."

Seen through Desh's lens, Danaris's potential as an entrepreneur and as an innovator is equivalent to, or even greater than, that of students at Harvard or MIT. Once empowered with one success at Sweet Grace, she might take on a bigger problem. Informed by her lived experiences, these will be problems that directly impact her community and can't be taught in a classroom or studied from afar.

For now, Danaris is bringing a new product, Dominican cakes, to a little-recognized market, the Dominicans in and around Lawrence. Through mentorship and workshops EforAll helped her better understand the value and potential for her business, expand her marketing, improve her unit economics, move out of the kitchen in her home, and ultimately secure the financing she needed to open her bakery in downtown Lawrence. She in turn serves as an example to, and a potential catalyst for, other entrepreneurs and innovators.

Desh brought money and passion to the work of EforAll, but, as is the case with many visionary entrepreneurs, he needed a partner to help him implement and expand on his initial idea. Someone who shared his vision but could turn those ideas into action while focusing on the day-to-day work. He found both in David Parker.

In 2010, in anticipation of its twenty-fifth class reunion, Harvard University sent David – a two-time Harvard alum and successful tech executive – an invitation to tell his fellow alumni about what he'd done over the course of his career. He dove into the task, listing six technology companies he had worked for or founded that had all achieved some level of success. These ranged from well-known businesses such as Tripadvisor and Delphi, to lesser-known ones like SoundBite Communications. SoundBite was seen as so promising in its day that it received investment within three weeks of first pitching the concept to a venture firm. That investment was based simply on an idea (which later turned out to be wildly optimistic) and the team's track record of previous successes. David's pedigree − Andover prep school/Harvard undergrad/Harvard MBA − certainly didn't hurt.

As he wrote about his career for Harvard, he had something of a revelation. "I really have been focusing on myself," he told us, remembering what was going through his head at the time. "What do I have as a result? I have financial success. I have a bunch of friends. Great people, but nearly all of whom are like me. I haven't done anything for other people."

Like Desh, David is also an unlikely hero in Danaris's story. Technology executives often become philanthropists later in their careers, but mid-career shifts away from the satisfying world of tech are fairly rare. Fortunately, David had an unusual level of introspection. He realized as he got further into his career that the ease with which he'd been able to achieve success troubled him. He was driven and smart about the companies he'd picked to work for, but he also recognized how much luck was involved. And how much of that "luck" was the result of the privileged world he so easily inhabited. He realized he would never have been able to build the career he did without the advantages with which he had grown up, and the safety nets that enabled him to take risks − from his extensive networks of like minded executives to the healthy bank account that would serve as a back stop against failure.

Recounting his business career for his Harvard reunion was a turning point for David. He thought about his family and its entrepreneurial roots. Though both of his parents had gone to the University of Pennsylvania, his father's father had been a blue-collar worker, and his mother was the granddaughter of immigrants. They'd both set an example of service to their communities and had worked hard for the success they achieved, success that was hardly guaranteed. This soul-searching led David to reach out to a few trusted advisors about what he might do next. Where might he point his energy in a way that would be more impactful to the world around him? As luck (or serendipity, as David describes it) would have it, one of the people he reached out to for advice was Desh Deshpande.

It didn't take long for David to see the potential in Desh's idea for EforAll. It would take a meaningful effort as well as the support of the broader networks that both David and Desh brought to the project (not to mention investment from Desh, David, and other early supporters).[i] But it was a vision worth fighting for. The people they would help were worth fighting for, too.

That conversation took place in 2010. Since then, EforAll has grown into a prominent organization, with business accelerator programs in Massachusetts (where EforAll was founded) and in Colorado. Their model is to focus on cities that are adjacent to existing entrepreneurial technology hubs – Lawrence, Massachusetts, near Boston and the highway 128 corridor; and Longmont, Colorado, near Boulder. This way they can leverage the mentorship and resources that have been built up to support these existing entrepreneurial ecosystems but in a new market and for a different set of entrepreneurs. Using this model, EforAll programs have supported hundreds of entrepreneurs and helped them create nearly 1,000 jobs for businesses that have gone on to raise more than $35 million in funding. EforAll companies generated approximately $25 million in revenue in 2019.[1]

David told us that he's never regretted – "not for a moment" – his decision to step out of the world of technology startups. What might have been hard to do earlier in his career became easy as he grew older and realized what was important to him: what kind of society he wanted to be part of. "Having EforAll entrepreneurs share their joy and pride and gratitude for our program's impact on them is the crowning achievement of my career ... the joy of the mentors, it makes me happy."

Danaris participated in the Lawrence EforAll accelerator in 2014, after attending a pitch competition and struggling through describing her story to a room full of strangers. She quickly became one of the stars of the program. Always with a smile and quick to look for ways to make those around her comfortable and welcome, Danaris has a knack for

---

[i] Seth and his wife are EforAll donors.

winning people over. "In my eyes, she had to overcome a crazy number of obstacles," said David who talks about Danaris with reverence. He knows her story is powerful because it's as unique as it is common.

At first, it seemed her most immediate problem was getting out of the house, where her business was bursting at the seams. The first time David visited her home, there were two children, two foster children, and a handful of employees all trying to coexist. But he soon realized there was a bigger issue holding Danaris back: she was selling her cakes for only $20. That price was barely covering the cost of the ingredients, let alone the time of the people who made them. The market for Dominican cakes was strong and she should be selling them for far more. This turned out to be correct, and a turning point for Sweet Grace. There were also the practical questions of licensing and food safety – this wasn't a business that could be operated out of a small space. "Her mentors and I kept pushing her, 'Let's get you out of this house and into a shared commercial kitchen,'" David said.

In January 2014, she posted on her EforAll profile: "I'm looking for a commercial location to rent to start my business out of my house."[ii] But there were no options for a shared kitchen in Lawrence at that time. It was Danaris's mother who suggested she consider buying a commercial property to move the business into. But her home foreclosure in 2008 weighed heavily on Danaris's mind; she was unsure how it would affect her ability to qualify for a mortgage.

Networks are powerful because they create a virtuous cycle for those in them. It's why they are such important tools for budding entrepreneurs, and why we talk about them so extensively throughout *The New Builders*. These networks are clubs of sorts, and for those lucky enough to be members, the rewards are access, help, and a certain stamp of approval. If you're in a network, you're to be trusted. You're "in the club." EforAll acts as this kind of ready-made network for the entrepreneurs it helps, and Danaris's story provides a powerful example of the direct mentorship and advice that comes from taking part in such a program. It also shows how putting yourself out there – taking a risk to join a group of people who aren't necessarily like you – can change people's perceptions of you.

[ii] At that time, EforAll was called Merrimack Valley Sandbox.

In Danaris's case, she came to the attention of Frank Carvalho. As a teenager in the late 1960s, Frank had come to the United States from Brazil and faced plenty of discrimination. At one point, he worked in a circuit board factory, where part of his job entailed dipping the boards in acid, a harrowing and dangerous task. One day as he reported for duty, a manager who didn't like foreigners gave him a glove with holes in it.

"I went out for lunch," Carvalho told us. "I never went back."

Frank is as driven as David and Desh, and like them he's a community builder. He became a business owner by buying an Espresso Pizza in Lowell, just a few towns over from Lawrence. He'd once washed floors in that same pizza shop. But his main career was as a banker, working in commercial lending. He spent more than three decades at Enterprise Bank, a regional power in New England. In 2012, he decided that central Massachusetts needed a community development finance institution. CDFIs, as they're called, were formalized during the Clinton Administration and exist across the country to fill in gaps left by the banking system. They're powerful tools for lifting up underserved communities and provide financing to people and projects often overlooked by more traditional banks. As such, they fill a critical gap in our rapidly consolidating banking system.

Using his deep ties in the community, the gregarious and determined Carvalho established Mill Cities Community Investments to help finance homes for the working-class communities surrounding Lowell and to help entrepreneurs create business plans to take to banks. In some cases, MCCI provides capital directly to entrepreneurs using grants and low-interest loans funded by the government, foundations, and a coalition of banks. In a region like that surrounding Lowell and Lawrence, MCCI offers a lifeline to struggling businesses and residents.

A powerhouse in Lawrence, Frank joined the EforAll board of directors, and he was there the night Danaris pitched her bakery idea. "I heard her beautiful story," he said later. Danaris describes him as "the best, the most generous. He is always there for anybody." The two immigrants became friends, and Frank spent many afternoons at Danaris's kitchen table, explaining to Danaris and Andres how to run the financial side of their burgeoning bakery operation.

One reason entrepreneurship still thrives in immigrant communities, he told us, is that "it's still seen as a way of providing for your family. A business owner is somebody that gains status in the community." Restarting entrepreneurship more broadly, he said, is a question of looking at the barriers that hold people back. "There are a lot of people who may have that dream but cannot make it reality. The barriers vary. It may be that people are discriminated against. There's a lack of education. Sometimes, when you are being put down, your self-esteem does not allow you to have the confidence."

Financial resources, of course, are a critical barrier as well. With many living paycheck to paycheck, saving for investment is often impossible, which is certainly how Danaris thought of it at the time. When her mother encouraged her to find a building to buy, rather than a kitchen to rent, they found an ideal location, on Essex Street in downtown Lawrence. It was occupied in part by a tax office and in part by a beauty shop. The tax office would vacate but the beauty shop could remain and pay rent and serve as the basis for a loan. If she could afford to buy the building.

The building owner wanted $170,000 for the property, but her bank told her that it was too much of a stretch – especially because of her prior foreclosure. The first time she went looking for a bank loan, a banker predicted she wouldn't have enough customers to pay the mortgage. "You wait," she told him. "I will have people. I will have people lined up, ready to pay cash for what I'm making here."

Eventually, Danaris was able to talk the building owner down to a more manageable $125,000. But the bank would still require a $38,000 deposit. With Frank's financial planning help, she had saved what seemed like a small fortune at the time, $8,000. But that would not be enough to cover the down payment on her own. Her mother and brother each gave her $5,000, and she kept saving. Frank helped her get her application ready for Eastern Bank. Danaris had a business to run at the same time she was trying to pull together the money for a down payment, and she was making more cakes than she ever had before. "I was working, like, 24 hours a day, making cakes," she said. By her telling, it felt like a miracle when she had $38,000 in her bank account. That loan, along with a small loan through MCCI for bakery equipment, allowed her to move out of her house and open her storefront. "She kept working, she kept saving, and she realized the dream," Frank recalled.

It was 2015, and Sweet Grace Heavenly Cakes was both five years old and brand new.

Late that year, she opened her doors. But success in business is rarely a straight-line path, and Danaris and the bakery struggled in their early days on Essex Street. On her first day open, she sold only $17 of baked goods. A religious woman, Danaris turned to her faith during these hard times. She asked God why He had given her the idea that she was going to grow big when she was selling so little? Frustrated but not deterred, she heard a clear answer: she needed to bake more and varied goods and be smarter about how her shop was set up. She expanded her product lines to include more products and became creative in the ways she displayed them. "That's when I realized: 'Your business is a process,'" she told us. "It's like a baby. The baby isn't born walking."

After the cake-making business was out of their house and not overtaking every aspect of their lives, her husband Andres started to come around. He had not just been skeptical at the beginning, he had been downright hostile to the idea of Danaris setting up her own business. Perhaps it was his depression from being laid off; perhaps it was his cultural background, which suggested that men in the family be the primary earners; perhaps it was some degree of jealousy. Whatever it was at the beginning, Andres eventually saw how hard Danaris was working and how that hard work was paying off. Not just in monetary terms – although after years of struggle that was nice – but also in terms of her stature in the community, and in her confidence. Eventually he quit his job to join her, learning the art of cake-making, and became the director of baking.

Things were turning around for the Mazara family. They took their first big vacation – to Dubai, no less – and with business booming, they secured another loan to expand into the space where the beauty shop had eventually moved out. By all measures, 2019 was a success for Danaris, Andres, and Sweet Grace. She was a businesswoman. She had a prosperous and growing business. Monthly revenue by mid-2019 had risen to more than $50,000, and Sweet Grace employed 16 people from the community.

Danaris started thinking about new ways to expand and new innovations. She had long wanted to work on a lower-calorie cake – something she felt would be very popular in her Dominican community. She lost weight herself and was worried about obesity among her peers. She thought about entering the wholesale business and was working on ideas for that expansion as well. She had become a true community leader and someone with stature and importance. As the year wound to a happy close, she was thinking about possibilities and looking to the future.

Sweet Grace Heavenly Cakes was a true American success story, updated for a new time. The poster child for EforAll, Danaris is featured in a video showing others the impact of their programming and sharing her journey. Frank Carvalho used Sweet Grace's story to lobby the Massachusetts governor for more funds for the communities of the central part of the state.

But none of this success, as much as it relied on the grit and determination of Danaris, was possible without the people who surrounded her to help in concentric circles of support: Desh, David, and Frank. Sweet Grace Heavenly Cakes was born in a generous spirit, which Danaris would carry on as she hired people to work for her – perhaps a few too many, as the pandemic wore on. Its success is the success not just of Danaris and the women who work with her, but also of the entire community, and the broader networks that helped her along the way and to which she now gives back as a mentor and advisor.

What might be most important about the story of Danaris and Sweet Grace is how "community" is defined and how overlapping communities can create a platform from which *New Builders* like Danaris can launch their ideas. Desh provided the initial money and had the vision to build a community of support for underserved entrepreneurs working in struggling markets. David took stock of his surroundings and decided to redefine his own community, not wanting to exist in a narrow world of people who looked only like him and had similar educational and work experiences. And Frank, inclusive by nature, saw the need for a broader financing base in central Massachusetts, taking it upon himself to start a bank to fill that gap.

A hallmark of *New Builders* – true of many entrepreneurs – is their willingness to give time, money, and resources to the interests of the long-term good of their communities. We see this in the ways Danaris is already giving back to her community in Lawrence and in the way that Desh, David, and Frank approach their work supporting *New Builders*.

All of them recognize that no one builds a business in a vacuum, that place matters. That, ultimately, the success of businesses of all types comes from a strong foundation and an economy that is broad, fair, and inclusive.

Endnote

1. https://eforall.org/impact/

CHAPTER ELEVEN

Crossing the Divide

Each year, Claire Cheff has a reunion with friends from her graduating class at Dartmouth. One is a nationally recognized pediatrician. Another is a leading science journalist. She loves her friends, but Claire often came home from these reunions questioning her life's path.

Claire's mother is a feminist with a PhD from Stanford, and her father a leading doctor in Salt Lake City. After graduating from college with high honors, winning a creative writing fellowship and admittance to the University of Montana's law school, Claire had visions of working on civil rights and changing the world's unfair systems.

Now, here she was with a husband, two kids, a small business in Montana, and a job as a public school teacher that was increasingly necessary to keep it all going. After years of being a high-achieving person, surrounded and influenced by the achievement-oriented culture of the Ivy League and the social pressures that go along with that culture, she was trying to unlearn those metrics of success. "If I compared myself to my Dartmouth friends, I felt very inadequate based on those standards. I was a public school teacher. I hadn't written books. I wasn't making six figures," she wrote later.[i]

---

[i] This chapter evolved from three trips Elizabeth and her daughters took with the Cheffs, and many conversations and emails with Claire and Mark.

The morning of her 40th birthday, she stood in the shower with tears running down her face. "Here I am, this 40-year-old woman," she thought. Her life wasn't what she'd imagined it would be. No one was telling her that she failed to measure up, but she was still struggling to convince herself that she had done the brave thing by not buying into the script of success.

It turned out that her birthday was a turning point. Over the next few years, Claire focused on the beauty and accomplishments of the path she *had* chosen. "I eventually found my way back to teaching on the Flathead Reservation in Montana, where I felt authentically challenged and was able to connect with students in exciting and life-changing ways. I chose a life of teaching and service – and it afforded me the summers to work alongside Mark in The Bob Marshall Wilderness," she wrote.

Together she and Mark, her husband, operated a small outfitting company located at the edge of The Bob Marshall Wilderness Area in western Montana, named for an early conservationist and affectionately called by locals as simply "The Bob."

Less than 3 percent of the land in the lower 48 states is protected as wilderness by the federal government. Enabled in 1964 by the Wilderness Act, US wilderness land by law can have no paved roads, no electricity, and no running water. In The Bob, one of the largest swaths of protected land in the US, you can't have as much as a wheelbarrow, much less a car, and the only way in is on horseback or foot. Wilderness areas have rangers devoted to protecting them, but over the years their number has been shrinking. In The Bob, what was once a force of dozens of seasonal rangers in the 1980s and 1990s has today shrunk to fewer than 10. They cover a wilderness area of one million acres that is surrounded by National Forest Land of another million acres. Practically speaking, it's the small businesses, like outfitters and mule packers, who keep the wilderness alive and help the increasing number of adventurous Americans navigate in and out.

Small business owners are often at the heart of a community's progress or preservation. We saw that in Kansas City, where Isaac Collins funds yoga classes; in Lancaster, Pennsylvania, where Steve Murray stood up to big business interests; and on a grander scale, as Desh financed EforAll chapters to support underserved entrepreneurs in Massachusetts and Colorado. In a deeply polarized society, small business owners operate in a space beyond the politics of the moment. If they own a physical location, they typically welcome people of all political persuasions, creating a space for people to connect, interact, and learn from one another. These business owners have a long-term interest in the health of their communities and, often, the stature that allows them to stand up to political pressure.[ii] Successful business ownership creates backbone. Not only do small business owners learn to have confidence that one client won't make or break their livelihood, but they become practiced at setting boundaries and striking reasonable compromise.

Grassroots entrepreneurs also are more apt to see the balance between the short-term and long-term. On one hand, Claire and Mark Cheff's outfitting business thrives when more people travel to the wilderness and awareness of the wilderness is something they fight for, because tourism is their livelihood. On the other hand, the future of their generations-old business is endangered if the land becomes overused and overrun. The Cheffs are not overtly political about issues like climate change, but they're quietly firm about what they see happening around them. In the case of climate change, they see more and more fires sparked in the increasingly drier summers. Roughly 72,400 wildfires have burned nearly seven million acres of land in the US each year since 2000, double the number of acres scorched by wildfires in the 1990s.[1,2]

But the ranchers, loggers, and outfitters around the Cheffs' campfires, as well as the Cheffs themselves, don't often slip into talk about politics. For them, it's about balancing conservation and livelihood. "If you take it down to the local level, people will vote for conservation almost every time," said Mark Alber, who owns a small sawyer business

---

[ii] The most famous recent example is that of Brad Raffensperger, Georgia's secretary of state, during the 2020 election. Though he was a Republican who had voted for Trump, Raffensperger denied national Republicans – including the president – who wanted him to throw out some of Georgia's votes. Insisting on the integrity of the electoral process he had overseen, he said, "I'm an engineer. We look at numbers. We look at hard data." Significantly, few of the media outlets recognized Raffensperger as what he also was: a small business owner. He owns two companies, Tendon Systems, LLC, a contracting and engineering firm in Columbus, Georgia, and Forsyth County, Georgia, and a small steel manufacturer. It's not surprising to us that a small business owner took a principled, reasonable, and middle-ground stand in the face of partisan political pressure.

called Miller Creek Reforestation. Sawyers are the experts who cut down trees in difficult situations, such as during forest fires when the tops of those trees are burning. Small business owners in Montana don't look like activists in a traditional sense. However, they are activists for a middle ground, the long-term, and a communal future.

Over the years, as Claire Cheff became more aware of her role, it dawned on her that while she wasn't working on systems change in a way that would be recognized by her professors at Dartmouth, she was making a difference directly in people's lives. And it was making her happier than a career as an activist might have, not to mention being a doctor, lawyer, academic, or some other profession that traditionally has more respect in the world.

Two years after her crying bout in the shower, her husband could stand in the corral with a horse's hoof in his hand and say that they both were satisfied with the life they were building. "I've watched her get more and more content," he said. "Some people chase success their whole lives, the way the world defines it, and then wake up and realize they've been chasing the wrong thing. They don't know what makes them happy."

Each of us faces varying challenges in defining what constitutes success. It's easy to feel like we don't add up in this always-on era, with social media streaming a near-constant reminder of just how amazing and seemingly perfect everybody's lives are. And with the pressure to be great at everything and to somehow manage to balance parenting, career, family, and hobbies, it's easy to forget that almost everyone around us is struggling with the same fears.

When Claire looks back, that year was a turning point. She took ownership of her life choices – her garden, home, family, impact as a teacher, and her role as an advocate for the wilderness, something that grew out of her stature as a small business owner. "It's really a call-ing," she would say a few years later, standing next to a tiny white cookstove in a camp near the confluence of the White and Flathead rivers. "You see what being outside does for people. The kids start to laugh again."

The Cheffs live in a wide open world, quite literally. And from that vantage point comes a unique perspective.

Big Prairie and Open Pastures

Guy Zoellner watched a group of horses cross the plain in front of the Big Prairie ranger station. Only one family had horses that moved that fast and smooth, bred as they had been from generations of Tennessee walkers and Arabian racehorses. Clearly he was watching the Cheffs.

As a backcountry ranger in the Spotted Bear District, Zoellner had an agenda. In 2010, he arrived at the historic Big Prairie Ranger Station, the oldest continuously operated station in the United States. Back then, he had a crew of 28 to keep the trails through this section of the Rocky Mountains clear.

Thousands of people hike, hunt, float, fish, and ride through nearly two million acres in and around The Bob. In 2020, traffic in The Bob spiked as the Covid-19 pandemic sent more people outside for recreation, and new, lightweight rafts made it easier to carry a raft for miles before setting it down in one of the clear glacial lakes or rivers that dot the landscape of The Bob.

With more people came real challenges to this rough and majestic wilderness. In particular, the fire danger mounted as the fire season became elongated and the impact of more people and more usage of the wilderness took its toll. Climate change and a long history of mismanagement by the US Forest Service were significant contributors.

Even as more and more people come to visit The Bob, fewer in Washington, DC, seem to care. Guy arrived in 2020 to an even smaller staff due to budget cuts. Five people to clear 500 miles of trails, traveling by foot and horse and using only the simple cross-cut saws permitted in the wilderness. Guy had done what he could internally to advocate for more. He and other rangers had pointed out to the higher-ups that outdoor recreation goes in waves. The pandemic had sent sales at outdoor stores such as REI and Patagonia through the roof. And the people who flooded into National Parks in the spring of 2020 would eventually find their way into the National Forests and wilderness areas. Such are the logical next steps in an adventurer's journey.

Working in The Bob, and in wilderness areas like it, was his life's work. Guy wanted more people to understand and experience the mountains, to reset from their busy lives and find beauty in the simplicity of being outdoors. But he knew that if the trails weren't clear, and if people didn't have safe access to the areas in which he worked, many of them couldn't, or wouldn't, come.

An Uphill Climb

Guy also worried about the dangers of an increasing number of people spread across a vast wilderness, much of it unmaintained. "We don't even know where these people are," he said, looking over a map that showed the Flathead and White rivers. If there were a fire, would he and the other rangers be able to get to people to evacuate them? Would visitors have the sense, let alone the skill, to get out on their own?

His advocacy fell on deaf ears, certainly those he lobbied in the federal government. So he and the district ranger tried a different tack, reaching out to a large corporation, AT&T, that they believed had a vested interest in maintaining access to the wilderness. A hundred years ago, AT&T had installed phone lines in the park, which had now fallen down in long stretches, causing system outages as well as strangling dozens of animals. But the rangers hadn't been able to get the company's corporate social responsibility team to engage. Their main interest seemed to be in putting up a billboard at the trailhead to take credit for any funding they provided. That was a nonstarter, Guy told them, it just wasn't how the wilderness worked.

Zoellner decided to line up the small business owners that make a living off The Bob to make his case. "The outfitters have so much more pull than the rangers," he said. "That puts a whole other kind of pressure on the government."

He still had that option in Montana, where the romantic image of cowboys and mule draggers can still pack a political punch. It's one of the few places where it still does.

The influence of small businesses in most local and national politics has been waning while at the same time the influence of larger businesses is growing. With its landmark decision in 2010, *Citizens United v. FEC,* the Supreme Court opened the floodgates to increased corporate power and influence in our politics and, by extension, into our daily lives. The *Citizens United* decision essentially uncapped the amount of money that corporations could give in political cycles and created a system where large business interests, already a major influence in Washington, dwarfed those of individuals and smaller businesses. The results were stark, if not unexpected. For example, in the 2012 election cycle, big businesses spent a reported total of $188 million on corporate lobbying. Small businesses spent $4.5 million.[3] Not surprisingly, candidates who spend the most money in elections win much more often. This was true in more than 90 percent of congressional races between the 2000 and 2016 election cycles, according to the election statistics site, FiveThirtyEight.[4]

One measure of the effectiveness of all this influence and spending by big corporations is the effective tax rate paid by large businesses. According to the Institute for Taxation and Economic Policy, the actual tax paid by profitable companies among the Fortune 500 was just 11.3 percent in 2018. Ninety-one of those companies took advantage of elements in the tax code that allowed them to generate tax losses despite being profitable. Those companies paid no federal income tax at all and included name-brand businesses like Amazon, Chevron, Delta Airlines, Eli Lilly, General Motors, Halliburton, and IBM.[5] In contrast, small businesses pay substantially more of their revenue in taxes.[6] The result has been a massive shift in the percentage of overall tax revenue share collected from large corporations, which has fallen by over two-thirds from 30 percent in 1950 to just 7 percent in 2019.[7,8] The result of this shift is that the burden of tax paying has shifted dramatically onto individual taxpayers and smaller companies.

Even the definition of what constitutes a small business has evolved, in ways that are detrimental to our understanding and tracking of actual small enterprises. In 2014, the SBA modified its definition of what constitutes a "small business" to be more expansive. These changes (updated again in 2016) had the effect of substantially changing what is officially considered a small business to include many firms that had previously been classified as larger companies. The SBA's definitions of small businesses vary by business sector, but now include, for example, children's clothing stores with revenue of $32.5 million and natural gas distribution companies with 1,000 employees. We're losing touch with the fabric of business in the United States by glorifying and prioritizing larger businesses.

Fights That Don't Exist

The economic implications of the shrinking small business sector are easy to track. Left almost unnoticed is the effect this decline in small business is having on our civil society, as a strong collective voice for the long-term interests of communities fades. We saw *New Builders* holding the middle ground in communities from Staunton to Minneapolis to Oklahoma City. In Montana, the role of small business is particularly striking, perhaps because most businesses in the state are small businesses. Deeply invested in the Mission Valley, the Cheffs have been ranching and guiding in western Montana for four generations. When the national media drops in, it often portrays a fight between the locals and the outside preservationists, as in the case of the American Prairie Reserve, an effort to buy land from ranchers to create a new protected grassland. Major donors to the private foundation include members of the Mars and Packard families. Outsiders frame the story as a conflict. Those actually on the ground see it differently. Some ranchers sell while others want to continue to graze their cattle and don't. It's a choice in priorities, not a conflict.

"Few issues are much of a political fight around here," Mark Alber said, as he sat with a beer after a day of fishing on the Flathead. Where the national media sees conflict, he sees a process of preserving land where there is consensus that it ought to be preserved. The same is true, he noted, with the Blackfeet Tribe's land just to the north, Badger Two Medicine. The Tribe recently won a federal court case ruling that mineral leases sold to a Louisiana oil company were done so illegally; they had the support of local loggers and ranchers.

"Every bit of wealth I have has come from the timber industry," Alber said. But he and his wife, Colleen, don't like an increased timber cutting budget without an increase in the tree planting and precommercial thinning budgets.

Issues such as forest management and land preservation are complicated in this part of Montana. On one hand, many communities have a strong libertarian streak. They like their freedoms, including the freedom to define the word *libertarian* for themselves. There's a knee-jerk reaction against the idea that the federal government might make land off-limits for logging. But those same loggers, many of them small business owners

like Mark and Colleen, are also strong community activists and conser-
vationists. It's a nuance that is lost to most outside observers, and one that
is reflected across the country in communities that are as varied in their
businesses as they are in their politics. The closeness that small business
owners have to their communities creates for surprising and unexpected
contrasts in their political and philosophical outlooks.

Mark Alber can run through a dozen issues that he thinks have been
oversimplified. The demonization of the logging business, for instance.
A couple of years ago, he wrote a 4,000-word op-ed for the *High Country News* that covered topics as varied as racism, employee benefits, and
economic development.[9] It was better argued than most of the much
shorter op-eds that grab national attention.

There is "hypocrisy in our national politics on both the left and the
right," he wrote.

> *As I write this, the smoke has just cleared from one of Montana's worst fire seasons.
> The state's new congressman, Republican Greg Gianforte, is planning a "Forest
> Jobs Tour" to promote the idea that the fires resulted from a combination of US
> Forest Service inaction and environmental litigation that has shut down public-lands
> logging and thinning. Absent in the discussion is that our Mountains are hotter and
> dryer than in the past, and our government cannot secure funding for pre-commercial
> thinning which would reduce a fire's severity. No one mentions the fact that, should
> a vast renaissance in thinning timber occur, none of the jobs would go to locals, since
> the H-2B guest-worker program – which President Donald Trump and Republican
> congressmen want to expand – already boasts 9,434 forestry workers, many of whom
> work on public lands adjacent to Western communities with soaring unemployment
> rates.*
>
> > *On the left, the concern with the rights of immigrants, documented and undocu-
> > mented, contrasts with an apparent indifference to the fate of native-born Americans
> > in places like Clearwater County, Idaho, or Superior, Montana. Disappearing are
> > the debates environmentalists once had about immigration and the impacts of over-
> > population. There is not enough discussion of how the millions of marginalized,
> > hungry people in the labor market suppress wages and displace American workers.
> > Some of the staunchest advocates for the public lands seem relatively uninterested
> > in the future management of those lands. And two important questions go almost
> > unasked: Why are so many rural Westerners, surrounded by public lands, some of
> > the harshest critics of the Forest Service? And why are they among the loudest voices
> > calling for transfer of federal lands to the states, or for their outright privatization?*

Alber shrugged. He tries his hand at advocacy here and there, but he's busy. Right now, he's toying with the idea of applying for a grant to clear unwanted plants from the area. He and Colleen might spend weekends backpacking through The Bob pulling out the noxious weeds that are starting to infiltrate, their seeds probably trekked or floated in with tourists. Colleen, meanwhile, is well aware of their role as small businesspeople. She pointed out that one of the other functions small businesses play in a community is as employers of first and last resort.

By no means is every small business an upstanding citizen in The Bob. In fact, Forest Ranger Guy Zoellner recently won a lawsuit against an outfitter who repeatedly violated the rules of his license. But Zoellner considers himself lucky. The National Park rangers down the road in Glacier National Park didn't have a small business community to draw on when they went to lobby for more funds for the National Park. By the end of 2020, the deferred maintenance on the National Park System, built up over years of neglect by both Democrats and Republicans, had reached an estimated $12 billion.

In the middle of the century, tourist businesses based near National Parks could be counted on to advocate for such investment. But the situation in Glacier mirrors that of other parks, where most of the concessions have been taken over by larger businesses. In 2013, Xanterra Parks and Resorts won a contract from the National Park Service from a smaller company, Glacier Parks Inc. Xanterra is owned by billionaire Philip Frederick Anschutz, who also owns oil, railroads, telecommunications, and entertainment companies. The entire contract for the National Park system is a rounding error on Anschutz's business interests. Xanterra executives expressed little interest in getting involved advocating for legislation to restore the parks. They didn't want to get involved, they said, because they doubted any legislation would ever pass.[10] (The legislation did in fact pass in 2020, as a result of years of lobbying by environmental advocates and complicated election-year horse trading in the Senate.)

National Wilderness Areas don't generate the kind of revenue that would attract big companies. Only a select few guides, like the Cheffs, are licensed to have camps in the wilderness over the summer. Every year, the mules pack in big canvas tents and cots, coolers and water filters, even the tiny stove Claire Cheff uses to make huckleberry pies. Mark Cheff makes peach cobbler over the campfire.

In Montana, small business owners can't afford to be either divisive or nonchalant. Land preservation is key to their survival, as tourism becomes an increasingly important part of their economy. Hunting is also an important economic force. And locals clearly see the need for industry, if for no other reason than to provide employment and much needed cash to help through the long Mission Valley winters.

Five years ago, Mark Cheff knew his wife felt like she'd fallen behind the promise of her twenties. Every year, she returned from her informal reunion with her girlfriends questioning herself. When his wife came back from those reunions, bothered, he reminded her of the impact one teacher can have on a student. Whether it was his reminder or something else, she seemed changed after her fortieth birthday. She grew more content as the years went by, while her friends became less so.

Asked why he does this work, which is hard, dirty, and sometimes dangerous, Mark cracked a joke. "The question is not so much why I do it. It's how I get out of it." After the laughter died down he paused. "I could be driving to an office sitting on the southbound 101 in Los Angeles. But at sunrise or sunset or whenever, when I'm crossing a stream, I think, this is not a bad commute."[11]

Three years ago, when his parents decided to sell their business to their children and grandchildren, he and Claire stepped up to acquire the rights to the camp and run the outfitting business. Mark Cheff was in his element, Claire says. And she's seen the effect of the wilderness on people. Girls braid their mother's hair. Kids play, untethered from their devices. Young men wrestle and practice swing dance moves together. She watches the guests come riding in, curious and sore after the long trek over the mountain, and ride out as advocates for the wilderness.

Guy Zoellner stopped by the camp to ask the Cheffs to attend a meeting on managing the flow of people into The Bob and the outfitters who bring them in and out. He is thinking of Mark, or one of his brothers, as the wilderness lovers he might need to help advocate for moderation. Back at the camp, the Cheffs know that it's Claire who is more apt to speak before a crowd. It might be like a children's book they loved, where a police officer and a dog give speeches on stage.

The crowds go wild; while the officer speaks, the dog performs tricks behind him, holding the audience's attention. Claire can articulate their position on conservation and dedication to wilderness preservation. Mark is the one in the background who doesn't necessarily like to draw attention to himself or speak publicly, but has deep generational knowledge and life experiences that give him credibility."

"I'm not the most articulate … ," Mark says.

"He'll be the one doing the tricks behind me," she responds with a laugh.

Endnotes

1. "Wildfire Statistics," *Congressional Research Service*, 2020, https://fas.org/sgp/crs/misc/IF10244.pdf

2. Claire Wolters, "Here's How Wildfires Get Started – and How to Stop Them," *National Geographic,* 2019, www.nationalgeographic.com/environment/natural-disasters/wildfires/

3. "How Money in Politics Affects Small Business," representUs, 2014, https://dv9jgklhamlge.cloudfront.net/wp-content/uploads/2014/08/SmallBusiness Factsheet.pdf?053245

4. Maggie Koerth, "How Money Affects Elections," *FiveThirtyEight,* September 10, 2018, https://fivethirtyeight.com/features/money-and-elections-a-compli cated-love-story/

5. "Corporate Tax Avoidance in the First Year of the Trump Tax Law," *ITEP,* 2019, https://itep.org/corporate-tax-avoidance-in-the-first-year-of-the-trump-tax-law/

6. "Effective Federal Income Tax Rates Faced by Small Businesses in the United States," SBA Office of Advocacy, 2009, www.sba.gov/sites/default/files/rs343tot.pdf

7. "Fact Sheet: Corporate Tax Rates," Americans for Tax Fairness, 2014, https://americansfortaxfairness.org/tax-fairness-briefing-booklet/fact-sheet-corporate-tax-rates/

8. "Policy Basics: Where Do Federal Tax Revenues Come From?" *Center on Budget and Policy Priorities,* 2020, www.cbpp.org/research/federal-tax/policy-basics-where-do-federal-tax-revenues-come-from

9. Hal Herring "The Changing Politics of Woods Work," *High Country News,* October 30, 2017, https://www.hcn.org/issues/49.18/timber-how-the-out sourcing-of-forestry-jobs-seeps-into-our-public-lands-debates

10. Interview with an anonymous source, Fall 2019.
11. Elizabeth MacBride, "What Happens When an Eastern Greenhorn Rides into the Wilderness with a Famous Montana Outfitter," *Forbes*, August 19, 2018, www.forbes.com/sites/elizabethmacbride/2018/08/19/why-we-ride-unarmed-into-the-bob-marshall-wilderness/?sh=25f059581dfe

CHAPTER TWELVE

Sum of Our Parts

On the basketball court of Robert E. Lee High School in Staunton, Virginia, Jahleel Pettiford's first dream lived and died. He was one of the stars on a basketball team that went all the way to the state finals. But when college coaches came recruiting, they only were only interested in the team's top player. Jahleel, the son of a single mother with an involved father, entered into what he calls "an unusual head space" as high school wrapped up and he was becoming an adult. One day, in church, he was meditating on how thoughts can turn into reality when he realized that he had the power to create change. He and a friend came up with the word "Növel" to describe this agency. It became an anchor of sorts, a calling. He started doodling it, first on white T-shirts that he had around, adding colorful, whimsical characters. His designs were wry and hopeful, and they made him feel better. The first day he wore his shirt to school, three different classmates offered to buy them.

Jahleel wanted to help other people his age cope with a world that seemed increasingly complicated, if not downright grim. They'd been acutely aware of the Unite the Right rally in 2017 when the KKK marched 45 miles away in Charlottesville, and a young woman was killed by a far-right protester. Doodling became a way for him to help himself and others look to a brighter future, and Növel reminded him that things can change for the better. "You may be down," he said. "But you're about to have a breakthrough."

As his senior year rolled by, his father seized on the only thing that seemed to be making his son happy. He gave Jahleel money for 200 black T-shirts, blank canvases for Jahleel's designs. Jahleel sold the shirts for $25, and almost immediately had a waiting list for orders. What began as an escape and a way to pass some time turned into the start of a new business. Then came a stroke of luck. Through connections he made through his job at the local YMCA, he found his way up the steps to an office on the second floor of an old brick building downtown, into the Staunton Creative Community Fund.

Jahleel found mentors at the Fund, which had been set up to help budding entrepreneurs just like him. They helped him get up and running and establish his business. But he was disconnected from other local resources because of the color of his skin. It's hard not to think about what someone with Jahleel's entrepreneurial spirit could have done had he grown up in Silicon Valley or New York, perhaps with his entrepreneurial interests drawn toward technology and not the arts, and with an idea that was more geared to investment.

That wasn't to be Jahleel's path, nor, perhaps, would he have wanted it to be. Fortunately, Staunton's community leaders were working on their own culture and the support systems that could support entrepreneurship at all levels in their community.

"That's the beauty of communities like the Shenandoah Valley," Debbie Irwin, director of the Staunton Creative Community Fund, told us. "We have high-tech growth startups ... we have game makers who sell millions of units of their games. We also have the Main Street entrepreneurs. Every single one of those entrepreneurs is pivotal to creating the community where I want to raise my kids. The beauty is in recognizing that all of those people have importance."

Staunton is one of many places in the United States that is renewing the startup spirit in America. It's now home to a group of big-thinking entrepreneurs and economic activists, dedicated to creating jobs with dignity, to building livelihoods for themselves, and to bringing beauty to their community. Among the long-term initiatives that helped Staunton and its neighboring community of Waynesboro renew their small business communities was a revolving loan fund, an angel investment network that has put $8 million to work and has funded over 20 businesses, a maker space for people and owners who like to tinker and want to build product prototypes, and a dedicated group of community-supporters who shop, build, and invest locally. Staunton's population, perhaps the most basic measure of a community's health, grew 5 percent between 2010 and 2019.

Staunton reminds us that the personal connections between organizers, investors, and entrepreneurs have manifold value. That there is an important connective cycle and rhythm to entrepreneurial activity. Entrepreneurs start businesses, which add to the economic vitality of a community. Communities grow richer, both in terms of wealth and in the number and strength of connections between people. Owners of small businesses become mentors and donors to the community, helping enable the next generation of entrepreneurs. It is a virtuous circle of economic development and of hope.

The story of communities like Staunton, and the cadres of entrepreneurs that exist within them, and give them economic dynamism, can get lost in the overarching narratives that are centered on superstar cities. However, the pandemic might have accelerated a trend that was already starting to emerge. An increasingly large part of their populations are no longer able to afford to live in the urban core.[1]

The pandemic has made working remotely more viable, and towns like Staunton could start to grow even faster, reversing the trends of the past 15 years. Places like Staunton, or neighborhoods in Minneapolis, or rural areas like Ronan, Montana, offer powerful lessons in how people come together and rally around a community. Money is one ingredient, but it's by no means the most important. Jahleel's business shows how little capital it can take, often less than $5,000, to launch what can become a real company. But it also demonstrates the importance of what surrounds that capital, the knowhow and mentorship that can help an aspiring entrepreneur with an idea turn it into something.

One of the most powerful elements of the new network of entrepreneurial support organizations that exist across the country are maker spaces, with an estimated 1,400 opening worldwide in the past 15 years.[2] The one founded by Dan Funk in Staunton in 2014 is just one thriving example. Run by volunteers, the Staunton Makerspace has around 70 members, each of whom pay $50 a month for access to the facility and programming. In their donated building, that is enough to pay for insurance, utilities, and to support about a dozen "guilds," groups of members who work on similar projects – from metalworking to textiles. Three local schools use the space as an external campus, giving students a chance to build and experiment. A 10-year-old boy who visited on a school trip once dragged his grandmother to the Makerspace just before Halloween, insisting that the people there would help him create the costume he had in mind – Genji from the game Overwatch.

The power of community was on display in Staunton as Covid-19 struck. In February 2020, one of the guild leaders had offered a class in making molds, which turned out to be fortuitous for hundreds of medical workers at nearby hospitals. By March, a plea had gone out from nearby Rockingham Memorial Hospital asking for help procuring protective gear. Dan knew the Staunton makers could download the 3D printer patterns available online to create face shields. "I think we can put some of these together," he told the hospital's executives. "Can you make 500 of them?" was the response. Inwardly quailing after agreeing to that amount, Dan hung up the phone.

One of the makers, Sean Psujek, a former biology professor who'd moved back into the area to be near his parents, had taken the class as well. "Look," he told his fellow makers. "I think we can make a mold, and resin cast the masks." They figured out how to speed up the curing process by placing the masks in toasters. In all, working at the Makerspace over the next two months, they turned out 1,500 masks to supply two local hospitals and local paramedics. "The contributions that kept us stable and growing were personal contributions from people like … Sean and dozens of others. The community played a critical role, and our friendships and connections here allow us to thrive," Dan said.[3]

Beauty Matters

The story of Staunton's modern-day rebirth begins 25 years ago and, as in many cities and towns across America, much of the story unfolded quietly, invisible to everyone except those who lived in the community or who were looking closely.

In the 1980s Staunton didn't have a big employer and wasn't a center of any economic significance. It did have Mary Baldwin College, but the school was tiny, with barely 1,000 students. In 1985, the owners of a 1960s-era shopping center created the Staunton Mall by enclosing and enlarging a former shopping center. In Staunton, as in other small towns and cities, the mall sucked customers out of the downtown core, which led to plans to raze the historic Victorian downtown to make way for parking and yet another mall.

Joe Harman grew up on a farm outside Staunton before leaving and going into a career in banking. By the early 1980s, he was thinking about taking a buyout at his job and slowing down. As he made weekend trips back to his hometown, he saw that it was changing and thought he could help bring some vitality back to the lagging Main Street by opening a business there. He did exactly that, first opening a jewelry store, and later a bed and breakfast called the Frederick House.

"Starting a business is, to me, pretty basic," he said. "You have to know who you're going to sell to, what you're going to sell, and the means by which you'll produce it."

Joe recounts this history from his living room in a townhouse just a mile-and-a-half outside of downtown, close enough that he can walk to the now-thriving downtown farmer's market. When he started his entrepreneurial journey in his hometown, it was a far different picture. Much of the downtown was vacant and the historic Victorian buildings were empty and starting to fall down. The ones that were still occupied had added modern storefronts, all steel and glass, devoid of the Victorian charm that hid behind a characterless veneer.

"Staunton was in decline," Joe said. "We had to reverse that."

Downtown Staunton still had some assets, as well as pockets of wealth left over from its days as a railroad town and a haven for Confederate loyalists and White supremacists after the Civil War. The cosmopolitan identity of the railroad town coexisted uneasily with Staunton's racist institutions. There was a Black hotel and a White hotel. Mary Baldwin College was, for a time, a school for only White women. And flipping through the pages of the yearbooks from Stuart Hall, a high school named for the widow of the Confederate General, J.E.B. Stuart, reveals that for the decades after the Civil War, it educated the sons of former Confederate soldiers. Woodrow Wilson, the US president who helped lay the foundation for the United Nations but who was also a White nationalist, was born in Staunton. His birthplace and presidential library anchor the small city.

In 1924, one of the town's defining features, the Stonewall Jackson Hotel, was built. A local businessman, A. T. Moore, sold bonds to raise money to construct the hotel, which was designed by a trendy New York City architecture firm, H. L. Stevens & Co. The commercial real estate boom and the fluid bond market of the 1920s helped lead to the crash of 1929 and the Great Depression. But before that, the easy flow of capital fueled downtown developments and gave people a chance to invest in local businesses without opening one themselves. "The new hotel, because of its size and location on one of Staunton's more prominent hills, served as a beacon to weary travelers entering the city from the East, South, and West," recounted a history of Staunton. The Stonewall Jackson name was a firm commitment to the city's Southern allegiances.

Old identities die hard.

When Joe Harman returned to Staunton, he became part of a small cadre of preservationists working to restore the architectural glory and economic vibrancy of the area. The group traveled to neighboring Lexington, Virginia, which had begun a renewal project a few years before. It was clear to the group that the beauty and texture of the brick row houses and narrow streets that run up and down the foothills would be crucial to the city's future. The fights in those early years could be grueling, such as when they convinced the City Council to pass a tax to pay for old-fashioned lamp posts and to bury the electric lines. "Nobody would call this fun work," Joe said.

By the early 2000s, Staunton had drawn the interest of a nonprofit that could serve as a potential anchor for a tourism boom. A world-class traveling Shakespeare troupe, the American Shakespeare Center, based near James Madison University, was considering a permanent home in Staunton. The city found a hotel company to redevelop the Stonewall Jackson, which in the 1960s had become a nursing home, and turn it back into a hotel. With state financing, Staunton had already built a parking garage that could serve the hotel and a potential theater for the Shakespeare Center. But the project needed money for the theater, which was to be an exact replica of London's famous Globe Theater, where many of Shakespeare's plays were first performed.

The Old Boys Network Put to Good Use

Small business owners and entrepreneurs often play a kind of hidden role in communities, as connectors and catalysts. Their stores, inns, restaurants, and office spaces host the conversations that make communities vibrant and serve as the catalyst for any number of new business ideas and ventures. Often, the entrepreneurs themselves play a key role.

Joe knew the only institution with deep enough pockets to guarantee a loan to build the theater was Mary Baldwin College. He invited a trustee of the school to lunch at the Frederick House to discuss the idea. In the dining room, Joe made his case. The trustee was intrigued, and after many meetings to line up a broad base of support, the college agreed to guarantee the $3.7 million loan that would make the project a reality.

The Blackfriars Playhouse opened in 2005, and downtown Staunton exploded with new energy and vibrancy, as tourists from Washington, DC, and further away were drawn to the city's revived cultural life.

Staunton's investment in tourism drew an urban, progressive core of community builders. But its position amid rich farmland makes it a gathering place for entrepreneurs who don't necessarily fit the mold of progressive urbanists. On any given evening in downtown Staunton, you're apt to run into agricultural entrepreneurs and back-to-the-land fundamentalists, there for a tour of nearby Polyface Farm, run by a family of celebrity farmers that was featured in the book *Omnivore's Dilemma*. The farm is dedicated to agricultural practices that respect animals and bring people closer to the food they eat. Polyface's appeal cuts across the political divides that mark many other facets of American life.

"Does middle ground exist between the calm talking-stick consensus circle of indigenous eastern tribal cultures and the mad scramble frenzy of western capitalism?" asked Polyface's head farmer, Joel Salatin, on his blog. In Staunton, the answer is yes.

But what the community needed next were initiatives that crossed class lines to reach people who had the energy, but not the resources, to start businesses. Chris Cain, an entrepreneurship advocate who worked in Staunton, relayed the story of Bill Hamilton, the city's economic development director, who envisioned a new form of financing that could connect the city with the surrounding county's rural areas and bring needed cash to business ideas.

With a $250,000 seed grant from the US Department of Agriculture, Bill launched the Staunton Creative Community Fund in 2008. Cain was an early director of the Fund. At the Creative Community Fund, anyone could walk in the door and apply for funding. Many walked out with seed capital. Among the businesses launched from the Fund is Queen City Music Studios. Founder Molly Rose Murphy took a business bootcamp that taught her the basics and helped her save $500 from her income as a musician; a state program gave her a grant for an additional $4,000. From that tiny investment, which purchased laptops and instruments for kids to practice on, Queen City Music Studios was born. Queen City offers space for musicians to teach and practice. "I've got a lot of good people in my corner," Molly Rose said. By the spring of 2020, Queen City Music Studios was working with a local investor on a plan to expand.

Jahleel had a different experience with the Creative Fund. He didn't receive investment, but he did get access to mentors and business advice. He thought about going to James Madison University, but even in-state tuition, at more than $18,000 a year, was prohibitively high. He believed that Növel had a real chance, and he wanted to be a business owner. So instead of college he took full-time retail jobs to make enough money to live on and to pay his tuition at a community college. "I'm working on the business and honestly, getting sleep," he said when we reached him at one point. "I'm doing the best I can."

Proudly Supporting "Lifestyle Businesses"

The Staunton Creative Community Fund is just one example of hundreds, perhaps even thousands, of similar organizations that exist across the country. Large and small, rural and urban, they focus on supporting small businesses and promoting economic development at a very local level.

In many ways, these models are throwbacks to the past, where community banks lent based on relationships and where funding for local efforts came from pooled community resources, like the savings of the local community, whose deposits formed the capital base for loans doled out by local banks. Generations ago, the Stonewall Jackson Hotel was funded this way, receiving its original capital from a group of local investors who pooled their resources to finance the construction of the building. Now this old idea was getting dusted off and revamped for a new generation of entrepreneurs.

As the environment for business has changed, and as small and local businesses have struggled, many communities have come together to support their small business base. "Small businesses are the heart and soul of our neighborhoods," Chris Cain said. "Whenever I hear people in government call them lifestyle businesses, it infuriates me."

In Minneapolis, for instance, the Midtown Global Market operates as an incubator for immigrant-entrepreneurs. In 2018, Minneapolis had the highest number of refugees per capita in the United States, with immigrants making up nearly 10 percent of the population.[4,5] The Market, as it is affectionately known, is part of a larger nonprofit called the Neighborhood Development Center, which aims to cultivate economic development from within neighborhoods, but to do so without displacing people. It offers culturally affirming business training and financing, among its broader set of entrepreneurial and business startup offerings.

Far across the country from Staunton, nestled against much higher mountains, the Arlee Community Development Corp. serves a community of Montana ranchers and Native Americans from the Confederated Salish and Kootenai Tribes with traditional community development projects, such as building infrastructure and organizing volunteer days. Gradually, the organization has become more focused on young people, healing some of the cultural traumas of life in Western Montana through literature and poetry. Claire Hibbs Cheff, the Dartmouth-educated teacher and owner of the outfitting company we described in Chapter 11, served as the poet-in-residence for two years.

Services for youth naturally expanded, and now include connecting them with resources for counseling on how to start a business and access funding. A regional team of experts in business planning, financial analysis, human resources, accounting, marketing, strategic planning, engineering, manufacturing process controls, automation, business valuation, and succession planning round out the free assistance.

The most effective local entrepreneurship organizations find ways to tap into a community's social and financial capital, pulling people together into a network of support built by and for entrepreneurs. But creating truly diverse organizations is profoundly difficult in communities where information networks don't already connect people.

It's said the most segregated hour in America is Sunday morning church time. Many of the funds, accelerators, and networks that we encountered are similarly segregated, not by deliberate design, but as a function of where they're started, whom they're meant to serve, and whatever divides already exist in the community. So it is in Staunton, which is making progress, but only slowly. "We've done a handful of things to try and create more diversity at the Makerspace, but it's f★★★★ hard," Staunton Makerspace founder, Dan Funk, said in an email to us. The Makerspace moved a few years ago to an old body shop near a predominantly Black community, but Black membership remains small.

The Stonewall Jackson Sign Finally Falls

The years when Jahleel was in high school were marked by a clash between the conservative elements of the community, especially strong in the surrounding rural county, and newer, progressive elements in town. Soon after the Unite The Right rally in Charlottesville, the debate began over the high school's name, Robert E. Lee, which had been adopted in 1914 at the urging of the Daughters of the Confederacy. Jahleel told us that he was able to see both sides of the debate, but he's well aware that out in the Shenandoah Valley that surrounds Staunton there are people who would prefer to spend their lives never encountering a person with his skin color.

"I chill in any kind of environment," he said. "[The tension] starts in the Valley, out in Gap and Riverhead. And you know what, you can have your opinions. You can't be mean about it, that's all."

But as the spring of 2020 turned into summer, the Black Lives Matter movement swept across the country. The community around the

Stonewall Jackson Hotel had changed. The name and everything it stood for had finally met its match. With little fanfare, the hotel company announced it was renaming the Stonewall Jackson "Hotel 24 South." The giant letters calling out the Confederate general's name, a landmark in the city for more than 100 years, came down.

Two years after he started his company, Jahleel was generating about $1,500 a month in sales, selling almost exclusively through Instagram. For the time being, he was living with his mom. When the pandemic hit, he dropped out of community college, because online learning just didn't work for him. He'd never heard of the Makerspace, likely because Dan and the other Makerspace founders had decided that advertising didn't work and that looking for new members took too much time, according to Dan.

For a while, Jahleel worked two jobs, one at a sporting goods store and the 2 a.m. to 9:30 a.m. shift at FedEx, in addition to fulfilling orders for Növel. He often found himself nodding off as he packed up shirts on the floor of his room. He was aiming to save $1,000 a month to move himself into an apartment large enough for storing inventory and laying out his shipments. He was discouraged, but he hadn't given up. "Business is business," he said. Perennially optimistic, he was sure that something would change. "I think this is the year to do it."

A new T-shirt design reflected his optimism:

Considering the way the world is, one happy day is almost a miracle. Throw your worries out the window. No more fears. Add some crude humor. Keep the song grooving. Then your dreams will become endless.

One of the mysteries surrounding the decline in entrepreneurship is why more young people aren't starting their own businesses. One answer is that our systems of capital aren't set up to support today's entrepreneurs. Another is the fact that today's entrepreneurs aren't connected to the networks they need to help their business ideas get off the ground. But as Jahleel's experience shows, the decline reflects a fundamental shift in the American economy. If you're not lucky enough to be born with wealth and connections, you start with a real disadvantage and with no safety net for failure. Because of this, too many fledgling *New Builders* don't emerge. As much as organizations like those we found in Staunton are doing to revive entrepreneurship and community, they aren't yet building enough of a net, or replacing what was once a crown jewel of America's entrepreneurial economy: the community banking system.

Endnotes

1. Noah Smith, "New York and San Francisco Can't Assume They'll Bounce Back," *Bloomberg,* August 10, 2020, www.bloomberg.com/opinion/articles/2020-08-10/new-york-san-francisco-u-s-cities-will-struggle-after-covid-19
2. Nicole Lou and Katie Peek, "By the Numbers: The Rise of the Makerspace," *Popular Science,* February 23, 2016, www.popsci.com/rise-makerspace-by-numbers/
3. Psujek recounted the story to us in November 2020.
4. Bob Shaw, "Minnesota Has the Most Refugees per Capita in the U.S. Will That Continue?" *Pioneer Press,* January 13, 2018, www.twincities.com/2018/01/13/the-not-so-welcome-mat-minnesota-winces-at-refugee-cutbacks/
5. "Immigrants in Minnesota," American Immigration Council, 2020, https://www.americanimmigrationcouncil.org/research/immigrants-in-minnesota

CHAPTER THIRTEEN

No One Develops on the East Side

J ill Castilla is president and CEO of Citizens Bank of Edmond, a small
institution located just outside of Oklahoma City. By banking standards, Edmond Community is modest. With total assets of just over
$300 million, it ranks almost exactly in the middle of the US bank-
ing ecosystem.[1] But to the people who live in and around Edmond, it
is *the* bank, established in 1901 as one of Oklahoma's first community
banks. When a developer in Oklahoma City ran into a brick wall trying
to obtain funding for a particularly important project, it was Edmonds
Community, backed by its employee shareholders and an intensely loyal
community, that received the call.

Jill had just driven under the giant railroad trestle on Broadway
Extension outside Oklahoma City when that developer, Jonathan Dodson, reached her on the phone. "I have a deal," he started. Jill knew that
the young developer had previous successes in the city, including the
rehab of an old theater, so she listened with interest as he described the
benefits of his latest project. He pitched to her an idea for developing
a former service station that would be leased by a health clinic, which
would in turn spur retail development in a second building. Eventually, he described, the project would include a fitness center, restaurants,

shops, and more. Then he uttered the words that had sunk his pitch with 25 other banks.

"It's on the East Side."

The East Side of Oklahoma City hadn't seen a private real estate development investment in 35 years. The retail landscape, if you could even call it that, consisted of scattered pawnshops, a Kentucky Fried Chicken, and a CVS. A locally owned radio station, occupying a modest building, was the area's only bright spot. There were no sidewalks and few bus routes. Elderly people could be seen traversing a busy highway in motorized wheelchairs to get to and from the grocery store.

The East Side of Oklahoma is a mostly Black, poor neighborhood that is also home to the state capitol and a large medical complex. Those buildings are castles in a sea of poverty complicated by a long history of hard-edged race relations. When Jonathan, who is White, called Jill, he was just the latest in a long line of developers who had tried and failed to make something happen for the residents of the East Side. Lenders were wary of the area, and *redlining* – the racist practice of banks refusing to loan money in certain areas – had long stood in the way of progress. The community, having lived through generations of being passed over, was hostile. But Jill sensed something in the conversation with Jonathan. There was an opportunity a long time in the making that was just waiting to emerge.

It Takes Money

Starting pretty much any kind of business requires capital. Even entrepreneurs scrappy enough to get their businesses off the ground without startup capital require it to scale. But *New Builders* face unreasonable obstacles in obtaining the capital they needed to bring their business ideas to life and to scale their operations. The Minority Business Development Agency (a division of the US Department of Commerce) described access to capital as "the most important factor limiting the establishment, expansion, and growth of minority-owned businesses."[2] Grassroots entrepreneurs are, by their nature, scrappy, and we've described countless examples of creativity and ingenuity in how they approached finding the capital needed to build their businesses – help from local bankers, access to funds from friends or family members, business competitions, community loan funds, or simply growing at a pace that could be supported by the revenue they were generating. As the story of the EastPoint Development shows, it takes more than ingenuity to overcome systemic, embedded racism.

Access to capital is a critical area to address if we are to help maintain entrepreneurial dynamism in our economy. This will be especially important in the years after the Covid-19 economic crisis. With fewer than 1 percent of businesses accessing venture capital and only about 20 percent of businesses obtaining bank financing, there is a large gap to close. Part of this gap can be filled by addressing shortfalls in our banking system. But to truly address it will require new financing models and new ways of thinking.

Not every New Builder will obtain capital through these new sources. There will always be a need for entrepreneurs to be scrappy and innovative in their approaches to funding their businesses. History is filled with entrepreneurs who were told over and over that their dream was unobtainable. That their product wouldn't sell. That they were chasing a dream that would never be realized. And our history is filled with entrepreneurs who pursued their business ideas despite being told over and over that the market would never buy what they were selling. Many succeeded despite what others thought at the time. The capital markets do not have a monopoly on recognizing good ideas and funding them. Markets are often efficient but certainly flawed. Some New Builders will continue to find ways to turn their ideas into businesses without the help of our financial system. However, too many are being left behind.

The Death of the American Bank

In 1994, there were 14,400 commercial banks in the United States. Today, there are around 5,000. Even more stark is the concentration that has emerged over the last 20 years. Before the 2008 financial crisis about 50 percent of capital controlled by banks was in the hands of about a dozen large financial institutions. Now that number is 80 percent.

The four largest retail banks in the United States – JPMorgan Chase, Bank of America, Wells Fargo, and Citi – control nearly half of all US banking deposits. This is a threefold increase from 1980, according to the Federal Reserve Bank of Minneapolis.[3] SBA loans to truly small businesses – loans of less than $150,000 – have declined by two-thirds since 2005. The SBA has responded largely by attempting to redefine its definition of "small business" rather than by addressing the underlying gap in access to capital. This has contributed to a systemic lack of access to banking services that is reaching almost crisis status in minority and disadvantaged communities. Minority-owned businesses are less likely to receive loans than their nonminority owned peers. They also receive lower loan amounts, pay higher interest rates, and are more likely to be denied loans.

Consolidation in the banking sector has been ongoing, especially since the mid-1990s when Congress changed the regulations around interstate bank ownership. The Riegle-Neal Interstate Banking and Branching Efficiency Act of 1994 removed many of the restrictions on opening bank branches across state lines that had been in place since the 1920s. This resulted in a merger wave among banks as they looked to expand to new markets and, in particular, to consolidate and grow their deposit base.

Tracking the trajectories of the country's four largest banks is illustrative of this trend, as they all grew significantly through mergers while often trimming payroll. In the late 1980s and early 1990s, North Carolina National Bank acquired over 200 smaller banks and eventually changed its name to NationsBank. In 1998, NationsBank bought Bank of America and the combined entity took on the Bank of America name. In 2004, it added FleetBoston in a $47 billion transaction. In the years between 2005 and 2007, it also purchased the credit card juggernaut MBNA (for $35 billion), as well as US Trust and LaSalle Bank (transactions of $3.3 billion and $21 billion, respectively). During the Great Recession of 2008–2009, Bank of America acquired the country's largest home loan originator, Countrywide Financial, for $4.1 billion and eventually the investment bank Merrill Lynch in a $50 billion transaction.[4] Bank of America counted almost $2.5 trillion in assets as of its 2019 annual report and produced net income that same year of nearly $30 billion, with 4,200 branches.[5]

JPMorgan Chase is even larger, with $2.6 trillion in reported assets and 5,100 branch locations. JPMorgan similarly grew through a series of acquisitions, including Chemical bank's purchase of Chase Bank (which retained the Chase name) and eventually Chase's purchase of JP Morgan Bank in 2000, and BankOne four years later. During the 2008–2009 financial crisis, JPMorgan Chase again increased its size and footprint, acquiring Bear Stearns and Washington Mutual (transactions of $1.4 billion and $1.9 billion for these troubled assets that had been victim to their lax practices leading up to the Great Recession of 2008–2009).[6]

Wells Fargo (which jumped into the top four with its merger in 1997 with Norwest Bank) and Citi, through a series of smaller acquisitions, followed similar trajectories. The drop-off in size, as measured by assets, after the top four is precipitous. Wells Fargo and Citi each control about $1.7 trillion in assets. The country's fifth largest bank, US Bank, controls less than a third of that total.[7]

Financial Giants

Together, our country's top four banks exert a massive amount of control and influence over the US banking markets. It's also worth noting that all four of these large banks have been fined over the past years for illegal banking practices. Big banks have meaningful power in our current economy, power they don't always use wisely.

The importance and outsized role of these banks was underscored and likely exacerbated by the 2008–2009 financial crisis. In reaction to the crisis, the Federal Reserve of the United States provided an unprecedented amount of liquidity into the market. This disproportionately benefited larger banks that had more ready access to Fed capital. While the large banks were deemed "too big to fail," smaller banks saw a marked increase in failure rates as they, along with the rest of the country, suffered the consequences of the economic downturn. Ironically, many of those banks had not themselves participated in the lax lending practices that larger banks, and, in particular, the larger loan processors such as Countrywide Financial (which was purchased by Bank of America) and Washington Mutual (which was taken over by the federal government and eventually sold to JPMorgan Chase), practiced.

Banks were forced to turn to the Federal Reserve for short-term liquidity in ways they never had previously. So much so in fact that the Fed instituted a new form of lending called the Term Auction Facility (TAF), under which banks competed in an auction for Fed funds. This move was unprecedented, but the Fed quickly found that it needed to increase both the size and frequency of its auctions to facilitate the level of liquidity required by underlying banks. By the end of 2008, the Cleveland Fed reported that its loans to depository institutions had increased by more than 1700 percent over the previous year.

This liquidity was accompanied by a move to increase regulation of the banking sector. This was an overreaction to the crisis with little understanding or regard to the secondary and tertiary effects the new regulation would have on the entire banking system, not to mention the downstream recipients of banking services. The result effectively turned banks – especially the nation's largest banks – into defacto utilities, unable or unwilling to take the risks necessary to provide loans to key parts of our economy. It also created a labyrinth of new rules and regulations that banks needed to comply with. Entire departments sprung up inside of banks to deal with the regulatory overhead.

The unprecedented capital inflow from the Fed wasn't enough to stave off large-scale bank closures caused by the underlying economic contraction in 2008 and 2009, in particular the housing crisis. According to the Federal Reserve Bank of Cleveland, more than 500 banks failed between 2008 and 2015 (by comparison, since 2015 up until the Covid-19 crisis, fewer than 10 bank failures were reported annually).[8] Not surprisingly the failures were concentrated at the smaller end of the banking sector with the vast majority of failures – over 85 percent – from banks with less than $1 billion in assets.[9] Still more small banks were consolidated into larger banks. The result is that more than one in four community banks have disappeared since 2008. Community banks comprised around 40 percent of assets and lending in 1994, a figure that has dropped to half that amount today, further evidence of the consolidation of the banking sector that is described above. Black-owned banks, already a small percentage of overall banks, have also been in decline, falling from 48 in 2001 to just 21 today. None has assets greater than $1 billion.

It's impossible to overstate the importance of our community banking infrastructure for financing the grassroots entrepreneurial economy. As former Federal Reserve Chairman Ben Bernanke described it, "Community banks [play] a critical role in keeping their local economies vibrant and growing by lending to creditworthy borrowers in their regions. They often respond with greater agility to lending requests than their national competitors because of their detailed knowledge of the needs of their customers and their close ties to the communities they serve."[10] Community banks play an especially important role in smaller and rural markets that have fewer resources and where businesses have limited alternative financing sources. Seventy-five percent of all community banks are located in communities with populations of less than 250,000, and nearly half are in counties with populations of less than 50,000 people.[11]

Some have tied the decline in community banking to the financial reforms put in place after the Great Recession of 2008–2009, and in particular to the Dodd-Frank Wall Street Reform and Consumer Protection Act.[12] Dodd-Frank was passed in 2010 and enacted sweeping reforms of the banking industry by establishing myriad new regulations as well as the oversight bodies to keep watch over them. This included the establishment of the Consumer Financial Protection Bureau, a new federal agency charged with protecting consumers from abuses related to financial products such as credit cards and mortgages. Without question, these moves added cost to the operations of banks, something smaller banks were less able to absorb. But the reality is a bit more nuanced than simply blaming a single (albeit sweeping) piece of legislation. True, the regulatory oversight imposed by Dodd-Frank was burdensome to banks – it was meant to be. The regulations were designed to stave off the kind of predatory lending and other poor banking practices that led to the financial collapse of 2008. Clearly, the "too big to fail" mentality that Congress adopted for our nation's largest banks, essentially giving them special status in our economy and allowing them to operate free from the concern that their actions might someday result in their closing down, did not extend to smaller, community banks. In fact it didn't extend to any banks other than the very largest.

In an influential and widely read 2015 paper on the subject of community banking, Arthur E. Wilmarth of the George Washington University Law School argued that it was actually the changes adopted in the 1990s that started the precipitous decline in community banking across the United States.[13] By disconnecting banks from their communities and by allowing – and later through the Fed's actions, encouraging – large-scale consolidation in the banking sector, Congress set the stage for the demise of our community banking system. Dodd-Frank simply added gasoline to the fire of a system that was already moving to favor larger, national banks over their smaller cousins. By further commoditizing loan products through an increasing array of regulation, Dodd-Frank plays into the hands of larger banks, which were already commoditizing these loans and automating the systems needed to process them. This stands at odds with the more relationship-based loans that are the hallmarks of community banks.

There is an important role to be played by large banks in financing the entrepreneurial sector of our economy. Those banks, especially the four largest banks that control such a significant portion of the lending market, should be encouraged to increase their investment in, and support of, local entrepreneurs. Nevertheless, a robust, local banking system provides critical infrastructure to grassroots entrepreneurs that simply cannot be replaced by larger, national banks. We heard time and again in our conversations with *New Builders* that local banking relationships played a critical role in their businesses. Local bankers took the time to better understand the needs of their companies and were willing and able to take on the risk necessary to finance their operations.

We didn't go looking for stories of how the community banking infrastructure helped entrepreneurs. Those stories found us.

Redlining Is Real, Even Today

When it comes to economic development in areas that have long been starved of investment, there are typically two key issues. The first, and perhaps most insidious, is that in many cases trust has broken down. Communities, developers, and financiers often find themselves at odds with one another. Because of long histories of mistrust, often there is little middle ground to be found. The other key issue is the lack of investible opportunities. The small businesses that could, together, create enough jobs to make a difference are too small individually to receive investment, and often aren't ready for it.

Most approaches to reviving areas like Oklahoma City's East Side are policy-based. Opportunity Zones, the preeminent current policy to steer investment to underserved areas that need it, were no help at all on the East Side. The funds raised to take advantage of Opportunity Zone tax incentives typically look for much larger investments, and individual investors motivated by tax incentives look for the least risky ways to make a return on their money. The breadth of Opportunity Zones means there are much less "marginal" districts, even in Oklahoma City, that still qualify. There is a pecking order to projects such as these, and Oklahoma City's East Side had historically fallen to the bottom of the list.

But as it turned out, the East Side's time had perhaps finally come. The key ingredients turned out to be passion, and relationships between people who had power and resources of the traditional kind, and people who had social capital.

"We desperately need more investment and entrepreneurship along northeast 23rd Street," said Oklahoma City Mayor David Holt.[14] "I think this will be a catalyst," he added, referring to the work that Johnathan Dodson was proposing to undertake. "I think [Jonathan's] extremely inclusive and empathetic approach in a historically African American district is innovative ... Some of it is the way he listens."

To really understand how the East Side project came to be is to understand how three key players in the project – Jonathan Dodson, Jill Castilla, and a local entrepreneur and activist named Sandino Thompson – were open to working across boundaries.

A stylish, talkative, and blunt man, Sandino Thompson left Oklahoma City a few years after college to work for a construction company in the southeastern part of the United States. "After a project that included rebuilding over 600 units of housing and seeing a devastated community come back to life, I started to think about how the communities I grew up in Oklahoma City could be a part of the renaissance," he told us.

Sandino returned to Oklahoma City in 2010 and started thinking about how revitalizing blighted real estate could be a path to reinvigorating the communities of Oklahoma City. He and Jonathan eventually met through city organizations and established a relationship. Slowly and cautiously.

"One day, I'm going to like being your friend," Sandino told Jonathan at some point, after one of Jonathan's earnest and, to use his description, "naïve" questions about racial dynamics.

Oklahoma has an inspiring and horrific race history. The Black community was particularly active in fighting Jim Crow laws in the early 1900s. In 1921, in Oklahoma City's sister city, Tulsa, White rioters looted and burned an affluent Black community, an area that had come to be known as "the Black Wall Street" because of its success and prosperity. Thousands of White citizens poured into the city's Greenwood District, destroying homes and Black-owned businesses, including two newspapers, hotels, and shops. As many as 300 people were massacred and the formerly prosperous community never truly recovered.

The East Side had developed in the 1940s and 1950s as a redlined Black suburb of Oklahoma City. Poverty grew entrenched even as Deep Deuce, Ralph Ellison's home and a center of Black music and culture close to the city's heart, slowly gentrified.

Sandino Thompson encouraged Jonathan Dodson to consider an inclusive approach to developing in Northeast Oklahoma City. He knew there would be obstacles, but was willing to put his reputation on the line to work together. That, as far as Jonathan was concerned, was powerful.

But after years of failed ventures, East Side neighbors were skeptical of outsiders. "If developers showed up in all their whiteness, there would be riots," said Erica Emery, one of two sisters from the East Side whose real estate firm, Monarch Property Group, is active in the city.

"Once or twice a month, I get a call from someone working on a project. They want a Black face involved," added Monique Short, Emery's sister.

Sandino knew collaborating with an outside developer carried risk. If the project failed – or worse, extracted wealth from the community – he'd be considered a turncoat. In Jonathan, however, he found a person with a heart for the work. The son of parents who worked in evangelical nonprofits, Jonathan started his career as a banker. But events changed his life's path, forcing him to consider what happened to people without the same power and privilege he had because he was a White man.

One day, he heard his boss at the bank tell an assistant: "If you don't have sex with me, you'll lose your job." Jonathan reported the executive, who was given a year off with pay. The female assistant was given two months to find a new job.

Jonathan resigned.

As his family's financial situation slowly deteriorated, he found unexpected generosity in a developer friend, David Wanzer. "On my 35th birthday, he handed me a contract and said, 'Why don't we tackle [this project] together?'"

In 2017, armed with what he thought was decent knowledge about how to get a deal done, he visited the East Side with Sandino Thompson. They located a two-piece property with potential – a shopping center and a former service station.

They needed to lease to area tenants to win local support for the project, but they didn't want those tenants to be displaced by gentrification if the project succeeded. Eventually, they came up with a lease structure they thought might work. In exchange for signing 10-year leases, tenants would earn equity in the property. If one wanted to cash out after the initial 10-year term had expired, the property would be reappraised, and money would be borrowed to issue a payout based on the then-current value. If Jonathan could find an investor or lender to put money into building, they'd also be supporting the growth and long-term health of local businesses.

He obtained the city's commitment for $2.6 million in economic-development financing on the $9 million project and found an anchor tenant, Centennial Health, to open an outpatient clinic as part of the project's Phase One.

With that solid capital structure in place, he started approaching lenders in late 2017. "We had done 15 deals as a development company. We had an anchor tenant," Jonathan said. "I thought this would be an easy project."

He thought wrong. Even though the city had agreed to fund $1.2 million in incentives for Phase One, which was $4.3 million in total, and although an equity partner and community supporter pledged an additional $600,000 for both phases, the bank rejections started piling up.

Several banks told him outright, "We don't lend money over there," meaning the East Side. Redlining, while illegal, is still prevalent in many places across the country. Others said they couldn't find comparable sales necessary to appraise the property, or suggested that Jonathan needed another guarantor. So he lined up a commitment from a wealthy friend. "He had more wealth tied up in single malt Scotch than debt on the loan," Dodson said.

The banks still said no.

As the months rolled by, Centennial Health tried to pull out, and one of Jonathan's other projects ran into trouble. "Out of a 10, I was a 10," referring to his level of fear, he recalled. Then, he remembered Jill Castilla, who runs a bank with a uniquely entrepreneurial spirit.

"That Evil Woman"

The Citizens Bank of Edmond understood risk and redevelopment. It had a long and well-regarded history, but by the time Jill joined in 2010 it was the worst-performing bank in the state. Many of the bank's problems were self-inflicted, from poor management practices, to bad collections and credit management, to cases of outright fraud. To make matters worse, the bank, which had historically garnered a strong reputation and working relationship with the local community, was suffering from a reputational crisis brought on by the change in management and practices. Change can be hard to accept, and Jill was in the middle of it.

"I went across the street after being at the bank for a couple of months to get my hair cut, and the lady cutting my hair asked, 'Why did you move back to Edmond?'" Jill recounted in an interview about the turn around.[15] "I said, 'To work at Citizens.' And she put her scissors down and said, 'Oh my goodness, you need to be careful because there's this evil woman that's come to work there that's destroying that bank.'"

That "evil woman" was Jill. Clearly, she had her hands full.

But she persevered and took a creative approach to solving the bank's economic problems. In hundreds of phone calls, she asked local customers to move their high-paying CDs *out* of the bank, relieving the bank of these expensive capital obligations. Slowly, the bank's ratios righted themselves. "When we were in trouble, when our backs were

against the wall, people came to us and said, 'What can we do to help?'"
Jill recounted.

Under her leadership, the community came around, and ultimately
she and they saved the bank, for which the largest shareholder is its
employees. "There's a special place in my heart for communities that
are pulling themselves up," she said.

After listening to Jonathan Dodson's pitch, she felt compelled to act.
"We'll find a way to get to *yes*," she said. After she thought it over, she
asked Jonathan to get Steve Mason, a local entrepreneur who had sold
an engineering firm and is active in development projects, to sign on as
an additional guarantor on the bank's debt.

"I have faith in our underwriting," she said. "I knew it was a good
deal."

About a month later, the bank approved a market-rate loan for $2.6
million.

Nothing has been easy since. Tenants have signed letters of intent and
backed out. "We had it leased three times over," Jonathan said. While
the project is generating enough cash to cover the debt service, it won't
be cash-flow positive until more units are leased.

By late 2020, despite the Covid-19 economic crisis, the first tenants
at the EastPoint project had moved in. The health clinic is open for
business. A restaurant called Family Affair will be reopening soon. Local
rapper Jabee is opening another restaurant. And Kindred, a bar in which
Sandino Thompson has an interest, has opened.

There's also an optometrist, a nonprofit – Oklahomans for Crimi-
nal Justice Reform – and an art gallery launching soon. Sandino plans
a co-working space for people in the creative economy. And there's a
fitness center, the first tenant up and running in Phase Two.

Erica Emery, of the Monarch Property Group, said she drove by not
long ago and said to herself: "There are Black people working out at the
gym. I'm like, 'Look at y'all.'"

There is plenty of work still to be done to ensure the EastPoint
project is sustainable. Jonathan Dodson is optimistic and thinking about
the long term. He says that he'll consider EastPoint a success when the
first tenants receive substantial checks for their equity. The Tulsa Race

Riot is still on their minds a century later, but they are fighting racism and segregation with the tools at their disposal, and helping their community turn over a new leaf.

The Forgotten Hero of Community Finance

Within the community banking system lies a special subset of banks that's worthy of highlighting in more detail. Community Development Finance Institutions (CDFIs) are a product of the Riegle Community Development and Regulatory Improvement Act of 1994. CDFIs were championed by President Bill Clinton as a way to increase support for community organizations and to promote community development. The Riegle Act created the formal concept of CDFIs as well as establishing a Community Development Financial Institutions Fund with the goal to "promote economic revitalization and community development through an investment and assistance program for community development financial institutions."[16] By focusing on traditionally underbanked markets, CDFIs fill a particularly important role in communities of color, rural communities, and other locations where traditional banking infrastructure isn't available. There are several types of CDFIs, ranging from credit unions to loan funds to a small number of CDFI-certified venture funds. Each of them must be private and have community development as part of their primary mission in order to be certified by the CDFI Fund. Certified CDFIs serve specific, underserved target markets, and provide technical assistance – known as development services – in addition to other traditional financing services. There is an overlap between community banks, many of which have missions of promoting economic growth in underserved communities, and certified CDFIs. There are around 1,000 CDFI-like banks in the United States that aren't certified but have similar missions.[17]

Community-minded banking dates back to the founding of the United States, and there are many examples throughout history of banks or bank-like entities being established for the purpose of supporting community development. Benjamin Franklin set up small business loan funds in the late 1700s and early 1800s to fund the endeavors of early American entrepreneurs. Later, the Freeman Bank was set up to provide financing to newly emancipated slaves. Starting in the 1960s with President Johnson's "War on Poverty"[18] and accelerating in the 1970s with the advent of Community Development Corporations, this portion of the US banking infrastructure focused on working in low-income urban and rural communities. Since its inception, the CDFI Fund has directly funded nearly $3.6 billion, provided $57.5 billion in tax credits through its New Market Tax Credit Program, and has guaranteed more than $1.6 billion in bonds through the CDFI Bond Guarantee Program. All in an effort to "increase the impact of Community Development Financial Institutions (CDFIs) and other community development organizations in economic distressed and underserved communities."[19]

CDFIs can and should play an increasingly important role in helping finance *New Builders*. CDFIs disproportionately support local and small businesses in their target markets and, with the increasing consolidation of the banking sector, provide critical access to capital in markets where banking infrastructure is lacking. However, it is important that CDFIs are not politicized. There are some signs that the program – although it works in areas across the country and with underlying entrepreneurs of all political backgrounds – is viewed as a "Democrat-supported" program. For example, CDFIs were left out of the initial Covid-19 relief programs passed by Congress in a deliberate compromise to appease Congressional Republicans. The result was that early access to Covid loan programs wasn't available to many smaller entrepreneurs. This, of course, was exactly the opposite of the help that was needed. Ultimately, Congress fixed this and the later relief bills brought CDFIs and other institutions serving smaller businesses into the fold. It serves as a stark reminder of the risks of a concentrated approach to finance, and the increasingly consolidated banking sector, has on access to capital for critical areas of our economy.

Fewer Loans and Higher Interest Rates

Why are smaller banks, community banks, and CDFIs so important to *New Builders*? Our traditional banking infrastructure is failing women and, especially, people of color. Study after study has documented the racial and gender gaps in access to bank capital. Much of this work has been sponsored by the Federal Reserve itself, which seems keenly interested in understanding these gaps, but still has a way to go in finding solutions to address them.[20] The Minority Business Development Agency has also published a number of reports documenting these disparities.[21]

Alicia Robb, formerly an economist with the SBA and Federal Reserve as well as a fellow at the Kauffman Institute, has looked deeply at these issues and has co-authored several key reports on the topic. Patterns haven't changed since the 1980s in terms of access to capital and higher denial rates, Robb says: "People of color are less likely to apply in the first place because they are afraid of being turned down." This trend holds true even after controlling for other underwriting factors such as income and credit score.

Alicia's research has shown that minority-owned firms are less likely to receive loans than nonminority firms. Additionally, they received lower loan amounts and are three times more likely to be denied loans. Minority-owned firms are also less likely to apply for loans in the first place, due to fears of being rejected, applying for loans at less than half the rate of their White counterparts, even after controlling for other factors such as the size of business. Finally, when minority-owned firms do receive a loan, those loans cost them more than loans to White-owned firms. Alicia's analysis of the data shows that minority-owned firms paid an average interest rate on their loans of 7.8 percent compared with 6.4 percent for nonminority firms.

The rise of wealth and income inequality – especially since the early 1990s and exacerbated by the Great Recession of 2008–2009 and now the Covid-19 recession – have significantly limited potential entrepreneurs with fewer resources from either self-financing their businesses or raising startup capital from friends and family members. For grassroots entrepreneurs, accessing capital from personal funds or through existing networks or extended families, or using other assets such as home equity or business loans, often isn't an option. For *New Builders,* this lack of access to personal capital is even starker. Simply put, White families across every income range and every level of educational attainment have more wealth than their Black and Latino counterparts.

On average White families have *10 times* the wealth of Black and Latino families.[22] In 2016, 15 percent of White families had a net worth of over $1 million, according to data published by the federal government. That compares to under 2 percent of Black families.[23] This speaks to a systemic and generational challenge among Black and brown business owners to access capital from their families and their communities. A number of *New Builders* made a point to explain to us an additional financial challenge many are faced with. As they achieved some level of financial success, they were expected to support those in their extended families yet to make the jump to greater economic stability, pulling on their resources and taking away from their ability to invest back in their businesses.

The Relationship Factor

There is so much potential to change the trajectory of grassroots entrepreneurship in the United States by increasing the access these entrepreneurs have to the financial resources they need to start and grow their businesses. There are signs of hope that more inclusive and innovative capital ideas are beginning to spring up. From technology platforms such as PayPal and Square starting to make funding available, to innovative partnerships between CDFIs and their local communities, to new forms of financing that fall between bank loans and venture capital, there appears to be a wave of new innovation starting to crest.

For the East Side of Oklahoma City, that hope is turning into reality through the unlikely partnership between a developer, community leaders, and a bank that was willing to look past generations of stigma and outright racism to make possible the first step in a road to development and recovery for an area that has historically lacked opportunity. There's a fundamental lesson here: long-term, systemic change always starts with relationships between people, and often the most profound changes start with people prepared to take risks to build those relationships.

Endnotes

1. https://www.usbanklocations.com/bank-rank/total-assets.html
2. Minority Business Development Agency (2017), "Executive Summary – Disparities in Capital Access between Minority and Non-Minority Businesses," https://archive.mbda.gov/page/executive-summary-disparities-capital-access-between-minority-and-non-minority-businesses.html
3. Federal Reserve Bank of Minneapolis (2020), "Rising bank concentration," https://doi.org/10.1016/j.jedc.2020.103877
4. B. Rajesh Kumar, "Mergers and Acquisitions by Bank of America," in *Wealth Creation in the World's Largest Mergers and Acquisitions* (Cham, Swizerland: Springer, 2018), pp. 259–270
5. "What Would You Like the Power to Do?" Bank of America Annual Report 2019, http://investor.bankofamerica.com/static-files/898007fd-033d-4f32-8470-c1f316c73b24
6. Matthew Johnston, "5 Companies Owned by JPMorgan Chase & Co," *Investopedia*, December 17, 2020, www.investopedia.com/companies-owned-by-jpmorgan-chase-and-co-5092490
7. Alicia Phaneuf, "Here Is a List of the Largest Banks in the United States in Assets in 2021," *Business Insider*, December 22, 2020, www.businessinsider.com/largest-banks-us-list?op=1
8. Michelle Park Lazette, "The Crisis, the Fallout, the Change," *Federal Reserve Bank of Cleveland*, December 18, 2017, www.clevelandfed.org/newsroom-and-events/multimedia-storytelling/recession-retrospective.aspx
9. "Smaller banks – bigger failure rate," Face the Facts USA, 2013, https://facethefactsusa.org/facts/most-banks-failed-during-recession-were-community-banks/
10. "The Importance of Community Banking: A Conversation with Chairman Ben Bernake," Federal Reserve System, 2012, https://communitybankingconnections.org/articles/2012/Q3/conversation-with-Bernanke
11. "Community Banks: Number by State and Asset Size," *Banking Strategist*, 2020, www.bankingstrategist.com/community-banks-number-by-state-and-asset-size
12. Marshall Lux and Robert Greene, "The State and Fate of Community Banking," *Harvard Kennedy School*, Mossavar-Rahmani Center for Business and Government Working Paper Series, no. 37 (February 2015), www.hks.harvard.edu/sites/default/files/centers/mrcbg/files/Final_State_and_Fate_Lux_Greene.pdf
13. Arthur W. Wilmarth, "A Two-Tiered System of Regulation Is Needed to Preserve the Viability of Community Banks and Reduce the Risks of Megabanks," *Michigan State Law Review*, pp. 249–370; GWU Law School Public

Law Research Paper No. 2014-53; GWU Legal Studies Research Paper No. 2014-53, SSRN, January 15, 2015, https://papers.ssrn.com/sol3/papers.cfm?abstract_id=2518690

14. Email interview with David Holt, Fall 2020.
15. How to Turn Around a Struggling Community Bank: Jill Castilla, President and CEO of Citizens Bank of Edmond," *PixelSpoke*, 2020, "https://www.pixelspoke.com/blog/social-impact/jill-castilla/
16. "Riegle Community Development and Regulatory Improvement Act of 1994," Congress.gov, 1994, https://www.congress.gov/bill/103rd-congress/house-bill/3474
17. Elise Balboa and Christina Travers "CDFIs & Impact Investing: An Industry Review," *LISC*, December, 2017, www.lisc.org/media/filer_public/8f/21/8f21577d-bcf1-4b23-a180-f59a581558b0/011118_resource_report_cdfi_impact_investing_final.pdf
18. UVA Miller Center (1964), "January 8, 1964: State of the Union," Lyndon B. Johnson presidency, https://millercenter.org/the-presidency/presidential-speeches/january-8-1964-state-union
19. Jodie L. Harris, director "Expanding Opportunity: The CDFI Fund's FY 2019 Year in Review," CDFI Fund, 2019, www.cdfifund.gov/Documents/CDFI_Annual%20Report%202019_Final%203.30.20_508_FINAL.pdf
20. Alicia Robb, Mels de Zeeuw, and Brett Barkley, "Mind the Gap: How Do Credit Market Experiences and Borrowing Patterns Differ for Minority-Owned Firms?" *FED Small Business*, 2018, www.fedsmallbusiness.org/mind-the-gap-minority-owned-firms
21. Robert W. Fairlie and Alicia M. Robb, "Disparities in Capital Access between Minority and Non-Minority-Owned Businesses," *US Department of Commerce Minority Business Development Agency*, January 2010, https://archive.mbda.gov/sites/mbda.gov/files/migrated/files-attachments/DisparitiesinCapitalAccessReport.pdf
22. Dion Rabouin, "10 myths about the racial wealth gap," *Axios*, July 23, 2020, www.axios.com/racial-wealth-gap-ten-myths-d14fe524-fec6-41fc-9976-0be71bc23aec.html?
23. Ibid

PART IV

FACE TO FACE WITH THE
FUTURE

"*The future enters into us, in order to transform itself in us, long before it happens.*"

Rainer Maria Rilke

CHAPTER FOURTEEN

A Secret of Silicon Valley

In the springtime of 2020, as the bad news mounted, Kathryn Finney was worried about the impact of the Covid-19 pandemic on the most vulnerable small businesses and entrepreneurs. Women and people of color, who disproportionately own smaller companies in high-touch fields like salons and restaurants, were shut down. Even in sectors that relied less on face-to-face interactions, businesses run by women and people of color, which as a group have lower capital reserves, were facing greater strain from the crisis. And the aid programs set up by the federal, state, and local governments were doing a poor job of addressing the critical needs of small businesses in general, and in particular the most vulnerable ones.

As an entrepreneur herself, and the founder of a business accelerator focused on women of color called *digitalundivided,* Finney knew how lonely and challenging it can feel to be on the front lines of a crisis with little in the way of support and help. Who, Finney thought, was going to let Black women entrepreneurs know that they mattered?

"You have women and women of color who are doing everything right. Then they get to the end, and there's nothing there for them," she said, describing countless conversations she was having, almost daily, with Black women struggling to keep their businesses afloat.

Finney had about $5,000 saved up – money put aside for a vacation with her husband and their five-year-old son. But with the pandemic accelerating, vacation was clearly no longer on the table. Instead, she came up with a new plan for those funds, one that would directly address what she was hearing from women all around her. Her idea was both radical and simple: she would give the money directly to founders, in small increments, to do with whatever they wanted. There would be no long application process, no extensive follow-ups to measure impact, and no strings attached. Along with $5,000 in matching funds from her husband's employer, Microsoft, she created what she called the Doonie Fund (named after her grandmother Kathryn "Doonie" Hale). The Doonie Fund would give away $100 at a time to support Black women founders.

What Finney did was write checks with the same ease and spirit that White men and privileged people have always written checks. The checks were small, but it was the act of trust, not the size, that turned out to be important.

Those small dollar amounts had a profound impact, as the number of applicants, totaling more than 1,600, showed. Their stories were compelling, describing how much the tiny sums mattered. Kathryn saw this impact in the feedback she received from entrepreneurs around the country. Melanie, from Modern Brands for Women: "Hey friends! I wanted to say how grateful I am that you are here in my little community of dreamers, doers, and encouragers...." And Julie, the founder of Champagne & Melanin: "I am excited to announce that I am a 2020 recipient of the Doonie Fund," which included a shoutout to Finney for helping Black women "stay in the arena."

Clearly, Finny was onto something.

One of the most important realizations coming from both the pandemic and the Black Lives Matter movement, both of which gained momentum that same summer of 2020, was not just about how urgently change was needed but also about what exactly needed changing. It's not underserved communities that need to transform, it's the existing systems that are failing those communities that do. The Doonie Fund, along with similar initiatives such as the Parentpreneurs Foundation, put the onus on givers and investors to let go of their need to measure impact in excruciating detail, forcing them to examine why they give in the first place. "We have a history as a country of not trusting, particularly, Black women. It's time to change that," Kathryn told us.

The Doonie Fund doesn't track its investments in the traditional sense, and the money isn't expected to be repaid to the Fund. The application asks for relatively little information, primarily confirming that the business actually exists and has a website, Instagram, or Shopify account. Importantly, the money isn't restricted for use in the business itself. Finney found that surprisingly often the investments women need to make are for things seemingly unrelated to the business directly, but that free up their time to focus on their company (paying a gas or utility bill, for example). Finney trusts recipients to use the money in ways that ultimately help them be successful. And she doesn't ask for them to justify it.

The idea that philanthropists and investors should focus on changing themselves rather than their recipients is a radical one. With more and more philanthropists acting like investors – looking to measure return on their philanthropic dollars in minute detail – perhaps it's time to take a step back and to rethink our motives.

"You have a group of people – for the first 400 years or so – whose economic value was not recognized," Finney said, referring to Black people in general, and Black women in particular. "How deeply is that concept embedded in America? How dare this person want money when their work should be free?" The United States has a long history of not valuing the labor of Black people. As slaves, their work was not their own, but existed for the benefit of their owners. This history has deep roots in our society and it has become clear to us in meeting so many *New Builders* that it continues to negatively affect the ways in which we support, fund, and treat *New Builders* – especially Black women.[i]

Sheila Herrling, a member of digitalundivided's board of directors, told us by email: "The notion of almost no barrier to entry, no conditions on how recipients could spend the money, and no reporting requirements – not by the recipient on how they spent it nor by digitalundivided

---

[i] It's worth considering that in 2022, America will have been free of Black chattel slavery for as long as it was legal here.

on whether it had an impact – was revolutionary. It challenged the power dynamics that exist in the vast majority of foundations and impact investing companies and their tendency to convey a sense of distrust through burdensome reporting requirements and restrictions on spending. The construct of the Doonie Fund was impactful simply by how it was structured – to empower the founder by saying '*I see you, I believe in you, do what you deem best with this money*, your financial and emotional wellbeing benefits us all.'" (emphasis added)

One of the critical lessons that we took away from our work with *New Builders* was just how much our support structures need to be rethought and updated. Our mindset needs to shift from an emphasis on changing entrepreneurs to changing the system. We need to shift the thinking of those who have power – a list that includes philanthropists, venture capitalists, journalists, and policymakers – to consider ways in which the current system and hierarchy limit the innovation and success of a large portion of our economy. It's not the fault of this next generation of entrepreneurs that they are being held back; it's our systematic failure to see them and to support them that is the root of the problem.

Small micro-grants are clearly not the answer. We aren't suggesting that $100 is enough to change the trajectory for most companies, many of which need and deserve support in much greater amounts. We tell the story of the Doonie Fund because it is a powerful example of how changing thinking can result in new and innovative ways to look at old problems. It's a powerful step in the right direction, even if it's only a small one.

No One Does It Alone

Throughout *The New Builders,* we've discussed how important community is to entrepreneurship. Grassroots entrepreneurs survive and thrive with the support of a much broader set of constituents. While we love to celebrate individualism in the United States, the myth of the solo-founder who persevered on her own to defy the odds and, through sheer grit and determination, created a thriving business, is exactly that – a myth. Every entrepreneur we talked to in researching this book, and for that matter, every entrepreneur we've met through our 20+ years as a venture capitalist and business journalist, had help along the way by networks of individuals who came together to provide advice, counsel, introductions, and support.

Great businesses are not started and do not thrive in a vacuum. Successful entrepreneurs and business owners almost all find significant help from their networks and communities. Fortunately, an increasing number of these networks are being created as people begin to realize just how important they are to the success of new businesses. Allowing more businesses to participate in and benefit from the help and learning of others ultimately results in a greater number of successful companies. In the US economy, business success is a virtuous cycle. Of course, individual businesses compete with each other, but ultimately the more successful they become, the greater the success of our overall economy.

All of the entrepreneurs we've highlighted in *The New Builders* have benefited in one way or another from the networks and communities to which they belong. Some of these networks are informal and many *New Builders* almost chanced into them – Carmen from Cocoa Belle's encounter with a helpful banker from Arkansas Capital Corporation, while she was on a customer delivery, for instance, or Wendy Hudson taking a job at the local bookstore whose owners passed the business along to her and also helped mentor her. Some benefited from community networks, such as the one set up in Staunton, Virginia. Still others, such as Danaris of Sweet Grace and Jasmine, of i-Subz, benefited from more formal networks that were created to help underserved entrepreneurs succeed.

In Silicon Valley, and tech entrepreneurship more broadly, these networks have existed formally and informally for decades. A popular form of these formalized networks are called *accelerators*. They help startups access capital, develop early products, generate initial interest and sales, and work on building their teams. It's an effective formula and there are now thousands of accelerator programs in the United States.[ii,1] Accelerator programs support companies by offering them mentorship, educational programming, and financial and other support, generally delivered through a short-term (approximately three-month) program.

[ii] Seth's firm, Foundry Group, is an investor in Techstars, one of the more well-known accelerator programs.

These programs typically happen "on-site," meaning that startup founders travel to the program location and live and work in the accelerator's facility for that period of time, although because of the Covid-19 pandemic much of the in-person programming has moved online.

Accelerators have a positive impact on the companies that participate. Their graduates raise money sooner, gain customer traction more quickly, and their businesses are acquired faster, according to studies from several academic researchers.[2] Accelerators also have a positive impact on startup activity regionally. Areas with an accelerator program have greater early-stage company financing activity, an effect that is true beyond just the companies that participate in the program itself.

This is important to *New Builders* because while accelerators have been popping up across the United States, they have tended to focus on yesterday's entrepreneurs, not tomorrow's. Based on their lineage and history, accelerators tend to play into the old way of thinking about business and entrepreneurship and are largely focused on technology companies and the largely White, male, well-networked founders who start them. While the last few years have seen some positive geographic expansion of accelerator programs, they tend to be concentrated in well-known technology startup hubs and major cities.[3]

As David Parker from EforAll explained, "We've intentionally or unintentionally built systems to keep the folks who have been successful, generation to generation, in that place. Meanwhile, we're erecting more barriers around the successful group. Folks with more money can go to better schools. That makes it unbelievably difficult to break in. There are so many people who are smart and work hard, but they can't break in. The question is, culturally, can we keep raising the consciousness of that elite?"

Fortunately, there are at least some signs that consciousness is being raised. Our exploration into the *New Builders* revealed a number of newer and innovative programs that are supporting a broader set of entrepreneurs. Some follow the more traditional accelerator model. Others are different kinds of networks and affiliations that are supporting women and minority-owned businesses in new and innovative ways. Several of the entrepreneurs we have highlighted in *The New Builders* have participated in these programs and their stories vividly show how they can help transform businesses and opportunities.

But this change is happening slowly and generally is taking place at the margins. This is to take nothing away from the amazing work these programs are doing, but to impact the entrepreneurial landscape in the United States on a large scale, significantly more *New Builders* must find the kind of help and mentorship that is offered to the relatively few, relatively fortunate tech entrepreneurs who are the denizens of today's supporting infrastructure.

Serendipity

Like many accelerator programs, EforAll, the accelerator started by Desh Deshpande and David Parker, matches companies with a network of mentors and combines that with a regular cadence of programming, educational content, and targeted help for each business. But EforAll focuses on a cohort of companies and entrepreneurs that are not typically targeted by accelerator programs. The result is that EforAll startups are impressively diverse, reflecting the nature of today's *New Builders*. Since EforAll's inception, their participating businesses have been 73 percent women-owned and 57 percent minority-owned. The majority, 52 percent, have been started by immigrants. And, attesting to the grit and character of those that participate in the program, 59 percent were previously unemployed. Almost a quarter of the businesses that EforAll supports are food-related. But the program supports businesses of all types and focuses on a variety of sectors.

"What we are really doing is creating entrepreneurs," says David, "The businesses that get started are the side benefit of doing that."

Desh and David designed a program that in many ways is the model for how to work with underserved entrepreneurs. Importantly, EforAll helps engage a broader entrepreneurial ecosystem to surround its entrepreneurs with resources to help make them and their businesses more successful. Depending on the business and the background of the participating entrepreneur, this might take the form of expertise in pricing and market analysis or connecting entrepreneurs to mentors with experience opening new markets. Often, this includes helping entrepreneurs access the capital they need to invest in their businesses and themselves. And, just as Kathryn Finney emphasized, EforAll's help comes "with no strings attached," as David describes it. "We exist to help these entrepreneurs become more successful in any and every way that we can."

Importantly, EforAll is designed not just to attract underserved entrepreneurs but also to consider the different needs of this community in the design of the programming itself (something that is often a barrier in the way that most traditional accelerator programs are set up). In EforAll's case, that means they sometimes run entire programs in Spanish, as many of their program participants are native Spanish speakers who struggle through classes and lectures conducted only in English. Mentor meetings are designed to accommodate working schedules as well as those of caregivers. Even before Covid-19, many were over Zoom or Facetime, and often took place during lunch, right after work, or immediately after kids were down for the night. The programs mix aspiration with practical advice and, unlike most traditional accelerator programs, aren't centered on a final pitch event focused on fundraising from venture capitalists. Instead, they take into consideration the much broader forms of funding needed by the types of businesses they support.

Desh summed up the aspirations of EforAll perfectly when he told us:

> My hope is that over the next few decades, we can develop a whole new ecosystem. It's just as exciting for them as it is for any of us. If you want to create an inclusive economy, you have to realize every problem is contextual. We need all kinds of people to solve all kinds of problems. The people who are creating small businesses have just as much pride. And with them, you create a vibrant world, and everybody's having fun.

He's not alone in that vision. As it turns out, there are pockets of people all over the country who are focusing their efforts on helping to support *New Builders* and the businesses they are creating, some of whom we'll meet below. They give us hope and inspiration for the future of American entrepreneurship. And more importantly, for *New Builders,* they offer the promise of changing the landscape of entrepreneurship to finally recognize the value and contributions that *New Builders* make to the vibrancy and health of our economy.

Focus on the Numbers

As we've previously discussed, Black women are the fastest-growing group of business owners in the United States, starting businesses at a rate of 4.5× that of all businesses.[4] But perhaps no group is more overlooked in terms of their potential impact on our economy. That much of the future of the entrepreneurial economy is in the hands of the demographic group that receives the least support – financial and otherwise – should set off alarm bells across our country. People of color in the United States are less likely to access capital from friends and family members, from institutional sources such as venture capital and private equity, and have more limited family wealth. Minorities in the United States are chronically underserved by the banking sector.[5] Black neighborhoods have far fewer banks than their White counterparts (27 per 100,000 people vs. 41 in White neighborhoods), yet have far more expensive bank-like businesses such as payday lenders. Even the traditional banks in Black neighborhoods are more expensive, for example, requiring higher account balances on average to avoid service fees – an average minimum balance of $871 compared with $626 in White neighborhoods.[6] The result is reduced access to the capital and related resources that these communities need to support their entrepreneurial efforts.

Access to capital is only one piece of the puzzle to solve if we are to better support *New Builders*. We've spent decades building the infrastructure to help one set of founders succeed. To build on our entrepreneurial success over the coming decades, this support network must expand.

Kathryn Finney, founder of digitialundivided, felt this challenge firsthand. A successful media entrepreneur, she participated in a traditional technology-focused accelerator in 2012. Not surprisingly, she was the only Black woman in her accelerator cohort. Feeling out of place – a familiar position – and recognizing the need and opportunity to create a new model to support a broader set of entrepreneurs, she set out to create a program that would focus on minority women business owners. She started with an organization that she called FOCUS100 – the first conference of its kind for Black female technology founders. FOCUS100 started as a day-long conference in 2012 and quickly expanded to become a multi-week accelerator program by 2014. It was a natural expansion – the original intent of the conference was to bring together Black women founders with a network of mentors (whom they termed *Focus Fellows*). The mentor relationships were the most powerful part of FOCUS100 and essentially took over the conference and expanded its reach. By 2017, digitalundivided had morphed FOCUS100 into an accelerator program designed specifically for Black and Latina women. The program (which they now call the BIG accelerator) brings together these founders for a 15-week intensive program in Atlanta that is focused on three key business areas: customer development, product development, and company development.

Today, digitalundivided has a team of 14, though Kathryn herself has handed the reins of the organization over as she left to focus full-time on building an investment platform. It occupies the Hurt Building, a historic landmark in downtown Atlanta, a fitting location that, once off-limits to people of color, now houses one of the most innovative programs in support of Black entrepreneurs in the country.

Kathryn is a leading figure in the movement to help women of color become successful entrepreneurs. She's a gifted conversationalist, establishing trust early and using it to drive her points home. Much of her drive comes from her grandmother, Kathryn "Doonie" Hale, who was the younger Kathryn's constant encouragement (and why she named the Doonie Fund in her honor). Kathryn graduated from Yale and has leveraged her social standing and business success to establish relationships with key figures in the US business landscape. Kathryn recruited Jamie Dimon, the CEO of JPMorgan Chase, and Melinda Gates as supporters of digitalundivided, for instance.

"It's a privileged position to think that the world wants you to do well," she explains. This was true for the first several hundred years that Black people were in the new world – they weren't paid for their economic output, which existed for the sole benefit of others. "We need to recognize how deeply that concept is embedded in America."

Black and Latina women, she says, are trained not to expect that the world wants good things for them. "There isn't trust for women of color [and] the narrative of self-care in our community is really new," she points out.

On the other hand, Kathryn is quick to point out that Black women, given their history and shared experience, often know how to operate with constraints and with limited resources. "[Black people] have never had resources at scale. We're going to do really well during this time [of Covid] because we're used to managing with little and getting by."

The design of the BIG accelerator is similar to that of other accelerator programs, but there are some subtle differences designed to work for the specifics of their demographic, much in the same way that EforAll has modified their program curriculum. The program itself meets more on nights and weekends to accommodate both work and family schedules. As a result, the BIG programs run for nine months (versus the more traditional three-month model). Programming itself has been adjusted to focus on specific areas in which the digitalundivided team has learned their participants need more training, such as pitching their business. They have a dedicated coaching model that is run in conjunction with the accelerator – Confident Founders – tailored for Black and Latina women.

There is quiet magic to the work of platforms such as digitalundivided. On the one hand, what they do makes great business sense and is in some ways quite obvious: pick an underserved market and build a superior product for it – that's what all great entrepreneurs do. On the other hand, the struggles of putting together successful programming for the populations they serve are daunting. That they've been so successful – and as a result, so well recognized in the industry and beyond – is a testament to the tenacity and focus of the people who drive the organization, and to their dedication to their mission. Along the way, they are redefining success so that it is measured by impact as well as by financial return.

Fortunately, digitalundivided isn't alone in its focus on women of color. Sistahbiz, based out of Denver, Colorado, is another example of the new networks that are starting to pop up to support *New Builders*.[iii] Sistahbiz's history – and very existence – shows the depth of the need in communities of color for meaningful support networks. As Sistahbiz founder and CEO, Makisha Boothe, describes it, "Many Black women feel pushed out of their 9-to-5 jobs and start businesses out of necessity. This creates unique needs amongst this group." Sistahbiz addresses these needs through monthly "Black Girl Therapy" meetings, monthly

---

[iii] Seth and his wife are financial supporters of Sistahbiz.

masterclasses, and coaching. It has a particular emphasis on what they call their "loan readiness," "growth readiness," and "building profitable full-time business" models – helping prepare companies in their network to seek financing and ultimately to use that financing to accelerate their businesses. "The Black community has a historically strained relationship with US banking institutions," Makisha told us. Sistahbiz often coaches the founders they work with through the process of building lender and investor relationships. She has also consulted with banks and lending partners about ways to build trust and increase access in the Black business community.

Sistahbiz brings together all of these pieces in an effort to create an ecosystem for Black women founders that both encourages and supports their efforts to start and grow businesses. This network has now been paired with a loan fund of $775,000 to support the funding of these businesses. Additionally, Sistahbiz managed a $160,000 relief fund set up in response to the Covid-19-induced financial crisis.

Makisha didn't start out with a focus on Black women. They found her. With the sheer volume and ferocity of the inbound interest, she realized she was onto something – an untapped need in her community that was calling out to her to help fill.

The success of these networks suggests that there is more potential in serving *New Builders* and underserved entrepreneurs than many have realized. As programs like EforAll expand throughout the country, they are finding that entrepreneurs have a nearly universal presence in American cities and towns. Entrepreneurship is not confined to elite enclaves of Silicon Valley or the Route 128 corridor surrounding Boston. But for every entrepreneur helped by EforAll, or who participates in a program run by digitalundivided, or finds support in a network like Sistahbiz, there are thousands who aren't being reached.

Two Times More Likely

In a recent analysis, the Center for American Entrepreneurship determined that 43 percent of Fortune 500 companies were started by either immigrants or the children of immigrants. These immigrant-founded firms employed 12.8 million people in 2016 and generated $5.3 *trillion* in revenue. Immigrants start businesses at roughly twice the rate of nonimmigrants and as such they are a critical component of our entrepreneurial ecosystem.[7]

But we don't make it easy for foreign-born entrepreneurs to set up their businesses in the United States. This has been the case for a long time, but increasingly so in the past few years, as the national dialogue around immigrants, and immigration more broadly, has taken a dark turn.

"The US has always been a destination for immigrant founders. But the ease of starting a business for an immigrant changed after the terrorist attacks of 9/11." explains Nitin Pachisia of Unshackled Ventures, an investment firm that focuses exclusively on immigrant founders.[iv]

More recently, immigrants – especially those from Muslim nations – were targeted by the Trump Administration. These restrictions dampened the flow of skilled foreign workers as well as the flow of refugees, both groups that are apt to start companies. As just one example, according to the US State Department, there are about 1 million foreign students studying in the United States at any given time, contributing to our economy, immersing themselves in our culture, and benefiting from our educational system.[8] The vast majority of these students are sent back to their home countries once they are done with their studies. This is a particularly acute challenge at the highest levels of our educational system. *The New York Times* highlighted this trend in an article published a few years ago that reported that in science, technology, engineering, and mathematics (STEM) graduate programs, over half of the students are foreigners. In the specialty field of computer science, this number jumped to 64 percent of doctoral candidates and 68 percent of those enrolled in masters programs. Lawmakers from both parties have proposed programs that would grant foreign students receiving graduate degrees from US institutions an automatic visa, but these proposals have not gained traction. Instead, policymakers are making it harder and harder for those not born in the United States to stay here. These additional hurdles faced by immigrant founders limit job-creation in the United States, as thousands of highly educated foreign-born workers leave to start businesses in their own countries or to work for companies back home.

[iv] Seth has a small investment in Unshackled's fund.

Nitin Pachisia and his Unshackled Ventures co-founder, Manan Mehta, set out to change that. Theirs is yet another story of opportunity formed from experience. Nitin was born in India and moved to the United States in 2005 to work for the international audit and consulting firm Deloitte & Touche. In 2012, after working for several startup businesses, he wanted to start a business of his own. But without a green card – to this day he still doesn't have permanent status – this proved to be far more challenging than he anticipated. "Twenty-three immigration lawyers told me that I couldn't start a company because of my [immigration status]," he remembered. That turned out not to be entirely true, something the twenty-fourth lawyer he consulted finally helped him fully understand. He could *start* a business; he just couldn't be *employed* by the business he started. This was an important nuance. For Nitin, it meant he could start a business but he would need to remain employed by the company that sponsored his work visa. If he could manage the time, he could work on his own idea on the side. That's not an uncommon place for many immigrant entrepreneurs to start, but it's a daunting task. As Nitin discovered, starting and building a business while dealing with immigration compliance and maintaining his day job, became unsustainable.

It was through this process that Nitin and Manan discovered what they believed to be the larger opportunity of helping immigrant founders get their ventures off the ground. They realized that many would-be immigrant founders were tied – shackled – to their current jobs because of their visa status. These would-be founders lacked the understanding of how to work within the immigration system to set up their ventures, and because they were unable to leave the job that was sponsoring them, struggled to raise startup capital for their ideas, unable to work on them full time.

These are common problems for immigrant entrepreneurs who, in Nitin and Manan's view, will ultimately start businesses either here or back home. "Sending job-producing immigrants back home is the worst kind of offshoring," Nitin told us, referencing the term used by many in business for the practice of US-based companies moving jobs to other countries to take advantage of lower labor costs. In this case, offshoring is forced by the US government and our systems that make it so difficult for foreign-born entrepreneurs to start companies here. The result is the offshoring of entire companies.

Because of their higher propensity to start businesses, the net effect of immigration on US employment is actually positive, contrary to the popular narrative that immigrants take jobs away from US-born workers. "Ironically, the result is exactly the opposite of the usual narrative," summed up Northwestern University Business Professor Ben Jones, a co-author of a recent study that looked at questions of immigration and job creation. "[I]mmigrants actually improve the economic outcomes for native-born workers."[9]

Despite this, there are relatively few firms like Unshackled that are focused on immigrant entrepreneurs – especially working at the very earliest stages of company formation to help foreign entrepreneurs who want to stay in the United States navigate the immigration and visa process and start their own businesses. Because of the fund's structure, these companies tend to skew to the technology sector – Unshackled's business model is that of a traditional venture fund. But increasingly, they are looking at ways to leverage their immigration expertise for businesses with growth potential outside of the tech sector. Through experimenting with different forms of financing and by recognizing that businesses of all sizes can present unique opportunities for their founders and employees, as well as to Unshackled Ventures and its investors, they are expanding their reach.

In Unshackled's case, through two funds and almost $30 million of capital, they have a 100 percent success rate in gaining immigration status for the approximately 40 founders they've worked with. Over a third of those founders are female, which puts them well ahead of the venture industry averages.

It's heartening to see groups such as Unshackled concentrate on helping immigrants. That they're not alone in this suggests that others are starting to catch on to the underserved opportunities that immigrant entrepreneurs present, to the innovation they can drive, the jobs they can create, and the value they can bring to the US economy.

Metcalfe's Law

As more accelerators focused on *New Builders* arise, and more funders see the potential in these underserved entrepreneurs, more winners will emerge in overlooked parts of the economy. Programs such as Camel-back Ventures in New Orleans, Opportunity Hub in Atlanta, the LatinX Incubator in Chicago, and the Hillman Accelerator in Ohio are emerging.[v] And a growing number of investment firms, especially those led by women and people of color, offer support and networking to diverse founders, turning themselves into small accelerators. Large companies are increasingly playing a role in spurring innovative founders outside the traditional White male, software-driven model. For instance, Microsoft and Melinda Gates's venture firm Pivotal Ventures jointly fund a number of women-led startups each year with substantial sums.

The network effects of these models – bringing more people together across like minded groups with the goal of aiding and supporting the next generation of entrepreneurs – will pay increasing dividends to society for years to come. Dr. Robert Metcalfe, a pioneer in internet and networking technology, describes the power of networks in what is now known as *Metcalfe's law:* a network's value is proportional to the square of the number of nodes in the network. Put another way, the power of any given network grows exponentially with the number of nodes on that network. Networks exponentially increase the power and potential of our entrepreneurial ecosystems. Silicon Valley has understood this power for years and used it to create an ecosystem in the technology world that is unparalleled. We have the imperative to do the same to address the needs of a much broader set of entrepreneurs.

Endnotes

1. Alejandro Cremades, "How Startup Accelerators Work," *Forbes,* January 10, 2019, https://www.forbes.com/sites/alejandrocremades/2019/01/10/how-startup-accelerators-work/?sh=a80bb3a44cd8Brookings

2. Benjamin L. Hallen, Christopher B. Bingham, and Susan Cohen, "Do Accelerators Accelerate? A Study of Venture Accelerators as a Path to Success?," *Academy of Annual Meeting Proceedings*, 1 (2014): 12955, www.research gate.net/publication/276895878_Do_Accelerators_Accelerate_A_Study_of_Venture_Accelerators_as_a_Path_to_Success

3. Sheharyar Bokhari, Andrea Chegut, Dennis Frenchman, and Isabel Tausendschoen, "Is Innovation Really in a Place? Accelerator Program Impacts on Firm Performance" (draft, 2018), https://mitcre.mit.edu/wp-content/uploads/

---

[v] Seth and his wife are financial supporters of Camelback.

2018/03/Is-Innovation-Really-in-a-Place_Accelerator-Impacts-on-Firm-
Performance_030518.pdf

4. "Women-Owned Businesses Are Growing 2× Faster on Average Than All
Businesses Nationwide," *American Express*, 2019, https://about.american
express.com/all-news/news-details/2019/Woman-Owned-Businesses-Are-
Growing-2X-Faster-On-Average-Than-All-Businesses-Nationwide/default
.aspx

5. Jacob Fabor and Terri Friedline, *The Radicalized Costs of Banking* (New America, June 2018), https://s3.amazonaws.com/newamericadotorg/documents/
The_Racialized_Costs_of_Banking_2018-06-20_205129.pdf

6. Ibid

7. "Immigrant Founders of the 2017 Fortune 500," *Center for American
Entrepreneurship*, 2017, http://startupsusa.org/fortune500/

8. "Number of International Students in the United States Hits All-Time
High," Institute of International Education, 2019, https://www.iie.org/
Why-IIE/Announcements/2019/11/Number-of-International-Students-in-
the-United-States-Hits-All-Time-High

9. Pierre Azoulay, Benjamin F. Jones, J. Daniel Kim, and Javier Miranda, "Immigrants to the US Create More Jobs than They Take," *KelloggInsight*, October
5, 2020, https://insight.kellogg.northwestern.edu/article/immigrants-to-the-
u-s-create-more-jobs-than-they-take

CHAPTER FIFTEEN

New Capital Models

S eth has devoted his entire career to financing early-stage businesses. As a venture capitalist for over 20 years, he has been a part of the system and the establishment. For most of this time, the industry paid limited attention to questions of equity and inclusion in what has histori-cally been a White, male-dominated industry. It has only been in the past several years that somewhat of a reckoning has started to take place – a reckoning about how little progress has been made around diversity in the venture business and about how narrow a slice of the business world venture capital actually addresses. We see this work as positive but also recognize that it is slow-moving and deliberate. It will take time. Our hope is to see this work accelerated with change coming both from inside the industry as well as from disruptors from the outside, challenging the status quo and doing exactly what the venture industry prides itself on: innovating.

The venture industry has created many great successes and has played a part in helping bring to life world-changing businesses. It's also been incredibly myopic in its thinking and insular in the way it has operated. The result is an industry that believes it is transforming the world, while at the same time operating in an incredibly narrow segment of that world. To have a front-row seat to the explosion of venture capital over the past decade provides what is perhaps a glimpse into the possibility for other forms of finance. It's easy for those inside the industry, who control the purse strings of billions, to see only to the horizon of their relatively small world.

Elizabeth came to this work – writing *The New Builders* – through a different path, that of a storyteller looking for entrepreneurs who didn't fit the Silicon Valley mold but who had as much talent and grit as those whose ideas were generating millions of dollars of funding. Even with this background, she didn't fully understand the changing face of today's entrepreneurs, the extent to which our systems of mentorship and finance are failing them, or the extent to which the landscape had shifted to make it harder for all entrepreneurs. As one of the few women writing about high finance, venture capital, and private equity in the United State and abroad, she also recognized many of the people she was interviewing, who were mostly men, seemed to resist looking out-side their narrow worlds, perhaps out of the fear of being motivated to change.

There are some hopeful signs. In our experience, the smartest, profit-driven people take a long-term view. The trends and numbers are clear – the future of the economy lies in a more diverse direction.

Financing at Scale

Large technology platform companies that power small business payments have the potential to touch a large number of businesses. Increasingly, companies such as Square, Stripe, and PayPal are rec-ognizing the business opportunities presented by helping grassroots entrepreneurs access capital to help stabilize and grow their businesses. To be clear, these programs have focused on existing companies – many have requirements that participating businesses have a certain longevity and payment history with the platform to qualify. But still, these are encouraging signs. Initially left out of the Payroll Protection Program implemented by Congress after the Covid-19-induced economic crisis, these platforms were later added and ended up serving as critical infras-tructure for funneling federal aid and loan dollars to small businesses around the country.

Square offers a great example of the power that technology platforms have to impact small businesses. Launched in 2014, Square Capital offers loans to companies ranging from as little as $300 to as much as $100,000. As of September 2020, Square Capital has advanced over $7.7 billion to some 420,000 small businesses. The average loan size is under $10,000. According to a 2018 company report, 56 percent of the loans issued through this program were to women-owned businesses and 36 percent to minority-owned businesses.

These "loans" are really cash advances, and as such the rates that are charged tend to be higher (in some cases significantly higher) than those charged by banks. But they do offer rapid access to capital, streamlined paperwork, and flexible repayment terms, which make them attractive for many businesses. These programs aren't the answer to the capital gap, but they are a starting point for broader access to capital for a wider range of businesses.

Paypal and Stripe have similar programs. Each provides much faster access to capital (often wired the day the funding request is made), as well as a simplified application and streamlined underwriting, especially when compared to traditional bank loans. And because the platforms are already connected to the merchant accounts of the businesses to which they are lending, they can profitably offer much smaller loan sizes and more flexibility than banks.

Our hope is that by leveraging technology, these and other financial institutions can offer more competitive rates to a broader set of companies. However, they're not a replacement for our declining community banking system and shouldn't be viewed in the same light. These technology platforms are geared to offering transactional services on a formulaic basis to existing companies. That's great for many companies that are already up and running, but it's not the same as the more relationship-based offerings that so many *New Builders* told us had such a meaningful impact on their businesses. These relationships come from local and community banks, not from the internet.

Funding through these platforms won't solve the startup capital gap, but they do have the potential to provide capital to a large number of businesses. While Square positions its program under their ESG (equity, social responsibility, and governance) umbrella, all of the platforms offering loans and advances of this type appear to be doing so as a profitable part of their business models. This is important because to reach the scale necessary to be truly impactful for America's small businesses, programs like these need to generate an economic return.

There is a harsh reality and a familiarity to the rise of technology platforms such as the ones described above. Their convenience and accessibility make them tough competition for highly regulated small and community banks, as well as for large banks, many of which have already retreated from small business lending. And these platforms typically charge interest rates that are higher than those available at banks, raising the cost of capital for entrepreneurs struggling to build their business. As large businesses now, these platforms also risk falling prey to the Milton Friedman dictum that companies should be managed to maximize short-term profits. Given the sway that large-tech businesses hold in our imaginations and in our political system, it's not clear that the rising large players in the financial services market will function well for the *New Builders* in the coming years. However, if they *were* to become leaders in the battle to help the *New Builders*, it would likely come from a mindset shift among their top executives and the largely White men in those executives' networks: that businesses started by women and people of color are not inherently riskier and not "ESG" investments. That even big public companies have a responsibility to help create a more inclusive and equal society, and that in doing so they will open up new and profitable business opportunities for their companies.

That kind of mindset and cultural shift is not impossible. Indeed, the hope that we may encourage and accelerate that shift was one of our motivations for writing *The New Builders*. But it is a tall order.

The Definition of *Investor* and *Financier*

Our financial system often sees lending to entrepreneurs, especially early-stage entrepreneurs, as much riskier than it actually is, and as something that is outside the norm, when in many cases it is not. This is true not just in the United States, but globally as well. In the 1980s, the Grameen Bank formalized a model of community finance in Bangladesh, where small groups of women pooled money and set up systems to lend capital to each other. Although many believed this to be an inherently risky endeavor, it turned out that money that was pooled this way – and that relied on lending to women – saw repayment rates that were astonishingly high. Grameen's founder, Muhammad Yunis, who was later awarded the Nobel Peace Prize for his work, figured out how to raise money from investors and philanthropists to distribute via these lending networks and by doing so created change and opportunity on a scale that most hadn't thought possible. Kiva, a San Francisco – based technology company, uses technology to enable donors (many of them individuals) to fund entrepreneurs around the world using a model that borrows from Grameen Bank. Loans sizes start at just $25, and once that money is repaid, funds are recycled to be lent out again.

In many respects, impediments to lending models like these have less to do with downside risk – investors losing their money – and more to do with the definition of "investor." Indeed, the term *investor* has seemingly come to apply to only a thin sliver of the actual world of investment. But as Kiva, Grameen, and others have shown, investors can come in all shapes and sizes and invest in amounts both big and small.

Connecting Investors with Main Street

We first came across the concept of community funding for Main Street businesses in Staunton, Virginia, highlighted in Chapter 12. Launched in 2008, The Staunton Creative Community Fund has loaned more than $1.2 million to businesses throughout the Shenandoah Valley, with loans ranging from $1,000 to $50,000.[1] While it's still a relatively small effort – there are only two staff members managing the fund – it has had an outsized impact and serves as both a model and an inspiration to other communities looking to jumpstart support for local entrepreneurs.

The premise of the fund is simple, but its power comes from that simplicity. By providing small loans to local businesses and entrepreneurs, The Creative Community Fund helps promote and enable entrepreneurship throughout the region. They also help local entrepreneurs access matching funds from the Virginia Individual Development Account (VIDA) program through which the state of Virginia will match dollars saved by qualifying entrepreneurs on an 8:1 basis. The Creative Community Fund has paired this financial support with programming for both established and growing entrepreneurs and serves as somewhat of a community hub for grassroots entrepreneurship in the area. As they describe it, they are "a safe place for dreamers and schemers to imagine the possibilities, ask questions, and get the funding they need in order to succeed."[2]

An entrepreneur in Salem, Massachusetts, is taking the idea of local support and investment further, and online. Nicholas Mathews is the CEO and co-founder of the local investment platform MainVest. Something between GoFundMe – the popular donation-based fundraising platform for individuals and businesses – and more traditional investment vehicles, MainVest enables ordinary citizens to invest in local businesses looking to fund their operations. Individual investment amounts are often as little as $100, but when paired with many other investments, offer a meaningful lifeline to local shops, restaurants, and businesses in need of investment capital. Typical funding campaigns on MainVest range from $20,000 to $100,000. Expected returns for each project are posted online, in the information that investors receive before making an investment.

Projects on the site tend to skew toward Main Street, consumer-oriented businesses. At the time of our writing, these included funding for a local arts venue, support to enable a local culinary institution to purchase kitchen equipment, and several breweries looking for money to expand their operations. It's the connection between investors and the businesses they support that appear to be driving interest in the idea – investors can actually go experience what they've helped make possible through their funding. This connection to place and to purpose, we believe, is a critical ingredient for programs that support grassroots entrepreneurs to be successful. It can serve as the driving force for mobilizing entire communities to support their local establishments.

Importantly, this local capital is reaching places in our economy that are often overlooked by other funding mechanisms. For example, according to Mathews, 58 percent of the businesses that have raised capital on MainVest are women-led and 38 percent are owned by people of color.[3] These are exactly the kinds of *New Builders* that need support and opportunity. MainVest isn't alone in helping to democratize investment in this way. It's one of a handful of similar companies and organizations working on innovations in Main Street investment and finance. Others include Ideazon, Fundopolis, and Crowcube, and new platforms are being launched regularly.

This kind of Main Street investment is a rapidly evolving sector of finance, brought about largely by the passage of the JOBS Act in 2012. Adopted in the wake of the Great Recession of 2008–2009, the JOBS Act was an effort to find new ways to fund small businesses and, more generally, to ease restrictions on private companies and allow for more flexibility in their financing options (including the length of time they could remain private, as well as the process for going public). The JOBS Act significantly changed the landscape for business financings and altered the rules around how private businesses could access capital. Importantly, it provided an exemption to Securities and Exchange Commission (SEC) registration requirements for certain types of transactions, allowing for the creation of online platforms, like MainVest and its peers, to offer individuals access to investment opportunities. There continue to be restrictions on the limits that individuals can invest based on income and net worth (the traditional mechanisms that the government has used to restrict individuals' ability to invest in private securities), but these restrictions were eased significantly by the JOBS Act, opening the aperture for who can invest in startups of all types.

It's still very early days for these new rules – especially the most inclusive part of the Act, the *crowdfunding* rules that were implemented in 2016 – and only a relatively small number of companies have taken advantage of raising capital in this way. According to the Securities and Exchange Commission, from May 2016 through December 2019, companies raised approximately $170 million through crowdfunding (via 795 completed offerings – an average of approximately $0.21 million each). But this is just a drop in the bucket compared to the $2.7 trillion that was raised by companies through other private offerings during that same period.[4]

This represents an area of great opportunity for Americans to open up investment in its grassroots entrepreneurial sector and extend the kind of dynamism that we see at the top end of the financial markets to a broader swath of our economy.

A Trailblazer 40 Years in the Making

Local investment and support for entrepreneurship are not new, however. Across the country, there have been many examples of grassroots financing supporting grassroots entrepreneurship, often in creative ways. In just one such example, a group of concerned citizens in New Hampshire came together nearly 40 years ago to create a funding platform for local businesses in their region. They envisioned a revolving loan fund that would lend to projects that benefited local communities, but that were unable to garner capital from traditional sources. By pairing these projects with investors who wanted to invest locally and see the impact of their work, they would create a virtuous circle to allow critical funding projects for businesses, housing development, and individuals – capital that would otherwise be unavailable to them. The result was a novel experiment at the time, but one that has had staying power, and, as a result, shows the potential of true community capital: the New Hampshire Community Loan Fund.

"The idea was to build a better New Hampshire. And to do so by building a more inclusive economy," explained John Hamilton, who was the Community Loan Fund's acting president from June 2020 until early 2021. "We help people invest their savings in ways that give back to their communities by enabling loans to fill the gaps where the mainstream financial system has said no."

Their first loan, funded by an investment from the Sisters of Mercy of New Hampshire, saved a manufactured-home park and pioneered a new model for manufactured-home communities. That $40,000 initial loan lit the spark that has now resulted in over $65 million in loans for similar projects across New Hampshire and has paved the way for similar programs across the country.

The Community Loan Fund is not a bank. It's more of a bridge – connecting people with capital to those in need. Its success and longevity shows the potential for this kind of model. Since its founding, the Community Loan Fund has invested over $360 million into New Hampshire businesses, communities, and individuals. The Community Loan Fund is supported by a network of some 650 investors, the vast majority of whom live in the state. Investments in the loan fund range from just $1,000 to more than $1 million and support loans ranging in size from as little as $5,000 to well over $1 million. The cumulative loan loss rate over

36 years is just 2.8 percent — remarkable by any measure, but especially considering that the Community Loan Fund loans almost exclusively to populations that have been turned down by more mainstream capital sources. Equally important, investor losses have been nonexistent. "Since our inception, the Community Loan Fund has never failed to repay an investor," Hamilton reported to us.

Community is central to the Community Loan Fund. It is core to their mission, and it's front of mind in every action they take and every business and project they fund, as well as in how they recruit investors and donors. "Because of our work's emphasis on community, we never use any acronym (NHCLF, CLF) or any shortening of our name other than Community Loan Fund," declares the Community Loan Fund's website.

The Community Loan Fund's success is driven in large part by the training, coaching, and business education it provides to loan recipients. This assistance encompasses an array of services and connections, from finance and accounting, to access to advisors and mentors, to access to a CEO peer group. It's more akin to the support a company might find if it went through an accelerator program. That the Community Loan Fund ties mentorship and network to lending highlights the importance of supporting *New Builders* with more than capital. It recognizes the need to think more holistically about new models that tie together broader support infrastructure with capital.

The form of lending pioneered by the Community Loan Fund is the counterpart to grassroots entrepreneurship — grassroots lending.

Community loan funds across the country often view their role in capital formation in this grassroots fashion. Instead of reviewing applications and determining underwriting risk, they work more closely with the groups they're trying to help to better understand their businesses and where investment dollars, along with other support, can be of greatest impact. The process focuses on how to get to "yes," versus reasons to turn applicants down.

Consider one small, diversified farm that was looking for investment money to expand their pork operations. The farm didn't actually have detailed enough financial information to support either the loan or the decision to invest in that portion of their business. The Community Loan Fund, through its assistance program, connected the farm with a technical accountant who developed an enterprise-wide analysis to identify products on which the farm was making money. In the end, it turned out that the farm was actually losing money on pork. The loan it was seeking was asset-backed, and perhaps another financial institution would have been fine blindly lending money to it, knowing that the investment was secured. In doing so, the farm would have been investing in a money-losing endeavor, the scale of which would have brought down its entire operation. Instead, the Community Loan Fund helped redirect capital to that portion of the farm's business – in this case, dairy and cheese production – that was actually making money. The result was the farm not just staying in business but expanding its operations, creating more jobs and more financial sustainability for the community in which it operates.

There are over 500 CDFI-affiliated community loan funds in operation across the United States, according to the federal government. Many, like the New Hampshire Community Loan Fund, operate as nonprofits. Their operations are funded entirely by the earnings they make on the loans themselves; the technical assistance side of their business is made possible by donations. That said, the limiting factor for scaling community loan funds is access to the capital needed to make loans. And while some of the capital that is lent comes from the federal CDFI Fund as well as from Community Reinvestment Act (CRA) credits, more individual and local capital is critical for helping these community funds to continue to operate. This is especially true as recent changes to the interpretation of the CRA regulations appear likely to reduce the incentive for banks to invest through community loan funds. Investing directly into community loan funds is one of the highest impact ways that readers who have the means to do so can help spur entrepreneurship in their local communities.

A Laboratory for Innovation

Few organizations have done more to study the challenges around democratizing capital access than the Ewing Marion Kauffman Foundation. In 2019, the Kauffman Foundation, with support from the Rockefeller Foundation, launched the Capital Access Lab with the goal of providing "risk capital to new investment models that do not resemble traditional venture capital or lending." Ultimately the aim is to increase capital invested in "underserved entrepreneurs who have been historically left behind due to their race, ethnicity, gender, socioeconomic class, and/or geographic location."[5] It's a small pilot at $3.5 million but because of the backing of the Kauffman Foundation, can serve as a larger catalyst for change across the funding landscape.

This effort supports an ongoing, quiet revolution happening in a small subset of the venture capital community that searches for a different approach to capital access. Firms such as Village Capital, Next Wave Impact, and Indie.vc are pioneering new ways of supporting entrepreneurs and are starting to change the narrative around how to invest profitably in businesses that fall somewhere between venture capital and bank loan – backable businesses.

The funding model favored by many of these firms is a hybrid between traditional equity investment and bank financing. Often described as revenue-based investment (or revenue-based financing – RBI or RBF), this "new" style of investing pays back investors a portion of a company's revenue until a set multiple of the original capital has been returned. It's considered a more company-friendly style of investing because the payback is flexible and set as a portion of sales rather than as a fixed amount, and because the survival of the company doesn't hinge on exponential growth. This allows companies to grow into their loans, instead of needing to quickly generate cash flow to cover a fixed payment. There are a number of flavors of this type of structure, which sometimes include partial ownership of the company for the benefit of investors (in that way, it has some attributes of traditional equity investing). Often, when RBF investments include an equity component, there are provisions that allow companies to buy down the portion of the company that investors own over time, based on how quickly they pay back the initial capital investment.

This type of investing has been around for decades but has only been applied more broadly in the past few years. In the oil and gas industry, RBF models have been commonplace for generations. The same is true in the entertainment industry. The New Hampshire Community Loan Fund has been providing businesses with revenue-based loans for decades. But the more widespread use of flexible financing models is certainly new and has the potential to meaningfully change the funding landscape for *New Builders*.

Almost all of the models we came across recognize the need for capital to be paired with mentoring and support, as well as the power of connecting entrepreneurs to a broader community of entrepreneurs from similar backgrounds and with similar stories. These capital pioneers are engaged in a quiet revolution, challenging the status quo of a funding system that has all but excluded large segments of business owners in our country and has resulted in a large capital gap. These new models provide a roadmap for change and give us hope that broader support for *New Builders* can be accomplished in ways that are scalable and that ultimately provide market-rate returns to investors.

Kim Folsom, Candice Matthews Brackeen, and her husband, Brian Brackeen, stand out as perfect examples of capital pioneers. They are focused on providing capital *and* network to underserved entrepreneurs, especially Black, female founders. And are finding early success in their models and are beginning to scale the reach and impact of their work. They've taken different approaches, but their similarities highlight some key elements that are required to succeed in helping *New Builders*. That they've been successful by using different approaches suggests that a breadth of models can be effective in supporting a new generation of entrepreneurs. But the work being done in this space hasn't yet achieved meaningful scale – certainly not when compared to the tens of billions of dollars that are invested annually in venture-backed businesses or the trillions of dollars that constitute the overall bank lending system in the United States.

New Builders Supporting *New Builders*

Kim Folsom's background instills confidence in her abilities. The founder of six different venture-backed technology companies, she has decades of experience in entrepreneurship. The experience of starting and growing venture-backed startups as well as that of raising capital as a woman of color made her realize just how much of a gap exists in the market for funding people like her. And, like Kathryn Finney from digitalundivided, her experience participating in multiple accelerator programs as the only Black female founder (actually, the only female founder *and* the only Black founder) taught her that little was being done to help mentor, fund, and grow these diverse founders. In her view, too many programs that focused on underrepresented founders were focused on the wrong types of businesses. Armed with that experience and her perspective on the market, she formed Founders First Capital Partners in 2015.

Using a format critical to the success of these new financing models, Founders First combines capital access with structured training, education, mentorship, and advice in an effort to prepare and support entrepreneurs in their businesses. This programming is delivered through a series of accelerator programs to address business challenges faced by diverse founders, and also through a formal advisory program that is a requirement for entrepreneurs that are backed by Founders First. Their focus is on businesses led by "diverse founders," which for Founders First includes women, ethnic minorities, military veterans, inclusive teams, and businesses located in low- to moderate-income areas. Founders First Capital works with a variety of diverse teams; however, a majority of the companies they work with are founded by women of color.

"People grossly underestimate what you have to go through as a woman of color to raise money from traditional sources," Kim told us. "We're trying to tap into that passion but at the same time solve the funding problem faced by these underrepresented communities and provide a method for differentiated, premium returns for investors."

The initial Founders First fund was small – just $1 million in size, backed by high-net-worth investors. That fund was able to invest in 10 businesses and provided proof of the working thesis that Kim had developed. With the launch of the accelerator, her reach broadened to hundreds of companies, many of which constitute potential fund investments as the platform grows. And the fund is growing. In late 2019, Founders First raised $100 million led by Community Investment Management, a large impact fund. This increase in scale puts Founders First at the very upper echelons of this emerging asset class and provides a significant platform from which to expand the reach and scope of their work.

Two thousand miles away, Brian and Candice Matthews Brackeen are looking for underrepresented founders to back. Based in Cincinnati, Ohio, their fund, Lightship Capital, invests in founders from diverse backgrounds – Black, women, LGBQT+, and other minority communities. The fund is focused on companies located in the Midwest, and like the other funds we've profiled, they look to match their founders with mentors.

Brian, who had been an executive at Apple, struck out on his own in 2012 with a Miami-based company called Kairos, which developed facial recognition software. "I was sitting at my desk one day, amid all those Silicon Valley perky things. I felt like my soul was being sucked into the neon lights above," he said. "I resigned that Thursday or Friday. I still believe in the mission of Apple, but I wanted to serve."

He came from a Black family that had always been builders. His great-grandfather was a doctor in segregated Texas, his grandmother ran schools in Haiti and Sierra Leone, and his grandfather was a Baptist minister in Philadelphia. To Brian, service meant building a company that would both innovate (Kairos focused on facial recognition that took ethnic diversity into account) as well as employ people. Candice was the founder of Hello Parent, an app that helps parents share information and advocate for diversity. Brian told us he ran into plenty of prejudice of what Black people were and were not able to do in business. Ironically, sometimes, people wanted him to have *more* of a hard-luck story.

"In fact, nearly 75 percent of Blacks are not poor," he wrote in a heart-felt Medium post. "The vast majority of us do not live in urban blight. That's 75 percent of us who do not live under the bigoted blanket thrown over us by politicians and the media, both conservative and liberal. Yet here we are, somehow obligatorily apologetic for our success because we didn't have a desperate circumstance from which to escape."[6]

After the two founders met and married, they both left their respective careers as company chiefs to become investors. Their fund, which initially set out to raise $25 million, eventually launched with $50 million. Brackeen told us Lightship was able to raise so much because companies and wealthy people who invest in early-stage finance were increasingly interested in diversity in their portfolios, yet another sign that investment in underrepresented communities is starting to become more mainstream.

A Call for Creative Finance

Many platforms working in this space operate as nonprofits. And while it's encouraging to see organizations such as Community Investment Management investing meaningful money into funding underrepresented businesses, it is barely scratching the surface of the capital that is truly needed to create transformation in these underserved markets. Perhaps this reflects our historical inability to see entrepreneurs from underserved communities as equals in terms of their business potential. It also reflects broader market realities. Because we don't support Black, brown, female, and older entrepreneurs well, we have created a self-fulfilling system that prevents us from helping them succeed, which then reinforces that decision as we see their businesses – often lacking the resources required to scale – become less successful. As this dynamic changes, the success of those businesses, and the ability to create more sustainable and profitable ecosystems to support them, will follow.

We've focused in his book on the potential of founders who are the most disadvantaged and who are entrepreneurial in large enough numbers that changing the system to make room for them could make a huge impact on our economy. But the bigger impact will come from internal change within people working in finance if more of them recognize the necessity of stepping outside of their existing networks and embracing new ways of thinking.

For us, the exploration of new capital models has been eye-opening. While there is plenty to be learned from the world of venture capital, there is even more to be learned from the world beyond it. Gaining a better understanding of the breadth of ideas that are already being put into practice to support a much broader set of entrepreneurial endeavors has caused us to rethink some deeply held beliefs about how the world of finance works. Many of these new ways of thinking still sit at the margins of our financial system. Impactful, clearly, to those they work with directly, but on the whole dwarfed by the larger systems of mainstream finance that surround them. *This* is the opportunity for our future – to rethink our old models and old ways of doing business and to pioneer new and innovative ways of financing the next generation of entrepreneurs. Whether our systems of finance need a revolution or an evolution is up for debate. But these systems must change. This is clear from our view from the inside. What's also clear is the potential role for those with power to lead this change. We shouldn't be asking *New Builders* to change how they build and finance their businesses. We should be asking *ourselves* how we can adapt to the new generation of people starting businesses today.

Endnotes

1. Staunton Creative Community Fund, "Starting or Expanding a Business Is Challenging. We're Here to Help," https://stauntonfund.org/
2. Ibid
3. "Want to Invest In A Post-Pandemic Boom?," *Times of Entrepreneurship*, 2020, https://timesofe.com/a-former-uber-exec-throws-a-lifeline-for-mainstreet/
4. "Facilitating Capital Formation and Expanding Investment Opportunities by Improving Access to Capital in Private Markets," a proposed rule by the Securities and Exchange Commission, Federal Register, March 31, 2020, https://www.federalregister.gov/documents/2020/03/31/2020-04799/facilitating-capital-formation-and-expanding-investment-opportunities-by-improving-access-to-capital
5. Capital Access Lab, "About the Capital Access Lab," www.kauffman.org/capital-access-lab/
6. Brian Brackeen, "I'm Not Black Enough for *Inc.* Magazine," #FacesofFounders, March 27, 2017, https://facesoffounders.org/im-not-black-enough-for-inc-magazine-337569d54a6b

CHAPTER SIXTEEN

Hope and Promise

Entrepreneurs envision a different future and then set out to create it. They don't do so in a vacuum or out of whole cloth. Generally, they aren't artists, writers, or philosophers, working in the abstract or on beauty for beauty's sake. Instead, entrepreneurs translate society's values into reality by meeting the needs and wants of the time with products, services, and experiences. Collectively, they create much of the economic energy that sustains our way of life. As individuals, they play a key role in the process of creativity and innovation, bringing their own ideas and experiences to bear. What they chose to work on and where they put their wild-spirit energy is a crucial question, especially in a country that has change and capitalism baked into its being.

But today's *New Builders* are different from the entrepreneurs who came before them. For the first time, the people often left out of the entrepreneurial narrative are walking onto center stage. If our finance and mentorship systems catch up to this new diverse reality, the *New Builders* will have a star turn on America's revolving stage. We believe that they will.

What does that mean for the future? *New Builders* have a visceral awareness of systemic unfairness. They aren't all successful, certainly, but they understand how an unjust system keeps good ideas and great entrepreneurs from getting the support everyone needs. They are likely to work outside those systems, even to upend them.

We saw evidence of that in the *New Builders* we interviewed, who are redefining success on their own terms. In every generation, entrepreneurs rise to the challenges and opportunities of the time. It leaves us asking: What are the challenges and opportunities of *this* time?

The answer has only emerged for us over the course of working on this book, hidden in plain sight. The pandemic, the crisis of climate change, and the political divisions that have emerged in the past few decades, culminating in the rise of dangerous populist politics, show us the need for a new and different future. At the same time, consumer desires are changing. The convenience, low prices, and rhetoric delivered by companies of huge size and and at times overbearing technology seem increasingly empty, and not enough. The middle ground, diverse gathering places, uniqueness and pluralism, all built through real connections between people, are the needs of our time.

What do a family of wilderness guides in Montana, the dogged real estate developers in Oklahoma City, a Dominican baker in Massachusetts, a young man in Virginia making T-shirts, and all the other *New Builders* have in common? They're working on building their businesses with connection to their communities and in the lost middle ground between big institutions and our cherished individual rights. The next turn of our economy, the place where the winners will be found, is likely to lie exactly there, in this middle ground.

The future might not be judged on the scales of the past. Size, wealth, and appearance were the lingua franca of the late twentieth century and the pre-pandemic twenty-first century. But different times call for new ways of measuring success. We believe communities will weigh heavily on those new scales. We deliberately focused in this book on *New Builders* working on Main Streets and in communities left out of the narrow economic expansion of the late twentieth century, But there are *New Builders* working on breakthrough innovations, in the arts economy, fashion, science, and elsewhere – in corners of the economy we haven't even thought of – to succeed in the new era.

It's up to us to support them.

See *New Builders* and See Ourselves

To wrap our hands around the changing nature of our economy, we need to understand who the *New Builders* are and to start seeing them. It's clear from the data that the trends we are seeing today – that an increasing percentage of new business owners are women, people of color, and older Americans – are permanent ones. In every aspect of our economy, but especially our entrepreneurial economy, we need to embrace this change and adapt to it, from the world of high-tech venture-backed start-ups to Main Street businesses and grassroots entrepreneurs. As a society, we need to rethink our relationship with local businesses, recognizing the collective power that comes from entrepreneurs of all kinds and the varied businesses they start and run.

To fully recognize *New Builders*, we need to fully recognize ourselves. Unlike many other countries in the world, America offered the promise of a better life for those willing to work hard and play by the rules. But this is changing. While the American Dream remains attainable to some, this vision of an egalitarian society, where hard work wins over status, is slipping away. Market economies such as America's offer advantages to those lucky enough to be born at the highest levels of society. For those whose family status offers them greater opportunities for education and advancement. For those whose skin tone gives them an advantage from birth. But the number of people from the bottom economic rungs who are able to reach the top rungs of that ladder has significantly dropped. Supporting all entrepreneurs, and especially supporting *New Builders*, offers an important way to start to reverse these trends. Especially coming out of the Covid-induced financial crisis, recognizing the breadth and depth of America's entrepreneurial landscape is a critical step toward strengthening our economy.

To get there, we need to recognize the potential of entrepreneurs outside the Silicon Valley mold, at the same time letting go of the idea that we can generate enough real and inclusive growth solely by pouring money into software startups. Dynamism and innovation happen in unexpected places and from people who aren't necessarily interested in starting and running fast-growth technology businesses. In fact, the next turn of our economy is likely to come from these overlooked people and places. That should be obvious, but after a half-century during which Silicon Valley has dominated the narrative of entrepreneurship, many people seem to have forgotten it. We believe *New Builders* working in different parts of the economy can grow important and large businesses if they have access to mentorship and capital. *New Builders* won't create another Silicon Valley, because the software innovations that drove Silicon Valley won't be replicated. But if we support *New Builders* the right way, as Silicon Valley was supported in its early days, they will create new centers of innovation and growth. The split between startups and small businesses is a false dichotomy that ends up steering more and more capital to fewer and fewer new businesses. This concentration of both capital and mindshare isn't healthy for our economy. It's also not healthy for Silicon Valley and the technology startups that it serves.

We can see the effect of this concentration in the statistics around venture financing more generally. On the surface, the world of venture-backed startups appears to be booming. According to data research firm PitchBook, in 2018, US-based venture-backed startups garnered $130.9 billion in financing. This figure was the highest total ever, surpassing the dot-com-bubble-fueled year, 2000. Nearly 9,000 companies raised money from venture capitalists that year. However, upon closer inspection, the data suggest the same kind of consolidation occurring broadly is happening among venture-backed companies. In 2018, 198 companies garnered over 60 percent of the financing dollars, according to Pitchbook. And while the total invested dollars has risen significantly in the past five years, funding into the earliest rounds (commonly referred to as seed financing) is down. Even among our most supported entrepreneurs, we're concentrating our money and effort on larger, later-stage companies at the expense of new business ideas.

Change Starts with Individuals, but Collective Action Is What Really Matters

We need to respect local businesses, recognizing the collective power that comes from grassroots entrepreneurs and the businesses they start and run. In America, we love to celebrate the lone hero – the person who, seemingly on their own, creates something out of nothing or saves the day. We lionize these people as almost mythical creatures. They are the people who, through sheer force of will and charisma, are able to change an industry or society. And to be sure, there are many successful entrepreneurs who have started and led companies that had significant impacts on American business. These people are often worthy of our admiration for having pursued their business passions despite many obstacles that were put in their way.

But no one does it alone. And even the outsized impact of a few of these mythical entrepreneurs – think people like Steve Jobs – was only possible because of massive systems of support that surrounded them, from Jobs's Apple co-founders to people like the legendary Apple designer Johnny Ive. Not to mention any number of the over 60,000 employees who worked at Apple at the time of Jobs's death. Steve Jobs, Andrew Carnegie, Joy Mangano, Jeff Bezos, Oprah Winfrey, Bill Gates, Margaret Sanger – the list of people our society lionizes for their entrepreneurial spirit is long and impressive. But all of these inventors and innovators ultimately built large businesses and thrived in the American entrepreneurial economy because of the help of a larger system around them, from their parents to their schools to the infrastructure of the country and the massive government investments that have fueled innovation for generations.

Collective support doesn't take away from individual achievement. It enhances it.

As Covid-19 emerged, our first response to save small businesses was to act individually. We were urged to buy local, to buy gift certificates, and patronize small businesses over chains. All those efforts are crucial. But that our first instincts ran toward individual action and not to ways in which we could more broadly and effectively support businesses en masse perhaps suggests that we're missing the bigger picture. We've grown fond of individual action. It's easy (assuming you have the money), it's immediate, and it makes you feel good. But real change lies one level above that, in realizing that individual action is most effective and can be best amplified through collective action that supports it.

This is true at all levels of community and government. Once a base of support is built into a community's mindshare, it continues to show up, as it did when Covid-19 struck and the hospitals near Staunton, Virginia, needed masks. Staunton's story shows it's not nearly as hard as we think it is. By coming together, individuals looking to effect change in their communities can achieve outsized results, the total of which is truly greater than the sum of its parts.

Safety Nets and Backstops

People with power and resources need to recognize that they have a privilege that enables them to take risks. The security that comes from the backstop of savings or the knowledge that family and friends have the wherewithal to soften the blow of a failed venture is easy to take for granted when you've always had it. But this security doesn't exist for large portions of our society. A reasonable social safety net, including broad access to health care, is a critical ingredient necessary to support our changing entrepreneurial economy. In our push toward libertarianism, we've forgotten some of the key ingredients that enable the risk-taking and personal responsibility that libertarians so cherish. The United States was founded on the principles of shared destiny and collective responsibility. It was through these communal actions that our early cities and towns were built and upon which the infrastructure that enables our modern-day economy was forged.

For us, this isn't a political argument for access to healthcare and a basic social safety net. It's an economic one. The exact parameters of whether and how we will continue to offer some level of societal protections for those who are either less advantaged or who take risks that don't pay off will have to be argued and decided by politicians. But without question, considerations of healthcare, of access to basic services, and the health and safety of their families were top of mind for many of the *New Builders* we spoke with. Tying healthcare to employment (and, most typically, to large-company employment) is one of the single biggest impediments to entrepreneurial activity that we know of. We simply can't regain our entrepreneurial dynamism without some consideration for how we administer healthcare in our country. And, just as robust bankruptcy laws promote risk-taking, so too does a basic social safety net that provides at least some back stop for those entrepreneurs whose business ideas don't work out. This isn't an argument for a socialist-style society. To the contrary, it's a recognition that to maintain our entrepreneurial and capitalist edge, we need to consider exactly who constitutes the next generation of entrepreneurs in our country and create policies that enable and encourage their entrepreneurial spirit, rather than stifle it.

Rebalance Regulations to Help Small Business

We need to restore the regulatory frameworks that once protected smaller businesses and consumers. They have been slowly eroded over the past few decades, and the result is an economy that is too far out of balance. For small businesses and the entrepreneurs who are struggling to find their way in the current economy, regulations geared to big business represent a meaningful impediment to starting and growing a business.

Together, small businesses employ nearly 40 percent of the American workforce. Collectively they represent an important economic force we've been too quick to overlook. As more and more Americans turn to the gig economy to either build a career or supplement their income, we need to recognize that the future American labor force will look quite different than the labor force of past generations. The declining power of small business in politics is a reflection not of our stated priorities – politicians love to tout their love for small business – but of the realities of how power is currently wielded and influenced. That's a deliberate choice made by society based on the systems of influence and lobbying we've set up. Those systems are clearly out of balance.

It's certainly convenient from a consumer perspective to think big and to shop big. But doing so to the exclusion of small business reflects that too many of us are losing our patience for the simple pleasures of strolling Main Street and of browsing a local shop. Perhaps Covid-19 will end up being a reminder of the human connections that are so important and that constitute the fabric upon which our communities are built. The frenetic pace many of us have tried to maintain, perhaps, meant we left too little time to enjoy those things that can and should be enjoyable. Shopping isn't always something to be checked off a list or done online. There can be pleasure from these things that we've come to make ourselves believe are just chores, but which allow us the opportunity to get out into our communities and to interact with our neighbors.

Despite the constant rhetoric about the importance of small business, government focuses on big. Big companies make headlines. Big companies bring in a larger number of jobs (at least at one time; not so when small businesses are taken as a group). Big companies can afford the lobbying and public relations often required to get attention from government officials. The result is that larger companies have an outsized say in crafting the rules and regulations that govern business activity. While this may be most obvious at the federal level, where big businesses are regularly given an audience to lobby Congress about their specific priorities, big businesses' resources also give them a disproportionately large voice at every level of government below that, including in more community-based institutions. This is a mistake. By excluding small businesses in community-building efforts, we ignore critical voices that contribute mightily to the vibrancy and dynamism of our economy at all levels. While these voices aren't a monolith – they don't all fall in line to one worldview or perspective – they represent a different perspective on community and on our economy that is critical for government officials to understand if they are to craft policy that encourages broad-based economic development.

It's worth repeating here that our argument for small is *not* an argument against big. On the contrary, our economy has always thrived with a certain balance between big and small. The economies of scale that come from larger enterprises and the convenience they offer to our society are real and not something we discount. Yet in recent years we've allowed large businesses to gain too much power. Owning a small business used to be a reliable pathway to the American dream, and something that was celebrated. Not because these businesses grew large but because there is value in small businesses themselves. We need to get back to that way of thinking. Of recognizing that businesses of all sizes contribute to our economy. Instead, the voices of small business owners are drowned out. We certainly don't need to eliminate larger companies from our business landscape – to suggest so would be nonsensical. But we do need to find this balance once again. Refocusing on the question of what it takes for all businesses to succeed, rather than trying to control the future by making the bets on the kinds of companies that could grow big, will help. Call it a true "think small" movement. By thinking small, we'll ultimately benefit our economy, our communities, and ourselves.

Create a Movement of Support for New Builders

Many of the new ways of thinking about how to invest in *New Builders* still sit at the margins of our financial system. Impactful, to those directly affected, but on the whole dwarfed by the larger systems of mainstream finance that surround them.

We need to encourage more people in our financial systems to put their creative energies into rethinking how we fund new business endeavors. While there is a lively group of people who invest in women and diverse founders, funding for founders such as these and through alternative funding models such as revenue-based financing has largely been the purview of *impact investing*. It's hard to overstate just how limiting it is to pigeonhole support for new and innovative forms of capital into this subset of the investment universe. Some $300 billion in funding has been allocated to impact investing, which is a great start. But this pales in comparison to the trillions of dollars invested more broadly in businesses across the United States. We can – and need – to start thinking more holistically about investments in companies operating in other parts of our economy and to recognize that the returns they generate are competitive with (and by some accounts, greater than) those generated by more "traditional" investing. If we continue to confine investing in women and people of color to the purview of "impact," we are inherently limiting them, as well as suggesting to these communities that they are somehow lesser.

Collaborative models offer glimmers of hope as well as a roadmap for how we might better support *New Builders* and their companies. Greater support for the CDFI banking system would be a great place to start. In that system, the infrastructure already exists to provide capital to grass-roots entrepreneurs, especially those who are women and minorities. But the system lacks the overall funding required to properly support these business owners. Supporting the economic vitality of the next generation of entrepreneurs in the United States shouldn't be a political issue. There is a clear economic argument for doing so that is getting lost in the mix. Government efforts shouldn't be distracted by the high-tech promise that was the last generation of change, but we can learn from Silicon Valley's growth and the way that government funding without too many strings attached helped enable individual entrepreneurs and entire entrepreneurial ecosystems.

More support for community banks and tighter controls on the consolidation of the banking sector are also important factors to consider as we look to bolster our entrepreneurial ecosystems across the United

States. Consolidation across our banking sector has reached unsustainable levels. Ironically, it may be the overregulation of banking that is to blame, as the costs of complying with rules put in place after the Great Recession of 2008–2009 have become too great for many smaller banks. There are relatively easy changes that would alleviate this burden but will require both leadership and forethought to implement – two things that are often in short supply among those charged with doing so. We hope they can find the strength, political and otherwise, to consider the changes that need to be made to better support a robust community banking system. At the same time, there are provisions in place, primarily through the Community Reinvestment Act, that require larger banks to extend and expand their banking services to communities that have historically been underserved by financial institutions.

Strengthening these actions by enforcing existing laws is another easy way to start.[i] Ultimately we believe that there is a strong economic argument for investing in these communities – something that banks like JPMorgan Chase have also publicly declared. But sometimes large institutions require a nudge in the right direction to get going.

Broadening Capital Ownership

Ultimately, the ability to create wealth in a capitalist economy comes from more than just earning a wage. Investment and the accumulation of capital assets are critical pieces to ensuring greater access to prosperity in our society. It's through investments in these appreciating assets – whether stocks and bonds or businesses – that we can provide a pathway to wealth in ways that simply relying on earning a wage can't. As a society, we should consider better and more far-reaching ways to achieve the goal of more broad-based participation in capital appreciating markets. People with access to capital will start businesses.

One idea that has been floated for years, and which has at various times been supported by politicians of both political parties, is for the United States to adopt a so-called *baby bond*. The idea is simple but powerful. Every child born in the United States would have an

---

[i] Over the past four years, interpretation of the CRA has gone in the other direction, and banks have been held to lower standards for investment in these communities.

investment account set up for them by the federal government. This account would grow tax-free through investments in a selection of low-cost investment funds overseen by the US Treasury. Money in this account couldn't be accessed until the child turned 18, after which the money could be used, but only for certain purposes (education, starting a business, etc.). At some point, the money would become freely available for account owners to do with as they please. If such an account grew at 7 percent annually (approximately the yearly overall market return since the end of the Great Depression), it would be worth nearly $17,000 when that child turned 18. If they waited to pull the money out – say to start a business – until they were 30, they would have nearly $40,000.

The beauty of these accounts is what everyone from Ben Franklin to Jack Bogle, the founder of Vanguard, has called "the miracle of compound interest," which is the multiplying effect of earning interest upon interest.[1] The other benefit is that it would encourage others – family and friends – to contribute as well. Even a small amount of contributed capital makes a significant difference. And having an account already set up for this purpose makes it easy for relatives to add to it. Contributing just $150 annually would increase the value of a baby bond account to over $22,000 at age 18, for example.

The cost of such a program would be relatively modest in comparison to the overall size of the US budget. There are approximately four million children born in the United States each year, meaning that the cost of the program would be in the neighborhood of $20 billion annually. Certainly a lot of money, but it represents less than one-half of 1 percent of the current federal budget. If that was too much for politicians to swallow, the program could be structured as a loan, where participants had to pay the original principal back when they turned 18. The point is to turn every American into an investor and to provide each child with a nest-egg on which they can build. Whether they use this money for education or to start a business or for some other purpose, an entire generation could reap the benefits of investing in themselves and such a program could provide critical capital infrastructure for our next generation of builders.

A shift in mindset toward opening broader investment in private enterprises will also help. With few exceptions, ordinary Americans have been unable to participate in most private investments. This started to change a few years ago as the JOBS Act began opening the doors to new investors and new investment opportunities by lifting a number of key restrictions on private investment while at the same time maintaining reasonable controls and protections. The result has been opportunities for those with more limited capital to invest in local businesses and in their communities. We should double down on these opportunities and create new pathways and partnerships between individuals and the businesses they could be supporting. We applaud the work that a number of platforms are doing to enable investors to invest relatively modest sums into businesses. These sums are banded together with investments from other individuals and together constitute a meaningful source of capital investment for the companies they support.

There are other interesting and innovative pathways that communities are developing to help support their local business communities. Local banks are putting together community loan funds that allow local businesses to access risk capital to start or expand their businesses. The federal government would be well served to anchor these community funds by offering matching funds that both encourage and enhance the power of local dollars raised. This could be administered through the existing CDFI program with relatively low incremental overhead. But the incentive it would offer to communities would be meaningful and, we believe, would accelerate the adoption of models that have been proven to effectively spur community investment and development.

Tax is another area where we can offer additional incentives to encourage local investment. There are already a number of tax incentives available for investments into certain types of businesses and into businesses operating in specific locations. These programs should be expanded to include more businesses operating in more areas, and the requirements streamlined so that more small investors can take advantage of these opportunities. State and local governments should match these incentives and set up programs to direct funds to businesses operating in targeted development areas.

Why Should You Act? Because Communities Matter.

We found *New Builders* working at the hearts of their communities, on businesses that have more value than it may seem to casual observers. Appearances can be deceiving and *New Builders* surprised us with their resilience and the depth of their vision to transform communities. Many people haven't valued Main Street businesses and grassroots entrepreneurs because today's business world doesn't have the right scales to measure their value.

What is clear from the stories of *New Builders* that we have told in this book is that community and place are critical parts of their startup journeys. Many have strong and deep ties to the people they work with, and many were helped along the way by communal infrastructure – whether a local banker, a locally sponsored co-working hub, local funding, or local mentors. Many look for ways to give back and to deepen their community ties, through volunteering at schools, mentoring other entrepreneurs, and advocating for local and small businesses. Their stories inspire us, and inspire other entrepreneurs to become *New Builders*.

We didn't set out to become passionate advocates on their behalf, but their grit, determination, passion, and drive drew us in. We were often struck by how much *New Builders* had overcome in their startup journeys. The Covid-19 crisis, hitting after we had conducted our initial interviews and just as we were starting to write up our findings, added another layer of complexity and urgency to the stories we were telling. As a group, *New Builders* have faced more than their share of obstacles in a system that has lately made it harder for most entrepreneurs from almost every background to succeed. Women, people of color, and older people in particular often don't fit the mold of a rigid business world.

But being overlooked is the secret power of *New Builders*. One reason we found many *New Builders* working on some of the hardest problems facing society today is that setbacks of the kind they have endured give them an uncommon perspective on what's important. One of the unfortunate consequences of success, especially easy success, is that it makes people less sympathetic to the struggles of others. The walls that separate the privileged from everyone else grow higher as a result. One of the *seemingly* inevitable consequences of running into those walls as an outsider is that it leads to a lack of trust of both other people and the world more generally.

Yet, we found *New Builders* working across divides to achieve their business goals and to carry people, and not just those who look like them, along on the journey. It's common these days to talk about building an inclusive economy, but across large swaths of society it is merely that, talk. *New Builders* and the people working to support them are an exception – they are turning talk into action. As Desh's vision for EforAll shows, an inclusive economy is not one that can be dictated top down. It must be built from the ground up, organically. *New Builders* are the invisible army in this fight, emboldened by the experience and empathy that comes from being outsiders.

New Builders are the future of our economy. They are building that future with a deep connection to their communities. This is the most important lesson we took away from our time with *New Builders*. Their commitment leaves us hopeful for our collective future.

Endnote

1. Adam Mayers, "John Bogle's 10 Key Rules of Investing," *Toronto Star*, February 5, 2014, www.thestar.com/business/personal_finance/2013/02/10/john_bogles_10_key_rules_of_investing.html

EPILOGUE

Just before we finished this manuscript, we checked in one final time to see how Danaris Mazara was faring. It was early 2021 and the Covid pandemic had been burning through the world for almost a year, taking an as-yet-untold toll on small businesses.

Tired, but determined and confident about the future, Danaris continued to display the optimism and grit we had come to know from her. But the reality of her past year was challenging that resolve. She pored over the numbers for the bakery, doing her books late at night, sometimes staying up until 2 a.m. or later in an effort to better understand how she could make things work. Although her business had reopened after the first pandemic lockdown ended, sales in 2020 were down 40 percent from the prior year. As the year wore on, things were getting worse.

On Thanksgiving Day 2020, Sweet Grace booked $400 in sales. A year ago, it had grossed $1,000. A $150,000 low-interest SBA loan in the springtime enabled her to hire back the 16 women who worked for her in 2019. Now, it was a balancing act. Sales, mortgage, payroll – trying to make sure there was at least some work for everyone. To cope with the reduction in sales, her entire staff was working reduced hours. Every week – every day, it sometimes seemed – someone would stop by the bakery or reach her on her cell phone to ask for work. "They say, 'I will do anything,'" she recounted. "I hate saying no." The work she had wasn't enough to keep her existing staff busy. With the reduced hours, some of her employees were relying on the food bank to fill their cupboards at home. And Sweet Grace in turn was donating to the food bank. A circle that was at once virtuous and vicious.

It wasn't the kind of economy taught in business school. It also wasn't what EforAll had preached. But the pandemic was an emergency, and Danaris and the community were piecing things together as best they could. She rarely spoke to Frank Carvalho, the Brazilian-born banker, or to David, EforAll's CEO. Where before she had been the student, now she was a peer and a community leader – someone whom other people turned to for help and advice.

There was no question, she said, that Sweet Grace would survive through the winter.

Frank retired from Mill Cities, the local CDFI, over the summer of 2020. The retirement had been long-planned after a brain surgery in 2015, but he'd delayed it because of the pandemic. "I've gone from 55 hours to 70," he said. He was running his pizza shop and advising small businesses on how to adapt to the pandemic, including by paring costs, negotiating with landlords, and changing their offerings to accommodate lockdowns. "I have bodegas doing delivery now," he said.

At EforAll, CEO David Parker was focused on fundraising, along with supporting a large network of entrepreneurs, many of whom were struggling through the pandemic and its consequences on their businesses. EforAll was starting to gain more attention and acclaim, winning financial support from the likes of Facebook and the Cummings Foundation. The entrepreneurs in the EforAll network needed help coping with many challenges presented by the Covid-19 economic crisis, including navigating various federal aid programs set up to aid struggling businesses. David knew that the United States would need a surge of entrepreneurship to restore economic growth once the pandemic subsided. Opportunity, for sure, but also something that would require new thinking and new ideas for supporting an ever expanding and complex network. Despite the pandemic – perhaps because of it – EforAll had grown, opening a program in nearby Worcester.

David knew that the economy would need thousands of Danarises to make meaningful progress against the economic tide. And he knew that these entrepreneurs were most likely to come from the ranks of people served by EforAll.

Desh, meanwhile, was juggling his work in India and the United States. In India, where his foundation supports startups and more traditional nonprofits, the scale was vast. His foundation distributed food and groceries, promoted a new app for Covid-19 monitoring, and donated 15,000 masks manufactured by micro-entrepreneurs, among other things. Reflecting on the pandemic and its economic effects, he explained that the "pandemic has widened the opportunity gap. It is even more important in the post-Covid world that we create opportunities for all." He then went on to describe how he was doubling his efforts to support grassroots entrepreneurship in both the United States and India.

Across the United States, people spent 2020 grappling with new realities and a renewed perspective on the importance of things closer to home. Infrastructure and institutions established generations ago had not adapted well when confronted by the Covid-19 pandemic. Everything from the healthcare system to the political system came under question. Even the computers that handle unemployment claims had staggered under the increased load. Everywhere there was a conversation about what businesses were worth saving, and if they were, how we could go about doing so. The federal government was spending trillions of dollars in the effort, but the effect of that spending, or even if those staggering sums would prove to be enough, won't be clear for some time.

Danaris and her employees operated through the early days of the pandemic mostly on faith and prayers – faith that the United States would come through. The weaknesses in America's infrastructure, newly apparent to many, had been clear to the Dominican community in Lawrence for some time. Back in 2018, the south side of Lawrence, where many Dominicans live, was hit by a massive gas explosion that killed one person and caused 80 separate fires. Two months later, 1,500 people still didn't have their heat back.[1] Danaris had evacuated, sent all her employees home, and then reopened as soon as possible, juggling her employees' housing dilemmas with the needs of the bakery. To reinforce the resilience of the Dominican community during that earlier crisis and make a case for funding small businesses, Frank had invited Massachusetts Governor Charlie Baker to visit Sweet Grace. Baker is a blue-blooded Republican from a wealthy family that has long been powerful in state and national politics. Elected in a firmly Democratic state, he is also a supporter of small businesses of all kinds.

As Danaris worked through the long fall and winter of 2020, she found herself looking back on that visit, memorialized in a picture of her and Governor Baker that hangs in her house. There she was, the Dominican woman once derided for practicing her English, standing next to this powerful man as an equal. The governor had gone out of his way to visit her bakery and hear her story.[2] Perhaps it was even on his mind when, around Christmas 2020, he signed a bill that provided $675 million in grants for small businesses to help them survive the winter.

Reflecting on that visit gave her hope. And a belief in herself and her community to make it through.

She found herself returning to a favorite Bible quote from 2 Timothy 1:7: *For God hath not given us the spirit of fear; but of power, and of love, and of a sound mind.* "If you have self-control, and love, you can be a powerful person," she told us.

Her hope is reflected in our own. As we checked in at the end of 2020 with many of the *New Builders* we profiled in this book, we heard similar refrains of optimism. That optimism left us with a strong belief in the promise of *The New Builders* and a sense that we will emerge from the pandemic with a renewed spirit of community and a will to rebuild. Together.

Endnotes

1. "Lawrence Gas Explosions Leave Many Without Heat to Fare the Harsh Winter," *NPR*, November 2018, www.npr.org/2018/11/25/670631099/lawrence-gas-explosions-leaves-many-with-no-heat-to-fair-the-harsh-winter
2. Interview with Frank Carvalho, December 2020.

ACKNOWLEDGMENTS

Writing any book is a labor of love. Writing one during a global pandemic posed particular challenges and offered the special gift of relationships built during a time of shared struggle. We are profoundly grateful for many people without whose help this book would not have come to fruition in this unprecedented time. Both of us are deeply passionate about the power of entrepreneurship to lift lives and communities. This passion grew as we came to know more people in the community of *New Builders* and sustained us through challenging hours of research, writing, and editing.

First and foremost, thank you to the *New Builders* themselves, who shared their stories and took time out from their businesses to help us understand their vision and passion. We met many on our journey writing this book and heard stories of many more. This book is for them and also for the army of *New Builders* working across the country, pursuing their passions, giving life to their ideas, and striving to make their communities more vibrant.

We had the great fortune of having a wonderful team surrounding us as we worked through early drafts of *The New Builders* and researching the underlying data we relied on to tell the stories of entrepreneurship in the United States today. Megan O'Connell provided invaluable help in managing the logistics behind the book. Everything from helping us make sure data were properly cited, to ensuring photo shoots were arranged for, to helping us create order out of the chaos that is fact-checking. This was essential to ensure the book you hold in your hands actually came together.

The team at *Times of Entrepreneurship*, including Shirly Piperno, Jean Benedict, Nina Roberts, Skyler Rossi, Kueh Wee Rock, Adam Schaffer, and Joel Berg, all stepped in at various times as Elizabeth co-wrote *The New Builders* while also launching a new media company during the year of a pandemic. Some stories from *Times of Entrepreneurship* became the basis for chapters of the book or otherwise helped inform our thinking and research.

At the very early stages of *The New Builders,* we found a wonderful advocate in Alice Martell, our agent, to whom we were introduced by John Dearie. Her immediate and visceral reaction to our idea bolstered our confidence and drive for this project. Along the way, she provided valuable feedback and helped us navigate the often-opaque world of publishing.

The team from our publisher was fantastic. Bill Falloon was the first person at Wiley to see our project and was a constant source of advice and encouragement. We benefited from the help of two wonderful editors – part of our extended Wiley team. Julie Kerr helped us through many revisions of the manuscript as it came together into its final form, enduring our continual questions and changes from large (moving entire chapters around) to small (writing and rewriting sentences that didn't quite feel right). Cheryl Ferguson was our copy editor, and it was her final eyes on the manuscript that helped bring it to its final (and grammatically correct) form. Our production editor, Purvi Patel, kept us on track, a big help as we decided to accelerate publication in the midst of the Covid pandemic.

Shannon Maier and Micah Mador provided research assistance for the "History of Entrepreneurship" chapter. That was back in the summer of 2019, just as we were getting started with our research. We were aided in our review of the data by the willingness of many primary researchers to talk with us. Some ended up being quoted in the book. Others provided helpful background and filled in important gaps in our understanding of the data. Thank you to Alicia Robb, Victor Hwang, Ross Baird, Ian Hathaway, Tom Nichols, and John Paul Lederach for sharing your insights and helping us better understand the data around the changing landscape of entrepreneurship in the United States.

A number of other people provided essential help and feedback to us throughout the process of bringing *The New Builders* to life. Elizabeth's long time friends Elaine Pofeldt and Holly Smith provided invaluable and practical advice on the process of writing and marketing a book. Nate Wong, at Georgetown's Beeck Center, helped us focus on the right title, as did Foundry Group portfolio company Suzy (through which we were able to test multiple titles across a focus group of several thousand people). Javelina, *Times of Entrepreneurship*'s marketing agency, provided guidance on how to create themes to connect entrepreneurial stories with analysis. Lori Ioannou and Barbara Benson at CNBC gave us an early platform for our ideas, which helped us realize how urgent the story of *The New Builders* was. Brad Feld and Charley Ellis made many helpful suggestions and comments to an earlier version of the manuscript and were the first people outside of our small editing group to read a draft. Entrepreneur Andy Rachleff and historian Margaret O'Mara provided great advice and counsel about the history and present-day realities of Silicon Valley. G. Nagesh Rao, who has pushed the conversation about small business and innovation for years in Washington, DC, also provided early feedback, as did Taylor Hall Debnam, a rising star in entrepreneurship and law. Penny Peavler and Brook Smith, two entrepreneurial leaders in Appalachia, and Erica Lucas and Melissa Vincent, similar leaders in the Midwest, and Elizabeth's friend Jen Collins, introduced us to many *New Builders* and helped us understand more about the issues they face. And Desh Deshpande, David Parker, and the entire team from Entrepreneurship for All were incredibly generous with their time and connections. Dina Sherif of the Legatum Center has been a long time friend and constant support in this and various entrepreneurial endeavors. David Smick was incredibly generous with introductions and help as we sought ways to get the word out about our book, recognizing immediately the importance of the topics we covered.

Support from the Ewing Marion Kauffman Foundation, the Walton Family Foundation, MIT's Legatum Center for Entrepreneurship & Development, the Beeck Center for Impact & Innovation at Georgetown University, and from filmmaker, philanthropist, and friend Abigail E. Disney provided invaluable support during this year. The insights and support of Sheila Herrling and John Heffern of the Beeck Center were helpful at many points along the journey.

Many journalists, entrepreneurs, and leaders in the United States, Middle East, and East Asia helped Elizabeth understand the power of entrepreneurship, including Loren Feldman, Christopher M. Schroeder, Ala' AlSallal (founder of the first online Arab bookstore, Jamalon), Fadi Ghandour, Ahmed Alfi, Maysa Jalbout, the many thousands of entrepreneurs attending the Rise-Up Summit in Cairo, the dedicated entrepreneurial community in Jordan, Ronaldo Mouchawar, Laura Hagg, Jihan at the Ghar Collective, and Trevor and Agnieszka Tynkiewicz-Gile and their team at the Liger Leadership Academy in Cambodia. Elizabeth and Seth would not have met were it not for the work of leaders working to create a better economy in Israel/Palestine, including Zahi Khouri, Ambar Amleh, Peter Abualzolof, Saed Nashef, and Kito de Boer.

Writing a book – especially while holding down full-time jobs – is an all-consuming effort. Late nights and weekends to start with. But a project like this also has a way of taking over mindshare and conversation, poking its way into discussions over dinners, walks, and whenever else the spirit might strike. Our families not only endured this constant in our lives for several years but embraced and encouraged it. Thank you!

Years into this idea, we find ourselves looking differently into the windows of storefronts and shops along Main Streets. Wondering as we pass someone on the street what business ideas they might be ready to bring to life. Looking with new perspective at those around us, now that our eyes are open to the reality of our changing entrepreneurial landscape. It's a change we embrace as, we hope, millions more will as well.

ABOUT THE AUTHORS

Seth Levine

A long time venture capitalist, Seth Levine works with venture funds and companies around the globe. His day job is as a partner at Foundry Group, a Boulder, Colorado–based venture capital firm he co-founded in 2006, which as of the end of 2020 had almost $3 billion in assets under management. Easily distracted and a passionate advocate for entrepreneurship, Seth also spends time as an advisor to venture funds and companies around the world.

The intersection of community and business has always been a driving force for Seth. He co-founded Pledge 1%, a global network of companies who have pledged equity, time, and product back to their local communities. He is on the board of StartupColorado, which promotes entrepreneurship in areas of Colorado outside of the front range. He is also a trustee of Macalester College in St. Paul, Minnesota, where he helped found their entrepreneurship program as well as a popular student hackathon (the "Macathon"). He also works with a number of funds and companies – especially in the Middle East and Africa – to help promote entrepreneurship and economic development.

A passionate cyclist, above-average skier, and general fan of all things outdoors, Seth and his wife live in Colorado with their three children. *The New Builders* is his first book, but you can find more of his writing at sethlevine.com.

Elizabeth MacBride

As an international business journalist for outlets including *CNBC*, *BBC*, *MIT Tech Review,* and *Quartz*, Elizabeth MacBride discovered a global movement of people who believe in the life-altering power of entrepreneurship. It is a path to agency, and as tech innovation continues to even the playing field, is a viable path to create whole economies. Elizabeth has reported from Cambodia, Dubai, Jerusalem, and Wales, among many other places, to capture the story of this global movement.

A military brat with a deep empathy for outsiders, Elizabeth also saw how unfairly the deck was stacked against people who weren't in powerful positions to begin with – those who didn't come from money, or who lived outside of big cities. The situation is especially pernicious against women and people of color, who are subject to systems that don't serve them well. She founded a new publication, *Times of Entrepreneurship*, to share the stories of those often-overlooked entrepreneurs.

She's also been an entrepreneur herself as co-founder of RIABiz .com and 200kfreelancer.com, and she was part of the founding team of Wealthfront, the first online investment advisor. Some of her writing and editing clients over the years have included Stanford GSB, the UN's Office of the Quartet in Jerusalem, Charles D. Ellis, and Abigail Disney. In 2020, she was journalist-in-residence at MIT's Legatum Center for Development & Entrepreneurship.

A writer, traveler, and seventh-generation Washingtonian, she lives in Alexandria, Virginia, with her two daughters.

INDEX